If Jesus Christ is truly human, then any account of human agents must reflect this obvious theological platitude. But how should we spell out the relevant inference? Most especially, given that Jesus is male and Jewish. Marc Cortez provides a clear and provocative answer. Written with apt caution and precision, this book is indispensable reading for both seasoned theologians and enthusiastic novices.

WILLIAM J. ABRAHAM,
Outler Professor of Wesley Studies and University Distinguished Teaching Professor, Perkins School of Theology, Southern Methodist University

Over the course of this extraordinary book, Marc Cortez engages some of the biggest questions of today while remaining thoroughly rooted in Scripture and tradition. He develops his constructive contribution to theological anthropology in conversation with an impressively wide range of contemporary voices. While never compromising his engagement with high-level thought, his book is exceptionably accessible and readable. Every Christian needs to wrestle with the questions engaged in this book: What does it mean to be human? How does Jesus Christ help us understand who we are? What does it mean to be made in the image of God? How does Jesus Christ help us understand gender and sexuality? What does Jesus Christ contribute to our conceptions of race and ethnicity today? And as they wrestle with these questions, they could have no better guide than Marc Cortez.

KRISTEN DEEDE JOHNSON,
associate professor of theology and Christian formation, Western Theological Seminary

Marc Cortez has done it again! Produced another brilliant study of theological anthropology! The publication of *ReSourcing Theological Anthropology* spotlights Cortez as a go-to author for insight on this important subject. Working from texts in John, Paul, and the author of Hebrews in dialogue with contemporary exegetes and systematic theologians, he builds a solid case that the New Testament views Jesus Christ not only as a complete and true human being but as the true human being; indeed, Jesus's humanity is the creational and teleological ground and goal for all other human beings. Cortez contends that Jesus is the "image of God" not only in his eternal relation to the Father but precisely in his concrete human identity given and achieved between Christmas and Easter. In keeping with his emphasis on the historical concreteness of Jesus's true humanity, Cortez boldly puts his theory to the test in his final three chapters on gender, race, and death. Students, pastors, and teachers will find in Cortez a reliable guide to take them safely through the maze of contemporary theories of theological anthropology. I recommend the book highly!

RON HIGHFIELD,
professor of religion,
Pepperdine University

If Jesus alone reveals what it is to be *truly* human, can there be an adequate anthropology that does not take its fundamental bearings from Jesus's specific humanity? Was Adam's humanity ultimately indecipherable, absent the revelation of the Second Adam? The specificity of Jesus's male, Jewish humanity might seem to pose a further quandary. Professor Cortez's lively and unfailingly gracious book is a delightful romp through such difficult questions, motivated by the joy of the Gospel.

MATTHEW LEVERING,
James N. and Mary D. Perry Jr. Chair of Theology,
Mundelein Seminary

Calvin famously claimed that there is no knowledge of self without knowledge of God. Barth amended the motion, insisting that there is no knowledge of God without knowledge of Christ. Cortez here extends the logic further, arguing that, theologically speaking, there is no knowledge of self apart from knowledge of the humanity of Christ. Christology does not simply supplement but constitutes the most important things we know about our own humanity. This is a bold claim, to be sure, yet Cortez clearly provides biblical grounding for it and anticipates the likely objections, thereby putting flesh on what many theologians thinly assume but never thickly describe—namely, how, why, and where Christology ought to inform anthropology.

KEVIN J. VANHOOZER,
research professor of systematic theology,
Trinity Evangelical Divinity School

Cortez is making a compelling case for a "comprehensive Christological anthropology," by which he means the normativity of the person of Jesus Christ for our understanding of human nature. Current on biblical scholarship, sensitive to contemporary issues such as gender, race, and sexuality, and exhibiting a remarkable analytical clarity, this is the perfect introduction to what is currently an exciting conversation in theology.

ADONIS VIDU,
associate professor of theology,
Gordon-Conwell Theological Seminary

RESOURCING
THEOLOGICAL
ANTHROPOLOGY

ReSourcing Theological Anthropology

A Constructive Account of
Humanity in the Light of Christ

MARC CORTEZ

 ZONDERVAN®

ZONDERVAN

ReSourcing Theological Anthropology
Copyright © 2017 by Marc Cortez

This title is also available as a Zondervan ebook.

Requests for information should be addressed to:
Zondervan, *3900 Sparks Dr. SE, Grand Rapids, Michigan 49546*

ISBN 978-0-310-51643-9

Cover design: Kirk DouPonce, DogEared Design
Cover photo: ⓢ *Giampietrino, The Last Supper*
Interior design: Denise Froehlich

Printed in the United States of America

17 18 19 20 21 22 23 24 25 26 27 /DHV/ 15 14 13 12 11 10 9 8 7 6 5 4 3 2 1

To my wife and daughters for giving me the time, space, and occasional Netflix binges I needed to make it through this book. To the dog for reminding me that sometimes it's enough just to run in the sun for a while. To the hedgehog for . . . I'm not sure. Hedgehogs don't do much.

Contents

Acknowledgments

IS IT BETTER TO MAKE a few acknowledgments at the beginning of a book and know that you will inevitably miss someone, or to skip the acknowledgments entirely and ensure that you miss everyone equally? Although the egalitarianism of the latter option seems appealing, I'll run the risk of the former anyway (mostly because my wife insisted that I had to).

By far the greatest debt of gratitude goes to those who commented on various parts of this project. Many thanks to Daniel Hill and Justin Zahraee, two of my doctoral students who faithfully read and insightfully commented on every chapter, somehow even managing to look on occasion as if they were enjoying themselves. My colleague Dan Treier similarly offered invaluable input throughout the process, often challenging my assumptions and conclusions in ways that improved the project immeasurably. Many thanks as well to Nick Perrin and Amy Peeler for their comments on my exegetical discussions. Each of these individuals helped make this book what it is. Although I should take full responsibility for any remaining errors, I won't. That's why I have doctoral students. So if you have any complaints about the book, feel free to contact Daniel and Justin. I can send you their email addresses and personal phone numbers.

I would also like to thank those who participated in the 2016 colloquium "On Christian Dying" held at Wheaton College and co-sponsored by The Wheaton Center for Early Christian Studies (Wheaton College), The Center for Scriptural Exegesis, Philosophy, and Doctrine (Mundelein Seminary), and the Chicago Theological

Initiative. I presented an earlier draft of chapter 8 at the colloquium, and the discussion of that paper as well as the other papers on the theology of death and dying helped refine my thinking in that area considerably.

Finally, I would like to thank my editor Katya Covrett for thinking that this book was worth writing in the first place, and for all of the patience and encouragement she has shown along the way. Thanks to my family, my friends, and the members of the youth group at First Baptist Church of Wheaton, Illinois. Without you, I might have still finished the book, but it wouldn't have been any fun.

Introduction

IT DOES NOT REQUIRE any great effort to find theologians claiming that Jesus is in some way central for understanding what it means to be human. As Mary Hilkert affirms, "Christians believe that not only the mystery of the divine, but also the deepest truths about human life and destiny, have been revealed in Jesus Christ."[1] John Zizioulas similarly claims that "the mystery of man reveals itself fully only in the light of Christ."[2] To express this idea, theologians have variously described Jesus as the *paradigm, pattern, norm, archetype, prototype,* and *ideal* of true humanity, among many other such terms.[3] Each of these suggests that anthropology depends on Jesus in some meaningful way. He is the one in whom humanity is both established and revealed. While we might be able to generate some knowledge about humanity from other sources, that knowledge will necessarily be highly circumscribed unless we

---

1. Mary Catherine Hilkert, "Cry Beloved Image: Rethinking the Image of God," in *In the Embrace of God: Feminist Approaches to Theological Anthropology*, ed. Ann Elizabeth O'Hara Graff (Maryknoll, NY: Orbis, 1995), 201.

2. John D. Zizioulas, "Human Capacity and Human Incapacity: A Theological Exploration of Personhood," *Scottish Journal of Theology* 28, no. 5 (1975): 433.

3. For examples of each of these, see Edward Schillebeeckx, *Jesus: An Experiment in Christology*, trans. Hubert Hoskins (New York: Seabury, 1979), 626 (paradigm); Brendan Byrne, *Romans*, Sacra Pagina (Collegeville, MN: Liturgical, 1996), 272–73 (pattern); C. Clifton Black, "God's Promise for Humanity in the New Testament," in *God and Human Dignity*, ed. R. Kendall Soulen and Linda Woodhead (Grand Rapids: Eerdmans, 2006), 181 (norm); Panayiotis Nellas, *Deification in Christ: The Nature of the Human Person* (Crestwood, NY: St. Vladimir's Seminary Press, 1987), 33 (archetype); Veli-Matti Kärkkäinen, "The Human Prototype: With Jesus, We See What We Were Created to Be," *Christianity Today* 56, no. 1 (2012): 28–31 (prototype); Dietrich Bonhoeffer, *Creation and Fall: A Theological Interpretation of Genesis 1–3*, trans. John C. Fletcher (New York: Macmillan, 1959), 37 (ideal).

can view it in light of the only one who can tell us what it really means to be human.

This christological intuition has been a part of Christian anthropology for some time now. In my previous book, *Christological Anthropology in Historical Perspective*, I surveyed a number of thinkers who took Christology as their starting point for understanding the human person, showing how this logic was at work in the theologies of Gregory of Nyssa, Julian of Norwich, Martin Luther, Friedrich Schleiermacher, Karl Barth, John Zizioulas, and James Cone.[4] To that list, we could easily add such important figures as Maximus the Confessor, Bonaventure, John Owen, Søren Kierkegaard, and Hans Urs von Balthasar, among many others. Anyone wanting to develop a christologically informed anthropology today would thus stand in a long line of similarly minded theologians.

However, at the end of that book I also noted that one of the challenges facing anyone seeking to develop a christologically informed vision of the human person today is the significant diversity that characterizes these earlier projects. While each shares the common intuition that Jesus meaningfully informs anthropology in some way, they differ markedly with respect to the christological intuitions that shaped their projects, the intellectual and cultural contexts in which they developed those christological insights, and the anthropological questions to which they applied their conclusions. Anyone wanting to explore the resources of a christological anthropology for understanding humanity today thus faces one of three options. On the one hand, we could "stay within the territory mapped by these case studies by adopting the same basic approach as one of our representative theologians."[5] This would allow us to sit at the feet of one of the great minds of the church— something I highly recommend. Rather than limit ourselves to a single approach, our second option would be "combining elements

---

4. Marc Cortez, *Christological Anthropology in Historical Perspective: Ancient and Contemporary Approaches to Theological Anthropology* (Grand Rapids: Zondervan, 2016).

5. Ibid., 232.

of these christological anthropologies in new and interesting ways."[6] Such an approach risks the incoherence that can accompany the *ad hoc* use of disparate theological conclusions, but it also provides the opportunity to develop the kind of creative synthesis that can produce new theological insights. The third option, of course, is to strike a new path entirely. Indeed, the diversity of these earlier projects "almost demands that we continue exploring the relationship between Christology and anthropology in ways that will certainly lead to new proposals today."[7]

Although I would argue that each of these offers a viable way forward for developing christological anthropologies today, this book follows the third path for the most part, though with elements of the second. Many of the figures studied in the previous book will make appearances in these chapters as helpful dialogue partners for thinking christologically about the human person. Unlike the previous book, though, which was an entirely descriptive endeavor, these will not always be uncritical conversations. Instead, this book strikes out in some new directions. It does so primarily by offering explicit answers to three key questions:

- *Why* should we think that Christology is fundamental for understanding anthropology?
- *What* are the theological issues involved in making that claim?
- *How* should we go about applying these christological intuitions to anthropological issues?

While the previous book demonstrated that many others have reflected on these questions, they tend to do so in ways that require the reader to tease out answers that are implicit aspects of larger theological arguments. This book will differ at least in making the biblical and theological arguments for a christological anthropology

---

6. Ibid., 233.

7. Ibid.

more explicit. At the same time, although the christological anthropology presented here will overlap at times with some of its dialogue partners, particularly the approach taken by Karl Barth, the answers I give to these three key questions also differ in important ways from each of them.

This means that people can approach this book in several ways. First, some may just be curious about what it even means to claim that Christology somehow informs anthropology. My own journey into this subject began in a similar place. When I first started reading in theological anthropology, I was struck by how often I would encounter claims like "Jesus reveals what it means to be human" with little or no explanation of what such a statement means or how it should inform our understanding of specific issues in anthropology. Hopefully this book will offer a bit more clarity than that, providing a resource to those who just want to know more about a longstanding theological intuition. However, the book can also be used as a resource by a second group: those seeking to develop their own way of thinking christologically about the human person. As I mentioned above, earlier approaches to christological anthropology have not always been clear about the specific biblical and theological issues involved in such an endeavor, requiring considerable effort to discern the implicit structures of their arguments. Although I cannot claim that this book will offer an exhaustive treatment of all such topics, which would be the work of a lifetime, it does clearly identify four key biblical and theological issues that any christological anthropology should be able to address. Some will certainly disagree with the conclusions that I draw over the course of those discussions, which will lead them to nuance their own christological anthropologies in importantly different ways. By identifying these as important issues to be addressed, though, I hope to have offered a clearer roadmap for developing such anthropologies than was available previously. Finally, of course, the book can be read as a work that seeks to make its own contribution to understanding humanity christologically.

WHAT IS A CHRISTOLOGICAL ANTHROPOLOGY?

Before we go any further, we should be clear about what it means to refer to something as a *christological* anthropology. This label can be relatively confusing given that there is a sense in which any anthropology that is meaningfully *Christian* will be somewhat christological. David Kelsey thus claims that what qualifies something "as authentically Christian theological anthropology" is that its beliefs are "shaped in some way by their beliefs about Jesus Christ and God's relation to him."[8] Although this is certainly true, we can still make a critical distinction between those who approach anthropology as though we can understand what it essentially means to be human apart from Christology and those who affirm instead that Christology is absolutely central to any adequate knowledge of the human person.

Consider, for example, the robust anthropology of the Old Testament. We already have in Adam and Eve a picture of unfallen humanity that offers an admittedly brief glimpse of God's creational purposes for his people. In addition, we have the history of Israel with its stories of faithful and unfaithful human existence, the wisdom literature and its rich depiction of everyday humanity in both mundanity and misery, and the prophets with their occasional glimpses of God's ultimate purposes for humanity, each of which offers considerable material for understanding what it means to be human.[9] Although this clearly qualifies as theological reflection on the nature of humanity, many would argue that none of this material depends on Christology in any direct way. On this basis alone, then, we would need to make at least some kind of distinction between a *theological* anthropology, which understands the human person in broadly theological categories, and a specifically

---

8. David H. Kelsey, *Eccentric Existence: A Theological Anthropology*, 2 vols. (Louisville: Westminster John Knox, 2009), 8–9.

9. See esp. Hans Walter Wolff, *Anthropology of the Old Testament*, trans. Margaret Kohl (London: SCM, 1974); J. Gordon McConville, *Being Human in God's World: An Old Testament Theology of Humanity* (Grand Rapids: Baker Academic, 2016).

christological anthropology, which contends that Christology plays a unique and necessary role in anthropology.

Even many Christian theologians identify with a theological rather than a christological approach to anthropology. For some, this simply follows the logic of the biblical material itself. The New Testament and the early creeds both seem to presuppose that we already know what it means to be human *before* Jesus arrives on the scene. Thus, for example, when the author of Hebrews declared that the Son had become one of us such that he was "fully human in every way" (Heb 2:17), he does not bother to explain what it means to be human, apparently believing that this has already been well established. Hebrews suggests that, rather than revealing what it means to be human, Christology assumes a preexisting understanding of anthropology, taking that as the starting point for affirming that the Son became human in the incarnation. Similarly, the Chalcedonian Definition emphasizes that the incarnation involves the Son becoming "truly Man," not bothering to articulate the anthropological content of that claim beyond the bare fact that it includes both soul and body. Here as well, there seems to be a presumption that anthropology precedes Christology and provides the necessary framework for understanding the nature of the incarnation. In addition to this biblical argument, we will see in the next chapter that several theologians think that unless we can understand human nature on its own terms (i.e., independently of Christology), we will inevitably undermine the intelligibility of the created order and the gracious character of grace itself. We cannot take time now to unpack the logic of that argument, but we need to see here that arguments like this support the necessity of distinguishing between broadly *theological* approaches to anthropology from more specifically *christological* ones. This does not mean that such approaches reject the significance of Christology for understanding the human person entirely. Instead, they typically claim that Christology provides *additional* insight into the nature of humanity, information that is not necessary for knowing that which is essential to being human.

We also need to differentiate between various kinds of christo-logical anthropologies. In my previous book, I argued that we can at least distinguish between *minimal* and *comprehensive* christological anthropologies, proposing the following as tentative definitions:

A *minimally* christological anthropology is one in which
(a) Christology warrants important claims about what it means to be human and (b) the scope of those claims goes beyond issues like the image of God and ethics.

A *comprehensively* christological anthropology is one in which
(a) Christology warrants ultimate claims about true humanity such that (b) the scope of those claims applies to all anthropological data.[10]

Thus, although both of these qualify as *christological* according to our initial distinction, they differ on the extent to which Christology shapes our understanding of the human person. One could argue, for example, that John Calvin offers an example of a minimal christological anthropology. He clearly uses Christology to warrant important claims about the human person, especially with regard to the *imago Dei*, but it does not seem to be the case that he orients his knowledge of the human person *entirely* around Christology. This differs significantly from the approach taken by someone like Karl Barth, who contends that anthropology must be "christologically determined" from beginning to end.[11]

My real focus in this volume is on providing resources for developing comprehensively christological anthropologies today. Consequently, unless I indicate otherwise, whenever I use the phrase "christological anthropology" in the rest of this book, I will have comprehensively christological anthropologies in mind.

---

10. Cortez, *Christological Anthropology in Historical Perspective*, 225.

11. Karl Barth, *Church Dogmatics*, trans. Geoffrey W. Bromiley and Thomas F. Torrance, 13 vols. (Edinburgh: T&T Clark, 1956–1975), I/2 (12); hereafter *CD*.

BUT, THE INCARNATION!

The first half of this book will devote considerable attention to explaining *why* we would or should affirm that human persons need to be understood christologically. For some, however, this seems entirely unnecessary because the incarnation itself so clearly establishes the anthropological significance of Jesus Christ. If the eternal Son assumed a complete human nature at the incarnation, joining that to the divine nature in a single person, how could we need any other starting point for understanding humanity? As important as the incarnation might be for Christian anthropology, however, this alone will not suffice to ground the claims made at the beginning of this chapter. Consider the fact that the person serving me coffee this morning also appears to be fully human. As far as I can tell, she is not some other creature. Yet I cannot imagine anyone claiming that we should view her, or anyone else, as somehow paradigmatic for the meaning of humanity itself simply because she is a particular example of that broader category. While the incarnation requires that Jesus be fully human, as opposed to only partly human, we will need something more to ground the further claim that his particular humanity has fundamental significance for understanding humanity in general.

We could address this problem by appealing to the idea that only Jesus exemplified *sinless* humanity. His humanity might thus give us insight into God's original purposes for humanity in a way that the humanity of my server cannot. However, appealing to Christ's sinlessness in this context is not as straightforward as it might seem. As we will see in chapter 4, we also need to account for the fact that Jesus lived in a broken world and that his human existence was shaped in at least some ways by the reality of sin (e.g., he suffered). Consequently, we will find that sin constitutes a challenge even for those who affirm Christ's sinlessness. Regardless, it is not clear that appealing to Christ's sinlessness alone will solve our problem since it would still leave us with a single, albeit perfect, instance of humanity. Even a sinless human person would not be able to actualize all of the potentialities of humanity. We have no reason to think that Jesus grew to be seven feet tall or that he could run a mile in under four minutes. He never developed breasts or gave birth. He couldn't speak French or play the clarinet. Given the impressively broad range of human potentialities, it is not clear how merely claiming that one particular instantiation of humanity is flawless would make it paradigmatic for understanding the rest.

Even more significantly, not only would appealing to the incarnation and Christ's sinlessness not answer the *why* question, but they both actually complicate things considerably since each suggests that Jesus's humanity differs from our own in significant ways. He alone is the one who unites both divine and human natures in himself, rendering him radically *unlike* all other humans. Similarly, however we understand Christ's sinlessness, this also puts him in a category of his own. He alone lived as a human being without sin (Heb 4:15). Rather than explaining why we should view Jesus's humanity as paradigmatic for humanity in general, both of these issues press in precisely the opposite direction by *distinguishing* his humanity from that of the rest of us.

Consequently, appealing to the incarnation alone will not suffice to ground the anthropological centrality of Christology. If we want to understand why people find this claim compelling, we will need to look further.

SOME INITIAL ASSUMPTIONS

As I pointed out in my earlier book, any meaningfully *christological* anthropology requires a robust Christology,[12] which means that any such approach immediately faces two risks. On the one hand, it might fail to provide any real christological framework, merely making vague appeals to some unarticulated concept of Jesus or the eternal Son as the ostensible basis for what is a largely nonchristological vision of humanity. On the other hand, it might become

---

12. Cortez, *Christological Anthropology in Historical Perspective*, 231–33.

so aware of the need for a robust christological foundation that its christological focus eliminates the opportunity for meaningful engagement with anthropological issues. Obviously, the ideal falls somewhere in between.

Throughout the course of this book, we will spend considerable time reflecting on questions that have traditionally been associated more with Christology than anthropology (e.g., the fallen nature of Christ), though we will see that these questions all have anthropological significance. This will provide considerable opportunity to develop a robust christological framework for this project. Nonetheless, we have neither the space nor the time to deal with all of the issues necessary for developing a comprehensive Christology. Instead, I will largely be assuming a traditional Christology, one that affirms the theological conclusions of the early councils and the shared christological convictions of most orthodox theologians. I will argue in places for conclusions that differ from more traditional positions, and those will provide the primary occasions for extended christological reflection in this book. The fact that I will pass over other christological issues without comment should not be taken as indicating that I disagree with them or find them uninteresting for anthropological reflection. Instead, such christological convictions form the background assumptions operative throughout the project.

I will also be assuming throughout fairly generic definitions of key terms like *nature* and *essence/essential*. Defining such terms with precision would involve us in extended philosophical and historical discussions, each of which has the potential to distract us from the focus of this book. Consequently, I will use "nature" and "human nature" to refer simply to whatever it is that an individual possesses or instantiates that is both necessary and sufficient to qualify that individual as a member of a particular class (e.g., "human"). At several points in the book, we will run into the question of whether such natures are best understood as concrete particulars (i.e., each human person is a particular human nature) or as universals (i.e., each human person participates in a universal human nature);

my intent is to avoid committing to any particular definition of "nature." Similarly, I will use terms like *essence* and *essential* to refer generically to whatever it is that an individual must have (e.g., a property or set of properties) in order to qualify as an instance of a broader kind. Thus, we will talk about that which is *essential* to being human, which simply means whatever it is that must be true of a particular being in order for that being to qualify as human.

WHAT, WHY, AND HOW?

The structure of this book flows around the three key questions mentioned earlier. Much of the first half of the book focuses on establishing *why* we should affirm that human persons need to be understood christologically. Despite the long history of understanding the human person christologically, however, the biblical basis for making this claim is not always entirely clear. Indeed, when we discuss the idea of a christological anthropology, people often raise the question of whether such an approach is adequate to the biblical material. After all, no biblical author simply states that we should look to Jesus if we want to understand what it means to be human. We *are* told that we should imitate Christ (e.g., 1 Cor 11:1; 1 Pet 2:21), but that is a far cry from claiming that his humanity is central to anthropology as a whole. Others will turn to statements about the Son as the image of God (e.g., Col 1:15), which chapter 3 will discuss in depth. Without further explanation, though, those texts alone will not make our case. It is entirely possible that this simply identifies Jesus as *an* instance of the *imago Dei* alongside others, not only establishing that he is fully human but also that he is paradigmatically human. Even if we concede that the Son alone is the *true* image of God, someone might contend that this is just one anthropological truth among many. While this would establish that the Son is central for understanding that aspect of humanity, they might still reject that this leads to affirming that Christology is fundamental for understanding humanity as a whole. We could go on. Lacking a clear biblical affirmation to support such christological claims, many will continue to wonder if this truly is the right way to understand the relationship between Christology and anthropology.

At the same time, though, we need to be aware that any attempt to explain *why* Christology should inform our understanding of the human person will also raise important theological questions. How can any single human reveal what it means for everyone to be human? Does this require us to take particular details of Jesus's like gender and ethnicity as anthropological norms? Is a christological anthropology inherently committed to the idea that the Son would have become incarnate even if humans had not fallen into sin? Does an approach like this rob the doctrine of creation of its significance by forcing it to be understood through the lenses of soteriology and eschatology? What is the relationship between the humanity we see in Eden and that which the Son assumes in the incarnation? What impact does the fall have on Jesus's human nature, and how does this affect whether we can view his humanity as paradigmatic for our own? We could go on. An informed christological anthropology must deal with these questions as it seeks to address *what* the theological implications of this approach might be.

We could easily deal with these questions in sequence, first addressing the biblical basis of a christological anthropology and only then asking about the theological implications of those biblical arguments. However, since many of these theological issues arise naturally as a consequence of the biblical discussions, I have taken a different approach. Each of the first four chapters deals with a specific biblical argument for the necessity of viewing the human person christologically, along with an important theological issue raised by that biblical discussion. Taken together, then, these chapters offer a robust biblical and theological argument for a christological anthropology.

Although I cannot claim to have addressed *all* of the biblical and theological issues involved in such an endeavor, these four chapters do identify some of the most important issues and demonstrate the kinds of biblical and theological moves necessary to justify and defend this approach to understanding the human person.

Chapter 1 takes the Gospel of John as its starting point, focusing specifically on Pilate's famous exclamation when he saw Jesus after he was beaten by the guards, "Behold, the man [*ho anthrōpos*]" (John 19:5). Although people often read this merely as a statement of pity or contempt, we will see that this declaration comes as part of an important Johannine theme that presents Jesus as the true *anthrōpos* who fulfills God's creational purposes for humanity. In the process, we will also see the significance of "new creation" in the Gospel of John and the central role that pneumatology must play in any adequately christological anthropology. We begin with the Gospel of John for two reasons. First, although the Gospels will necessarily play a prominent role in any christological anthropology as we seek to understand the significance of his life and ministry for understanding humanity as a whole, many fail to address the Gospels with any rigor when establishing the biblical ground for their christological anthropologies. Instead, they focus almost exclusively on Paul's theology for this purpose, implying by their silence that the Gospel writers have little to contribute for establishing this core truth. By starting with a closer look at John's anthropology, we can see that Paul is not the only one to view Jesus's humanity as having paradigmatic significance for humanity as a whole. Second, without establishing the legitimacy of a christological anthropology in the Gospels themselves, it would be difficult to justify using their material to provide much of the content of such an anthropology. We could easily give the impression that we were foisting an essentially Pauline framework onto the gospels and misappropriating that material. This first chapter thus establishes the legitimacy of approaching the anthropology of the gospels from a christological perspective.[13]

---

13. If we had space to offer a comprehensive biblical argument for christological anthro-pology, we would also need to demonstrate how this works in the synoptic gospels, probably by exploring either how they view Jesus as the true exemplar of humanity (e.g., the *imitatio Christi* tradition) or how they present him as the true Israel (see, for example, N. T. Wright,

However, the fact that John presents Jesus as the true *anthrōpos* who fulfills God's creational purposes for humanity raises an important theological question about the relationship between nature and grace in a christological anthropology. From one perspective, we can understand this claim as suggesting that the humanity we see in Jesus just *is* the definition of what it means to be human. From the beginning, God always intended humanity to find its *telos* in Jesus such that the consummation brought about in and through Jesus is intrinsic to humanity's essence. We cannot understand what it means to be human from any other vantage point. Yet others contend with equal seriousness that we must make a clear distinction between *nature* and *grace* when discussing the human person, seeing the latter as the elevation of the former. If this is the case, then we *can* understand what it essentially means to be human apart from Christology (nature), even if we maintain that God elevates humanity to a supernatural state through Jesus Christ (grace). The second half of this chapter will thus focus on an important contemporary debate about the nature/grace relationship and how this shapes a christological anthropology.

Having established the importance of a christological anthropology in the Gospels, chapter 2 offers the first of two studies in Paul's theology. Here we take up an issue already introduced in the previous chapter: the relationship between Adam and Christ. Although Paul famously addresses this topic in Romans 5:12–21, this passage focuses exclusively on Adam as the representative of fallen humanity, making it difficult for this passage to serve as a starting point for reflecting on how Christ relates to Adam with respect to God's creational purposes. Consequently, chapter 2 will focus instead on Paul's earlier discussion of the Adam/Christ relationship

---

The Climax of the Covenant: Christ and the Law in Pauline Theology [Minneapolis: Fortress, 1992]; Peter J. Leithart, *A Son to Me: An Exposition of 1 & 2 Samuel* [Moscow, ID: Canon, 2003]; Scott Hahn, *The Kingdom of God as Liturgical Empire: A Theological Commentary on 1–2 Chronicles* [Grand Rapids: Baker Academic, 2012]; Seth D. Postell, *Adam as Israel: Genesis 1–3 as the Introduction to the Torah and Tanakh* [Cambridge: James Clarke, 2012]). For our purposes, though, it will be sufficient to establish that we can ground a christological anthropology in the gospels as well as the theology of Paul.

in 1 Corinthians 15. Here we will see that although Paul still talks about Adam in relation to the fall (esp. 15:20–23), his discussion of how the "spiritual" body of the resurrection differs from the "natural" body of Adam (15:35–49) suggests that Paul views the Adam/Christ typology as relating to Adam before the fall as well. If so, then 1 Corinthians 15 echoes the logic of the Gospel of John, suggesting that God's eternal purposes for creation always included Jesus coming as the fulfillment of those purposes.

This inevitably leads to a theological question we did not address in the first chapter: Would the eternal Son have become incarnate even if humanity had not fallen into sin? If Paul presents Jesus as the second Adam in relation to Adam *before* the fall, this might provide support to those who think that the incarnation itself is intrinsic to God's plans for creation. Although such supralapsarian Christologies have been in the minority traditionally, it has become increasingly common for theologians to argue for this position. Consequently, the second half of this chapter explores the questions involved in understanding the "incarnation anyway" debate and the extent to which this conclusion is necessary for a christological anthropology.

Staying on the subject of Paul's anthropology, chapter 3 focuses on the *imago Dei* and Paul's declaration that the Son is "the image of the invisible God" (Col 1:15). The image of God has long been one of the primary ways in which theologians have connected Christology to anthropology, viewing Jesus as the ultimate expression of this fundamental anthropological truth. This chapter thus offers an opportunity to reflect on a seminal issue in christological anthropology, while also offering some resources and perspectives that may be new to many. The chapter begins by arguing that we should view the image as *formally* central to theological anthropology despite objections to the contrary. We then shift to the *material* content of the image, focusing on the relationship between the *imago Dei* and the ancient concept of what constitutes an "idol." Here we will see that *divine presence* is fundamental for understanding the image of God. All of this prepares us to address the christological reorientation of the image exemplified by Colossians 1:15. Though some scholars have argued that this verse does not refer to the *imago Dei* tradition at all, we will see that there are good reasons for rejecting this argument and continuing to view this verse, among others, as connecting Christology and anthropology through the language of the *imago Dei*.

The theological issue raised by this discussion has to do with the relationship between the eternal Son and the incarnate Jesus. What exactly does Paul have in mind when he declares, "He is the image of the invisible God"? Although the immediate referent is clearly "the Son" in 1:13, and elements in the immediate context suggest that Paul has the *eternal* Son in mind (esp. 1:16–17), other aspects of the passage suggest that the identity of "the Son" includes the history of incarnation and redemption (esp. 1:13–14, 18–20). We find a similar tension in Hebrews 1:1–4, where the author also describes the "Son" using the language of both eternity and history. This discussion has important ramifications for christological anthropology since it informs whether we are saying that the paradigm for humanity is the *incarnate Jesus* or the *eternal Son*. This in turn has the potential to shape the ways in which we can, or even should, appeal to the historic life of Jesus revealed in the gospels as a basis for understanding humanity in general.

In chapter 4, our final biblical/theological study again shifts away from the Pauline material to address the relationship between Christology and anthropology in the book of Hebrews, with a primary emphasis on its first two chapters. Here we find that the author of Hebrews presents Jesus as the eternal paradigm of humanity, revealing true humanity to us, but the author does so in ways that emphasize the eternal significance of Christ's incarnate life. In other words, Hebrews reiterates the argument of the previous chapter, that *Jesus* is the paradigm of true humanity, clarifying that this has been true from eternity past (1:1–4) and that it remains true in the future (1:5–14). Thus, Hebrews greatly emphasizes the full humanity of the Son, who can be our true and faithful High Priest because he became one of us and suffered alongside us (2:5–18).

However, if we say that Jesus is our anthropological paradigm specifically in his incarnate humanity, we have to address the *quality* of the humanity we see revealed in his life and ministry. From one perspective, Hebrews seems to affirm that Jesus's humanity was perfect and unmarred by sin. Because he was without sin, he can serve as our faithful High Priest (4:14–16) and unblemished sacrifice (9:14). This leads many to conclude that in the incarnation the Son assumed an *unfallen* human nature like that of Adam and Eve before the fall. Yet Hebrews also emphasizes that Jesus's humanity was affected in at least some ways by living in a broken world. He was tempted, he suffered, and he even died (2:14–18), all of which are realities that we generally associate with human existence shaped by sin. Consequently, many argue instead that the incarnation involved the Son's assumption of a *fallen* human nature. In other words, Jesus became "fully human in every way," which includes entering into our sinful state and experiencing the same temptations and struggles as all other humans since the fall. This is what allows him to be our *merciful* High Priest, truly empathizing with those who struggle similarly. We thus see two perspectives on the kind of humanity revealed in Jesus, each of which distinctly shape christological anthropology.

With chapter 5, the book begins to move in a new direction. The studies of the first four chapters required a series of interpretive and theological judgments, all of which have implications for christological anthropology. Yet it would be easy to miss some of those implications in the complexity of the individual discussions. In this chapter, we will gather together those various insights, outlining the implications for christological anthropology in eleven theses. Although I will argue that these theses do not comprise a particular "method" for christological anthropology, as if they are a series of steps that we can apply with rigorous consistency to particular anthropological issues, they can be viewed more loosely as methodological principles that can and should guide any such endeavors.

With those eleven principles in hand, the final three chapters of the book offer a series of focused studies on using Christology to inform our understanding of specific issues in anthropology today. With just three short chapters, we obviously cannot attempt anything as robust as developing a comprehensive christological anthropology. Instead, the goal with these chapters will be to see how our christological theses shape the way we deal with specific issues. Each chapter will thus consider how various theologians have approached anthropological issues from a christological perspective, offering a critical analysis of their conclusions on the basis of the theological judgments made in the first four chapters. Since I will occasionally draw from the same dialogue partners used in my previous book for these chapters (e.g., Gregory of Nyssa and James Cone), the discussions will seem to overlap in places. Yet the focus here is considerably different. In the prior project, the goal was simply to *understand* what these various authors were doing in order to discern the ways in which theologians have developed christological anthropologies in the past. Here our goal is to *assess* the anthropological proposals presented by various theologians, determining where their insights may need to be revised accordingly.

The sixth chapter offers the first such study, focusing on what a christological anthropology has to say about the nature of gender and sexuality. Here our dialogue partners will mainly be a number of feminist theologians who wrestle with how to understand the significance of Jesus's *maleness* in light of the apparently normative status of his humanity for both men and women. Three key questions arise in this context. First, what is the relationship between Jesus's maleness and the *imago Dei*, especially in light of Paul's apparent limitation of the image to men alone (1 Cor 11:7)? Second, what is the role of the resurrection for understanding Jesus's maleness? According to some theologians, the radical transformation of Jesus's humanity in the resurrection requires us to bracket all claims about the significance of his sexuality, resulting in a rather apophatic approach to christological anthropology. Third, what are the implications of Jesus's maleness for understanding gender and gender essentialism? Many feminist theologians argue that Christology challenges traditional views of gender, some going so far as to claim that Jesus's sexuality requires the radical subversion of gender itself. Others take the same christological starting point and conclude instead that Jesus's maleness supports traditional notions of gender essentialism. Through all three discussions, we will see how a number of theologians have used Christology to understand human sexuality, providing us with a considerable opportunity to reflect on the adequacy of their respective conclusions.

With the seventh chapter, we shift our attention to race and ethnicity. Here as well we face questions about the particularity of Jesus's human existence, though here the question has to do with the status of his *Jewishness* and its significance for understanding humanity in general. After taking some time to understand the modern concept of race and its historical roots, we will focus primarily on the christological accounts of race offered by James Cone and Virgilio Elizondo, though in dialogue with the more recent contributions of theologians like Willie Jennings, Kameron Carter, and Brian Bantum. Cone and Elizondo both argue that we need to begin with the particularities of Jesus's historic existence if we are going to take his humanity seriously. They thus criticize an earlier neglect of Jesus's Jewishness that has characterized much of Western theology, arguing instead that his Jewishness provides the key for understanding the nature of race and ethnicity today. As we will see, though, they do so in ways that raise their own troubling implications. Bringing their insights into dialogue with that of more recent theologians will help us discern a better path toward developing a christological account of race today.

Rather fittingly, the eighth and final chapter will focus on the issue of death. Quite a few modern theologians have argued against the traditional idea that human death is a consequence of sin, maintaining instead that death is an intrinsic aspect of any finite creature. Although these theologians use a broad range of arguments to support this conclusion, this chapter will focus specifically on the christological form of the argument offered by Karl Barth. For Barth, the unavoidable starting point of any christologically adequate discussion of death must be this: even Jesus died. While Barth recognizes that the Bible routinely associates death with sin and judgment, he contends that all of this is colored by the fact that humans have universally experienced death after the fall. Only in Jesus do we see that death is fundamental to God's purposes for humanity, the necessary limitation that grounds our radical dependence on God for meaning and identity. This topic not only allows us to reflect on one of the most powerful and tragic aspects of human life, but it will also provide the opportunity to reflect on the limitations of a christological anthropology as we determine whether this approach faces inevitable challenges when addressing certain kinds of anthropological questions.

CHAPTER 1

Ecce Homo

Jesus as the True *Anthrōpos* and the Nature/Grace Debate

WE BEGIN OUR STUDY by looking at one of the more intriguing passages for developing a christological anthropology: "When Jesus came out wearing the crown of thorns and the purple robe, Pilate said to them, 'Here is the man [*idou ho anthrōpos*]!'" (John 19:5). After Jesus's beating at the hands of the Roman guards, he stands before Pilate once more, and Pilate declares these famous words, which translate into Latin as *ecce homo*. What could this possibly mean? Did Pilate merely intend to humiliate Jesus with these words, pointing out his pitiable condition? Or maybe Pilate wanted to mock the Jewish leaders, highlighting the inanity of fearing such a wretched figure. Possibly he even sought to elicit sympathy from the crowd, drawing attention to Jesus's misery to provoke the crowd's compassion and to prevent further punishment. Interpreters have proposed each of these as a way of understanding *ecce homo*, viewing the phrase as focusing on Jesus's miserable condition.

But what if there is more? John is notorious for the subtlety of his rhetoric, often placing words in the mouth of a speaker that have both an obvious, surface meaning as well as a deeper meaning that only comes out upon a closer reading of the text. In one famous example, Caiaphas declares, "It is better for you that one man die for the people than that the whole nation perish" (John 11:50). This statement has a clear, prima facie meaning, one that offers a pragmatic argument for sacrificing Jesus to prevent further harm to the nation, alongside a deeper meaning about his atoning death that only seems obvious to those already familiar with the story. Is it possible that Pilate's *ecce homo* is another example of unintentional witness in John? I will argue in this chapter that not only is it possible, but that if we read *ecce homo* in light of the broader story of the *anthrōpos* in John, we will see that John uses this incident to portray Jesus as the true human who comes to inaugurate the reality of the new creation. As the *anthrōpos*, Jesus is the one who fulfills God's creational purposes for humanity.

However, this way of understanding *ecce homo* introduces us to a related theological issue. If we say that Jesus is the true telos of humanity, the eschatological end that God had in mind from the beginning, it seems to follow that we must also maintain that this telos is intrinsic to the meaning of humanity. In other words, we cannot fully understand what it means to be human until we have seen true humanity revealed in Jesus. This approach has a number of important theological supporters, yet many worry that such a view conflates what it means to be a human creature essentially (nature) with the ways in which God elevates humanity to a higher telos in Jesus (grace). Said somewhat differently, should we not maintain a distinction between the *natural* (the essence of what it means to be human) and the *supernatural* (that which comes as a gift of God's grace)? If so, as a natural entity, we should be able to understand much of what it means to be human independently of the incarnation, even though the latter remains fundamental for understanding God's eschatological purposes for humanity. Although this might sound rather abstract, it gets at the heart of what it means to be human. Indeed, the issue has been described, somewhat hyperbolically, as one of the two "hottest debates in theological anthropology."[1] In the second half of the chapter, then,

---

1. Joshua R. Brotherton, "The Integrity of Nature in the Grace-Freedom Dynamic: Lonergan's Critique of Bañezian Thomism," *Theological Studies* 75, no. 3 (2014): 537.

we will need to wrestle with the issues raised by this debate and determine the best path forward.

PILATE'S UNINTENTIONAL WITNESS

As I mentioned, interpreters commonly read *ecce homo* as merely an ironic statement emphasizing Jesus's pitiable condition.[2] We find a similar comment in 19:14, "Behold your king!" (ESV). There as well Pilate does not seem be offering any theologically robust statement about who Jesus is or why he is significant for the rest of humanity. Instead, he uses irony to make the opposite point: Jesus's human condition is so low and wretched that the leaders should give him no further thought. Yet, many wonder if this does justice to the full meaning of Pilate's words. The interplay between "behold the man" (19:5) and "behold your king" (19:14) suggests that more is in view than mere mockery; otherwise the two statements become largely redundant in the narrative.[3] Even the introductory "behold" suggests the need for careful reflection. The term inherently calls attention to what follows, but it has also been referred to as "the great 'Stop-Look-Listen' signal of the Gospels."[4] If this is the case, then "behold the man" and "behold your king" both call on the reader to pause for a moment of deep reflection about what those phrases might mean. If this is the case, then John portrays Pilate as someone who spoke the truth "accidentally,"[5] and *ecce homo* serves to draw our attention to this deeper truth.[6]

---

2. Charles Panackel identifies five versions of this interpretation. Pilate is (1) ridiculing the Jewish charges based on Jesus's obvious harmlessness; (2) expressing contempt for Jesus; (3) making a compassionate appeal based on Jesus's condition; (4) declaring how impressed he is by Jesus; and (5) stating his intention to release Jesus (*Idou o Anthrōpos [John 19:5b]: An Exegetico-Theological Study of the Text* [Rome: Pontificia Università Gregoriana, 1988]).

3. It is possible, of course, to see Pilate as merely reiterating his mockery with slightly distinct phrases in two different contexts. Nonetheless, it still seems reasonable to ask if the later phrase is a mere repetition of the ideas contained in the earlier one or whether something significantly different is in view with the earlier declaration.

4. Panackel, *Idou o Anthrōpos*, 294.

5. C. K. Barrett, *The Gospel according to St. John: An Introduction with Commentary and Notes on the Greek Text* (New York: Macmillan, 1955), 541.

6. Köstenberger thus lists John 19:5 as "a possible instance of double entendre and Johannine irony" (Andreas J. Köstenberger, *A Theology of John's Gospel and Letters*, Biblical

The Story of the *Anthrōpos*

Before we explore options for understanding this deeper truth, it will help to appreciate that Pilate's *ecce homo* comes as the final piece in a larger motif John has been developing throughout the gospel. Although the term *anthrōpos* is rather nondescript, John uses it in distinct ways. Indeed, John employs the term far more than the other Gospel authors, frequently in narratives that are particularly important for establishing the identity of Jesus.[7]

The first uses of *anthrōpos* occur in the opening chapter, where the individual identified by the term is actually John the Baptist (1:6), the *anthrōpos* sent from God. Yet even here we catch a glimpse of the true significance of the *anthrōpos* in the Gospel since John the Baptist comes as witness to the one who will bring light and life to all *anthrōpōn* (1:4, 9). Then, at the end of the chapter, we find Jesus declaring to Nathaniel that he will someday see the angels of God ascending and descending on the "Son of Man [*anthrōpos*]" (1:51). This phrase introduces another important theme in the gospels, one that raises its own complex set of issues. For our purposes, though, we can set that discussion to the side. Although many have argued that Pilate's declaration should be understood in light of the Son of Man sayings in John,[8] several scholars have offered convincing arguments to the contrary.[9] Rather than seeing Pilate's *anthrōpos* as

---

Theology of the New Testament [Grand Rapids: Zondervan, 2009], 532). Scholars have long noted John's use of irony and rhetoric to convey messages in subtle ways. See esp. Earl J. Richard, "Expressions of Double Meaning and Their Function in the Gospel of John," *New Testament Studies* 31, no. 1 (1985): 96–112; George Johnston, "Ecce Homo: Irony in the Christology of the Fourth Evangelist," in *Glory of Christ in the New Testament: Studies in Christology in Memory of George Bradford Caird* (Oxford: Clarendon, 1987), 125–38; J. G. (Jan Gabriël) Van der Watt, "Double Entendre in the Gospel according to John," in *Theology and Christology in the Fourth Gospel: Essays by the Members of the SNTS Johannine Writings Seminar* (Leuven: Leuven University Press, 2005), 463–81.

    7. Panackel, *Idou o Anthrōpos*, 2.

    8. Panackel identifies the Son of Man interpretation as "the most representative" (ibid., 315).

    9. See, for example, Rudolf Schnackenburg, "Die Ecce-Homo-Szene und der Menschensohn," in *Jesus und der Menschensohn: Für Anton Vögtle* (Freiburg im Bresgau: Herder, 1975), 371–86; Dieter Böhler, "'Ecce Homo!' (Joh 19,5) ein Zitat aus dem Alten Testament," *Biblische*

an abbreviated form of "Son of Man," these scholars rightly contend that the *anthrōpos* in John has its own significance, albeit one that is clearly related to the Son of Man tradition. Thus, what is important for us to recognize here is that already in the first chapter of John we have a story about a significant individual who will descend from heaven, dwell in the flesh with God's people, bringing life and light to all *anthrōpoi*, and who bears the title "Son of Man."

This story unfolds even more clearly when we turn to those uses of *anthrōpos* that refer directly to Jesus, many of which raise questions about his identity.[10] In John 4, the Samaritan woman identifies Jesus as an *anthrōpos* who displayed remarkable knowledge (4:29). Although this could seem like a relatively innocuous use of the term, meant only to denote that she had spoken with "some guy," the intent of the story is to leave the reader wondering, "Who is this *anthrōpos*?" John returns explicitly to that question in the story of the man healed at the Pool of Bethesda. After being healed, the Pharisees interrogate him, wanting to know, "Who is this *anthrō-pos* . . . ?" (5:12). Then, while the people are debating his identity, the Pharisees challenge the officers for failing to arrest him, to which they responded, "No one ever spoke like this *anthrōpos*" (7:46 ESV). Shortly thereafter, Jesus declares that he is the *anthrōpos* who brings truth from God (8:40). In each instance, John uses *anthrōpos* in the context of questions about his identity while also continuing to associate him with the "light" and "life" he brings into the world.

These themes develop further in the later chapters of John. In front of the Pharisees, the man born blind declares that Jesus is the *anthrōpos* who restored his sight (9:11), which leads to a debate about whether this *anthrōpos* is really from God and whether it is possible for a sinful *anthrōpos* to perform such miraculous signs (9:16). The Pharisees challenge the man born blind, demanding that he declare this *anthrōpos* to be a sinner (9:24), and the story escalates in the

---

Zeitschrift 39, no. 1 (1995): 104–8; Andrew T. Lincoln, *The Gospel according to Saint John*, Black's New Testament Commentaries 4 (New York: Hendrickson, 2005), 466.

10. Panackel identifies eighteen instances of the term referring directly to Jesus (Panackel, *Idou o Anthrōpos*, 3). Some of those instances, however, are debatable (e.g., 3:27).

following chapter with the Jewish leaders threatening to stone Jesus for being an *anthrōpos* who claimed to be God, again raising the question of Jesus's identity with respect to the Father (10:33). All of this leads to the famous conclusion of chapter eleven, in which the Jewish leaders determine that this *anthrōpos* who has performed so many miraculous signs (11:47) needs to die in order that the whole nation might survive (11:50; see also 18:14). These latter verses are particularly important for our purposes since they also involve *anthrōpos* in a statement that functions as an unintentional witness to a greater theological truth.

This brings us to the climactic conclusion of John's story of the *anthrōpos*. Throughout the gospel, John's readers have wrestled alongside the people and their leaders to discern the identity of this *anthrōpos* who brings light and life to God's people. Finally, the Jewish leaders hand him over to Pilate, and he demands to know the accusations they have against this *anthrōpos* (18:29). Then, after Pilate makes several attempts to dodge the situation, he finally brings Jesus back before the Jewish leaders and utters the final *anthrōpos* in the gospel: "Behold the *anthrōpos*." *Ecce homo.*

The *Anthrōpos* as the New Adam

Given both this prolonged emphasis on the *anthrōpos* in John and indications in the text itself that suggest the phrase denotes more than it appears on the surface, scholars have proposed a number of different ways to understand the underlying meaning that John wants his readers to take away from this passage, the most common of which are these:

1. It is an abbreviation of *Son of Man*, and should be understood in light of that tradition in John and the rest of the Gospels.[11]

11. E.g., C. H. Dodd, *The Interpretation of the Fourth Gospel* (Cambridge: Cambridge University Press, 1953), 436; Barrett, *The Gospel according to St. John*, 541; Wayne A. Meeks, *The Prophet-King. Moses Traditions and the Johannine Christology* (Leiden: E. J. Brill, 1967), 69–72; Francis J. Moloney, *The Johannine Son of Man* (Rome: Libreria Ateneo Salesiano, 1976), 205–7.

2. It presents Jesus as a particular instance of broader Hellenistic myths about a *heavenly* or *primordial* man who descends from heaven into the lower reaches of the world.[12]

3. It points to Jesus's full humanity in a context that emphasizes his deity and thus the phrase is an indirect witness to the *hypostatic union* itself.[13]

4. It is an *intratextual reference* to some OT text which provides the appropriate background for understanding the reference.

The first three options have drawbacks. I have already mentioned some important criticisms of the Son of Man option. Although John refers to the Son of Man throughout the gospel, he does not use *anthrōpos* as shorthand for that concept elsewhere.[14] It thus seems unlikely that John would expect his readers to discern an appeal to the Son of Man tradition on the basis of this word alone. The second option, which involves seeing Jesus as the *heavenly/primordial anthrōpos*, might be viewed as conducive to the argument of this book since it would potentially present Jesus as the paradigm of true humanity. Yet Schnackenburg rightly points out that nothing in the context suggests that John has such Hellenistic myths in mind.[15] And although John clearly places a high value on the importance of the incarnation, Raymond Brown speaks for many biblical

---

12. For examples of this view, see Carl H. Kraeling, *Anthropos and Son of Man: A Study in the Religious Syncretism of the Hellenistic Orient*, Columbia University Oriental Studies, v. XXV (New York: Columbia University Press, 1927); Dodd, *The Interpretation of the Fourth Gospel*, 437; John Marsh, *The Gospel of St. John*, The Pelican Gospel Commentaries (Harmondsworth: Penguin, 1968), 607.

13. Rudolf Bultmann, *The Gospel of John: A Commentary*, trans. G. R. Beasley-Murray (Philadelphia: Westminster, 1971), 659; D. A. Carson, *The Gospel according to John* (Grand Rapids: Eerdmans, 1991), 598; George Eldon Ladd, *A Theology of the New Testament* (Grand Rapids: Eerdmans, 1993), 252; D. Moody Smith, *John* (Nashville: Abingdon, 1999), 34.

14. Lincoln, *The Gospel according to Saint John*, 466. Böhler thus contends that if John wanted to refer to the Son of Man here, he would have had to use the entire phrase υἱός τοῦ ἀνθρώου as he does elsewhere (Böhler, "Ecce Homo!," 105).

15. Rudolf Schnackenburg, *The Gospel according to St. John* (New York: Seabury, 1980), 3:451–452. See also Schnackenburg, "Die Ecce-Homo-Szene und der Menschensohn"; and G. Sevenster, "Remarks on the Humanity of Jesus in the Gospel and Letters of John," in *Studies in John: Presented to Professor Dr. J. N. Sevenster on the Occasion of His Seventieth Birthday* (Leiden: Brill, 1970), 185–93.

scholars when he says that such an interpretation "is unlikely."[16] John never uses *anthrōpos* to refer directly to the incarnation,[17] and many contend that the phrase focuses instead almost entirely on Christ's humanity.[18]

The fourth option has received the most attention in recent years, with scholars offering different suggestions for the appropriate background text.[19] Given the importance of establishing clear textual links in any intertextual allusion, though, Dieter Böhler rightly highlights the significance of 1 Samuel 9:17 as the one place in the Septuagint where we find the entire phrase used explicitly.[20] In that text, God reveals the one he has chosen to rule over Israel: "This is the man [*idou ho anthrōpos*] I spoke to you about; he will govern my people." Here God himself is the one who declares the *ecce homo*, using it to identify his chosen king. Read against this background, Pilate becomes the one who unintentionally performs the same function, making John 19:5 an anticipation of the later declaration in verse 14.[21]

John N. Suggit strengthens this association by arguing that the purple robe and the crown of thorns similarly have the function of unintentionally bearing witness to Christ as king.[22] Yet Suggit extends the reference further, looking back to the creation and fall narratives themselves. In the Targum of Pseudo-Jonathan, we find the following as a comment on Genesis 3:7: "And they knew they

---

16. Raymond E. Brown, *The Gospel according to John* (Garden City, N.Y: Doubleday, 1966), 876.

17. Schnackenburg, *The Gospel according to St. John*, 3.257.

18. See esp. Panackel, *Idou o Anthrōpos*.

19. For example, Meeks argues for Zech 6:12 (Meeks, *The Prophet-King*, 70–72), Raymond Brown suggests Num 24:17 (Brown, *The Gospel according to John*, 876), and Derrett proposes two texts in Isaiah (J. Duncan M. Derrett, "Ecce Homo Ruber [John 19,5 with Isaiah 1,18; 63,1–2]," *Bibbia E Oriente* 32, no. 4 [1990]: 215–29).

20. See also Lincoln, *The Gospel according to Saint John*, 466.

21. John N. Suggit, "Jesus the Gardener: The Atonement in the Fourth Gospel as Re-Creation," *Neotestamentica* 33, no. 1 (1999): 161–68. According to Suggit, John routinely uses the repetition of key concepts/phrases for emphasis, thus concluding that the two phrases here work together to emphasize that Jesus is the true (human) king promised by God.

22. Ibid., 334.

were naked, stripped of the clothing of onyx (i.e., translucent as a finger-nail) in which they had been created."[23] Suggit draws on other Jewish texts to point out that there is a long tradition of seeing Adam and Eve as clothed with glory in creation, which was then stripped from them at the fall. This provides the context for understanding the image of Jesus being "clothed in the purple robe which is the mark of the glory of man at his first creation."[24]

Suggit's reading thus provides a bridge between Böhler's emphasis on kingship in 1 Samuel 9:17 and the creation/fall narratives. In Genesis 1:26–28, we have God creating the *anthrōpos* in his image and giving him dominion over the rest of creation. Later, after God has made Adam and Eve the garments of skin, God declares, "Behold the man [*idou adam*]" (Gen 3:22 ESV). The Septuagint does not use *anthrōpos* here, possibly under the influence of the shift from *adam* as a generic term for humanity to *adam* as a proper name for the first human.[25] Litwa adds further support from an early Latin work, *The Life of Adam and Eve*. The phrase "Behold Adam!" (*ecce Adam*) occurs in this work as well (13:3), though in a different context. In this account, the phrase comes when God presents Adam before the angels, thus making the *ecce Adam* into "an extremely lofty statement highlighting Adam's divine glory which he had with God (to use Johannine language) 'before the world began' (John 17:5)."[26] Litwa contends that this narrative draws on the interplay in the creation narratives between *adam* as a proper name and as a generic term referring to all humanity, thus allowing us to read John 19 as directing our attention to the one who came as the true *anthrōpos*, the second Adam. Others likewise contend that the *ecce homo*, particularly in a context permeated with hints

---

23. John Westerdale Bowker, *The Targums and Rabbinic Literature; an Introduction to Jewish Interpretations of Scripture* (London: Cambridge University Press, 1969), 121.

24. Suggit, "John 19," 334.

25. Matthew David Litwa, "Behold Adam: A Reading of John 19:5," *Horizons in Biblical Theology* 32, no. 2 (2010): 129–43.

26. Ibid., 138.

of royal destiny, serves to echo these creational themes and identify Jesus as the new Adam.[27]

In the next section, we will see that the Adamic background of Pilate's claim becomes even more likely once we see the ways in which creation and new creation function as fundamental motifs throughout his gospel.[28] "Even as Pilate declares, 'Behold, the man,' on the story level, on the discourse level the implied author is signaling that Jesus is the center of creational renewal."[29]

Creation, New Creation, and the Outpouring of the Spirit

Although John does not use the explicit "new creation" language that we find in Paul (e.g., 2 Cor 5:17; Gal 6:15), many scholars argue that it is one of John's fundamental theological motifs.[30] John signals this interest in the prologue with "in the beginning" (1:1—*en archē*),

---

27. Others who identify a "new Adam" motif in John include John Fenton, *Passion According to John* (London: SPCK, 1961); J. L. Houlden, "John 19:5: 'And He Said to Them, Behold, the Man,'" *The Expository Times* 92, no. 5 (1981): 148–49; Gerald L. Borchert, *John 12–21: An Exegetical and Theological Exposition of Holy Scripture* (Nashville: Holman Reference, 2002), 250; Litwa, "Behold Adam"; Jeannine K. Brown, "Creation's Renewal in the Gospel of John," *The Catholic Biblical Quarterly* 72, no. 2 (2010): 275–90. Sevenster ultimately rejects this proposal because "the characteristic terminology" associated with this concept elsewhere in the New Testament, "that of Jesus, the perfect man, the new man, the second Adam," is missing here. (Sevenster, "Remarks on the Humanity of Jesus in the Gospel and Letters of John," 193). But he neglects the possibility that *anthrōpos* just is John's language for this.

28. Thus understood, the connection with the Adamic narratives probably qualifies as more of an "echo" of Genesis rather than a direct allusion (cf. Stanley E. Porter, "Allusions and Echoes," in *As It Is Written: Studying Paul's Use of Scripture*, ed. Stanley E. Porter and Christopher D. Stanley [Atlanta, GA: Society of Biblical Literature, 2008], 29–40; Richard B. Hays, *Echoes of Scripture in the Gospels* [Waco, TX: Baylor University Press, 2016]).

29. Brown, "Creation's Renewal in the Gospel of John," 281–82.

30. For example, Raymond Thomas Stamm, "Creation and Revelation in the Gospel of John," in *Search the Scriptures; New Testament Studies in Honor of Raymond T Stamm* (Leiden: Brill, 1969), 13–32; John Painter, "The Enigmatic Johannine Son of Man," in *Four Gospels 1992: Festschrift Frans Neirynck* (Louvain: Peeters, 1992), 1869–87; Paul Sevier Minear, *Christians and the New Creation: Genesis Motifs in the New Testament* (Louisville: Westminster John Knox, 1994); Jan A. du Rand, "The Creation Motif in the Fourth Gospel: Perspectives on Its Narratological Function within a Judaistic Background," in *Theology and Christology in the Fourth Gospel: Essays by the Members of the SNTS Johannine Writings Seminar* (Leuven: Leuven University Press, 2005), 21–46; Köstenberger, *A Theology of John's Gospel and Letters*, 336–54; Brown, "Creation's Renewal in the Gospel of John"; Mary L. Coloe, "Theological Reflections on Creation in the Gospel of John," *Pacifica* 24, no. 1 (2011): 1–12; Carlos Raúl Sosa Siliezar, *Creation Imagery in the Gospel of John* (London: T&T Clark, 2015).

a clear allusion to the creation account that continues with his emphasis on the "Word," which "evokes the recurring Genesis language of 'God said' in the creative activity."[31] The emphasis on "light" and "life" in the prologue and throughout the rest of the gospel suggests an echo of the creation account, indicating that the Word is not only the one through whom these things came into being at the beginning, but he is also the one who comes now to restore light and life to God's creation.[32] This creational motif continues throughout John, with some arguing that John structured the entire gospel around the creation narrative.[33] Although Sosa Siliezar rightly warns against pressing such structural arguments too far, he helpfully points out the ways in which John inserts clear allusions to creation at key points in his narrative.[34] By framing the narrative around the story of creation and new creation in this way, John prepares his readers to hear echoes of the Genesis narratives even in texts where the connections might not be as immediately apparent.[35] Scholars have thus explored the possibility that we might hear such echoes in the language of a "new birth" (3:3–5),[36] the seven signs,[37] references to the garden (18:1; 19:41) and Jesus as the gardener (20:15),[38] and

---

31. Brown, "Creation's Renewal in the Gospel of John," 277.

32. Köstenberger, *A Theology of John's Gospel and Letters*, 341–49. For good background on these terms, see Craig S. Keener, *The Gospel of John* (Grand Rapids: Baker Academic, 2010), 381–87. Siliezar Sosa notes that the prologue "evokes the Genesis account" with these terms even though he makes no direct reference (Siliezar, *Creation Imagery in the Gospel of John*, 48). Coloe argues that the very structure of the prologue is shaped by the creation narrative (Mary Coloe, "The Structure of the Johannine Prologue and Genesis 1," *Australian Biblical Review* 45 [1997]: 40–55).

33. See esp. Thomas Barrosse, "The Seven Days of the New Creation in St. John's Gospel," *The Catholic Biblical Quarterly* 21, no. 4 (1959): 507–16.

34. Sosa Siliezar, *Creation Imagery in the Gospel of John*.

35. Thus, although I find Sosa Siliezar's argument helpful for seeing how John makes strategic use of clear allusions to the creation narratives, he presses the argument too far when he contends that John intends for *only* these clear texts to be read against the background of the creation narratives. Sosa Siliezer himself seems to allude to something similar when he contends with reference to the prologue that John intentionally selected terms like *life* and *light* "in order to link creation to the story that follows" (ibid., 50).

36. Köstenberger, *A Theology of John's Gospel and Letters*, 350.

37. See esp. Brown, "Creation's Renewal in the Gospel of John," 286–88.

38. John N. Suggit, "Jesus the Gardener," 161–68; John Painter, "Earth Made Whole: John's Rereading of Genesis," in *Word, Theology and Community in John* (St Louis: Chalice, 2002), 65–84;

Jesus breathing the Spirit on the disciples (20:22), among others. It is also quite possible to read John's description of the resurrection as the inauguration of a new creation, which would mean that his narrative is framed in important ways by creation (prologue) and new creation (resurrection).[39]

All of this provides additional justification for hearing the *ecce homo* as connecting John's *anthrōpos* with Adam. Yet John also hints that this new *anthrōpos* transcends Adam in important ways. The first hint, and it is no more than a hint, comes in the opening verse of John: "in the beginning" (*en archē*). Although we have already noted that this phrase draws our attention back to the creation account, it actually presses further to a "beginning" that lies beyond creation. John thus prepares the reader to view the one who will come as the true *anthrōpos* whose story predates and transcends that of Adam himself.[40] We see a similar move with respect to the creational vocabulary in John. We have already seen that terms like *light* and *life* have strong connections to the creation narrative, but we might also say the same about *darkness, shines, all things, world*, and more, each of which echoes the creation narratives.[41] At the same time, though, each term gets subtly transformed as John locates them in the context of this new narrative, suggesting that these differences "already indicate that John is referring to something beyond creation."[42] In a subtle way, then, John offers a story in which Jesus brings about more than just a recapitulation of creation; instead, he presents Jesus as one who has come to take

Ruben Zimmerman, "Symbolic Communication between John and His Reader: The Garden Symbolism in John 19–20," in *Anatomies of Narrative Criticism: The Past, Present, and Futures of the Fourth Gospel as Literature*, ed. Tom Thatcher and Stephen D. Moore (Atlanta: Society of Biblical Literature, 2008), 221–35; Brown, "Creation's Renewal in the Gospel of John," 286–88.

39. Derek Tidball, "Completing the Circle: The Resurrection according to John," *Evangelical Review of Theology* 30, no. 2 (2006): 169–83; Craig R. Koester and R. Bieringer, eds., *The Resurrection of Jesus in the Gospel of John*, Wissenschaftliche Untersuchungen zum Neuen Testament 222 (Tübingen: Mohr Siebeck, 2008).

40. Köstenberger, *A Theology of John's Gospel and Letters*, 338.

41. See esp. Sosa Siliezar, *Creation Imagery in the Gospel of John*, 48–50. See also Painter, "Earth Made Whole," 67–68.

42. Sosa Siliezar, *Creation Imagery in the Gospel of John*, 49.

the story in new directions, fulfilling the work of creation in a way that transcends what we had before.[43]

However, the most important way that John presents Jesus as the new *anthrōpos* who transcends the creational state of humanity comes with John 20:22 and the outpouring of the Spirit.[44] That John intends this verse as an allusion to Genesis 2:7 is virtually undisputed.[45] Just as humanity came into existence when God breathed the Spirit into his creatures, John portrays Jesus as the one who inaugurates new humanity by breathing the Spirit into his followers. This was almost certainly intended as well to bring to mind texts that refer to the life-giving Spirit in new creation contexts (e.g., Isa 44:3–4; Ezek 36:25–28; 37:9; Joel 2:28–29). Breathing the *pneuma* into the disciples does not merely restore what humanity had at creation, though it does not do *less* than this, but it also signals the breath of new life as one of the fundamental realities of the new creation.[46] Coloe contends that the very structure of John points toward the new creation significance of Jesus bestowing the Spirit on the disciples.[47] She begins by arguing that the prologue is shaped

---

43. It is important to notice here that John never suggests that this should be viewed as introducing "a dichotomy between original creation and some sort of replacement for it" (Brown, "Creation's Renewal in the Gospel of John," 275). Instead, John paints a picture in which Jesus comes as the true *anthrōpos* who raises creation to new heights.

44. One of the more difficult questions involved in understanding the giving of the Spirit in John 20:22 is, of course, its relationship to the outpouring of the Spirit on Pentecost in Acts 2. Since that is not directly relevant to the argument of this chapter, though, we will not be dealing with that issue here.

45. Brown, "Creation's Renewal in the Gospel of John," 282. See esp. Sosa Siliezar, *Creation Imagery in the Gospel of John*, 153–73. Using the same verb as found in the LXX, John says that Jesus also "breathed" (ἐνεφύσησεν) on the disciples so that they might "receive the Holy Spirit" (John 20:22). Given that the verb used here is relatively unusual, it seems likely that John has chosen it intentionally to echo Gen 2:7 (Brown, "Creation's Renewal in the Gospel of John," 282).

46. If this is the case, it would suggest a close parallel with the way Paul talks about the Adam/Christ typology with respect to the Spirit. In 1 Cor 15:45, Paul describes Adam as becoming "a life-giving being (*psuchē*), language that more closely approximates what we find in Gen. 2:7, while Jesus, as the last Adam, became a life-giving Spirit (*pneuma*). Paul thus uses *pneuma* in a context that also alludes to Gen. 2:7 as a way of suggesting that Jesus's relationship to the Spirit both corresponds to and transcends what we have in creation.

47. Even though I am not entirely convinced by the structural aspects of Coloe's argument, she still offers suggestive insights into the ways in which John echoes the creation narratives at key points and how this prepares the reader to discern creational motifs throughout the narrative.

by the creation account, but with one important difference—it has no parallel to the Sabbath. To her this suggests that John views the work of creation as being unfinished in some way, thus deferring the true Sabbath until the completion of God's creational plans. According to Raymond Brown, this helps explain Jesus's declaration that his purpose is "to do the will of him who sent me and to finish his work" (4:34; cf. 5:36) as well as the idea that God himself is still working (5:17).[48] We might also point to the raising of Lazarus, which involves producing life simply by speaking, as an instance of Jesus performing actions that echo the creation narratives.[49] On this account, Jesus did not come merely to restore a work of creation that was already complete in the beginning and only needs to be returned to its original state. Instead, John presents creation as something that somehow needs to be completed in and through Jesus Christ.[50] Consequently, in John's narrative, when Jesus finally declares on the cross "it is finished" (19:30), that comes as a statement that he has now completed the "work" God started "in the beginning."[51] The final chapter of John thus "signifies the start of a new creation."[52] Jeannine Brown draws a similar conclusion by focusing on the dual reference to "the first day of the week" (John 20:1, 19), by which John signals "that re-creation begins at the resurrection of Jesus Christ."[53] She argues further that we see hints of this new creation emphasis in the fact that Jesus twice greets the disciples by saying, "Peace (*shalom*) be with you," and concludes that in the broader context this greeting signals that the eschatological *shalom*, the fullness of God's plans for his people, has finally arrived.

---

48. Brown, *The Gospel according to John*, 2.908. See also Lincoln, *The Gospel according to Saint John*, 498. See also Brown, "Creation's Renewal in the Gospel of John," 285–86.

49. Thanks to Nick Perrin for this suggestion.

50. Painter, "Earth Made Whole," 77–79.

51. "Given these narrative connections in John between chaps. 4–5 and 19:28, 30, along with the focus in Genesis 1 on the work of God in creation . . . it is probable that the Johannine notion that Jesus comes to complete God's work echoes the creation story of Genesis" (Brown, "Creation's Renewal in the Gospel of John," 285).

52. Coloe, "Theological Reflections on Creation," 6.

53. Brown, "Creation's Renewal in the Gospel of John," 283.

Throughout the gospel, we see further indications that the out-pouring of the Spirit in the new creation transcends that which was originally available. According to John, the Spirit not only descends on Jesus, but he also *remains*. For John, the relationship between Jesus and the Spirit seems both intimate and inseparable. Yet Jesus will later describe the relationship between the Spirit and his people in much the same way. The Spirit "lives" (remains) in them and will continue to be in them (14:17). Indeed, John makes the permanence of the Spirit's indwelling quite clear when he declares that the Spirit will "be with you forever" (14:16). The permanence of the Spirit in this new creation stands in sharp contrast to the Spirit's presence in creation in the beginning. Although we must affirm that the Spirit was essential to God's creational purposes, only with the new creation do we have assurance of the Spirit's permanent presence with God's people in his creation forever. We might even be able to say something similar about the epistemological effect of the Spirit's outpouring. According to Jesus, this is one of the primary benefits of receiving the Spirit. He is "the Spirit of truth" (14:17; 15:26) who allows us to see and know Jesus (14:19; 15:26) and who will teach us "all things" (14:26; cf. 16:13). Although we cannot state with any real confidence what humans might have known in some hypothetical universe in which we never moved beyond the original state of creation, it does not seem too much of a stretch to think that this language implies that the Spirit moves us into an epistemological state that transcends creational realities.

The outpouring of the Spirit also brings about a participation in the life of God and God's people that seems to transcend what we see in creation alone. Jesus proclaims, "On that day you will realize that I am in my Father, and you are in me, and I am in you" (14:20). The "day" Jesus refers to is the time in which he will pour out the Spirit on God's people. Thus, the disciples' experience of the Spirit is precisely that which allows them to experience the Son's intimate union with the Father through their union with the Son. We find a similar idea without the explicit reference to the Spirit a bit later when Jesus prays that the disciples might experience the same kind of unity that Jesus experiences with the Father (17:11, 21). Here again we must engage in a bit of speculation given the scarcity of our knowledge about humanity in the creational state. Yet, although Genesis 1–2 describes humanity as living in unbroken fellowship with God and one another, the language of John at least hints at something that goes further. It suggests a unity and intimacy of relationship that only comes when we receive the Spirit as a result of the work of the Son such that the Spirit *remains* with us and incorporates us into the life of God and his people in new ways.

Throughout the gospel, then, John combines an emphasis on Jesus as the new Adam with an equally strong focus on Jesus as the one who pours out God's Spirit on God's people in fulfillment of the new creation promises. Consequently, as the *anthrōpos* Jesus is not just the return of Adam, as though he merely reconstituted the state of humanity in the garden, but he is both the one who inaugurates the *new* creation in fulfillment of all that God intended from the beginning and the new Adam who is the eschatological culmination of God's plans for humanity, the telos that defines the essence of what it means to be human. In the next section, though, we will see that this portrayal of Jesus as the new Adam raises important questions about the relationship between nature and grace and the extent to which humanity is intelligible apart from the revelation we have in Jesus.

THE NATURAL, THE SUPERNATURAL, AND THE END(S) OF HUMANITY

The first half of the chapter focused on the way John portrays Jesus as the true *anthrōpos*, the one who comes to complete God's creational purposes for humanity. Yet we can understand the phrase "creational purposes" in two ways, and both ways have different implications for understanding the relationship between Christology and anthropology. According to one approach, the eschatological consummation of humanity that we see in Jesus Christ simply *is* the meaning of humanity. Humanity has no proper telos other than eschatological consummation. Consequently this finality is *intrinsic* to the definition of humanity. Even if humanity had not fallen into sin, God would still have brought humanity to this state of eschatological consummation in some way, and it is *only* from this perspective that we see what it means to be human.[54]

A second way of understanding God's "creational purposes," however, distinguishes between what humanity is in creation (*nature*) and what humanity becomes through eschatological consummation (*grace*). The first tells us what humanity is *essentially*—that which is necessary to be human rather than some other kind of creature—while the latter reveals the *elevation* of humanity through grace. This approach still affirms that God's eternal purposes for humanity have always included eschatological consummation, but it maintains that this is *extrinsic* to the definition of humanity since it is something that God gives to humanity as a work of grace in addition to the grace of creation.[55] Unless we make a clear distinction between what humanity is by nature and what humanity becomes by grace, we will inevitably confuse these two orders of existence with the tragic consequence that we undermine both the gratuity of grace and the intelligibility of human nature. Consequently, we must not try to understand humanity from the perspective of eschatological consummation alone; we must also discern what humanity is in its essence—namely, in abstraction from what God calls humanity to be through grace.

The intrinsic option clearly supports the project of christological anthropology, locating the meaning of humanity in the telos we see in Jesus. The extrinsic approach, though, raises important questions about whether christological anthropology is misconceived

---

54. Whether this means that the incarnation itself would have happened irrespective of the fall is a question we will take up in the next chapter.

55. Feingold objects to the label "extrinsicism" because it suggests a view in which there is no "real continuity or affinity between our nature and its supernatural destiny" (Lawrence Feingold, *The Natural Desire to See God According to St. Thomas and His Interpreters*, 2nd ed. [Ave Maria, FL: Sapientia, 2004], 339). I am using the label instead to denote any view denying that eschatological consummation is fundamental to the definition of humanity.

from the beginning. Instead of a single, grace-based perspective for understanding humanity, we need two distinct perspectives: the *natural* and the *supernatural*. In this part of the chapter, then, we will take a closer look at this discussion, starting with the nature/grace distinction itself and why many think the distinction is necessary to protect the gratuity of grace and the intelligibility of human nature. Then, we will consider a number of responses to those concerns and why an *intrinsic* account of the nature/grace relationship is still worth pursuing.

Extrinsicism and the Nature/Grace Distinction

The extrinsic view begins with a fundamental distinction between *nature* and *grace*. According to Edward Oakes, *nature* typically denotes "what is essential to something's identity."[56] To have a human *nature* is to have whatever it is that is essential for being human rather than some other kind of creature. *Grace*, on the other hand, refers to something that "is *not* essential, that is, what is *grat*uitous, to the entity in question but comes to it as something extra, unexpected, or not required for a nature to be a nature."[57] We should notice here that this distinction does not require us to think that *nature* exists independently of God. Since nothing exists apart from God's work in creating and preserving the universe, *nature* must be viewed as a gift as well. Yet once God brings something into existence, it has a certain set of properties essential for it being the kind of thing that it is, which includes a certain set of capacities that allows it to accomplish ends appropriate to those capacities. That is its nature. Grace involves anything that goes beyond these essential characteristics.

A second distinction involves the difference between *nature* and *supernature*. Theologians often reserve the *nature/grace* distinction for things directly related to the salvation of fallen human persons.

---

56. Edward T. Oakes, *A Theology of Grace in Six Controversies* (Grand Rapids: Eerdmans, 2016), 1.

57. Ibid., 1–2.

The *nature/supernature* distinction, on the other hand, uses the same essential/nonessential distinction to describe the elevation of humanity to its supernatural end.[58] Consequently, this distinction draws on the idea that even in creation there were some ends humans could achieve by their natural capacities (e.g., natural happiness) and others that required an additional gift of grace (e.g., beatific vision). No matter how well they use their natural capacities, humans cannot accomplish supernatural ends through natural means. Consequently, their natural state needs to be elevated to the supernatural state by an additional gift of grace to achieve God's ultimate intention for humanity.

Both of these distinctions lead directly to the idea of a "pure nature" (*natura pura*), which is the idea of humanity apart from this elevating grace. Although it is possible to understand the *natura pura* as being the state of Adam and Eve in the garden, people commonly affirm that God created *and* elevated humanity at the moment of creation. However, even if there was never a time when Adam and Eve existed apart from this elevated state, it remains possible to think about what it means to be human apart from the additional gift of grace. Indeed, on this account it is *necessary* to have some concept of their natural state if we are going to understand the supernatural state as truly gratuitous. Otherwise we would collapse nature into grace and begin to think of the supernatural end as something humans can accomplish through the exercise of their natural capacities alone. Consequently, the *natura pura* "is a theoretical construct, but it is nonetheless an important one to make."[59]

The distinction between nature and grace results in a corresponding distinction between the natural and supernatural *ends* of humanity. Since the natural state has its own properties and capacities, there must be some natural telos that corresponds to the outworking of those natural properties (e.g., natural happiness). The

---

58. Kenneth Oakes, "The Question of Nature and Grace in Karl Barth: Humanity as Creature and as Covenant-Partner," *Modern Theology* 23, no. 4 (2007): 598.

59. Neil Ormerod, "The Grace-Nature Distinction and the Construction of a Systematic Theology," *Theological Studies* 75, no. 3 (2014): 520.

supernatural state, on the other hand, has its own telos, one that cannot be achieved through the actualization of natural capacities but must be received as a gift of grace (e.g., beatific vision). Although it is hypothetically possible that God could have created humanity and left them in the natural state, without calling them to a higher, supernatural telos, in reality God has called all humans to this higher end. From the beginning, then, this supernatural end has been the true telos of humanity.[60] Nonetheless, the natural telos remains at least conceivable as the hypothetical telos that would have been ours if God had chosen not to call humanity to the supernatural telos. A more contentious question arises when we consider whether humanity still has a distinct natural telos even now. According to some of Thomas's interpreters, the answer is yes.[61] When Adam and Eve fell, losing the grace necessary for their supernatural telos, they remained human, retaining the natural properties and capacities essential to being human. Those capacities became disordered by the fall so that humanity was no longer able to use them rightly, but these capacities remain essential to being human, and they provide humans with natural ends that can still be pursued to some extent even now.

A final question involves whether humans have a natural desire for their supernatural telos.[62] Those holding to the extrinsic view tend to affirm the Aristotelian principle that desires must be proportionate to ends.[63] In other words, all creatures intrinsically (and often unconsciously) want to reach their telos, the fulfillment of their being. Consequently, if we have natural desires (i.e., desires that are intrinsically part of being human), they must correspond to natural ends (i.e., things we can achieve using natural capacities). This means that we cannot have a natural desire for a supernatural end. Although it is possible that we have a *natural* desire for God

---

60. This does not mean that all humans will actually attain this end any more than all acorns will grow into oak trees. A creature's telos is the finality of what it *can* become.

61. E.g., Feingold, *The Natural Desire to See God.*

62. Thomas Aquinas, *Summa Theologica* I-II, Q. 109, A. 2.

63. Aristotle, *Opera omnia*, 40:431b.

(i.e., knowing God to the extent possible by means of our natural capacities), we cannot have a natural desire for things like deification or the beatific vision. Instead, even the desire for such ends must come as an additional gift of grace.

Putting all of this together, then, we arrive at the conclusion that humanity must be viewed and understood from two perspectives. On the one hand, we have the natural order in which we see that which is essential for being human in distinction from other creatures. On the other hand, we have the supernatural order in which we see God's ultimate purposes for these human creatures. Yet, as we will see in the next section, this is precisely what the intrinsic view rejects.

Henri de Lubac and the Essentiality of the Supernatural

Henri de Lubac sparked a firestorm in the middle of the twentieth century with the publication of *Surnaturel*, a critique of the extrinsic position.[64] According to de Lubac, the extrinsic view portrays grace as something optional, an extraneous addition that humans could have done just fine without. This runs contrary to the picture of humanity we see throughout the Bible, especially in Christ, in which the supernatural telos defines the essence of humanity. Consequently, the extrinsic approach results in a view of humanity "cut off from his transcendent finality."[65] Instead, de Lubac argued, we should affirm that the supernatural telos of humanity "is inscribed upon my very being."[66] Joseph Ratzinger similarly argued that this supernatural telos is "the core of his very essence" such that "it constitutes what is

64. Henri de Lubac, *Surnaturel* (Paris: Aubier, 1946). See also the further clarification and expansion in Henri de Lubac, *The Mystery of the Supernatural*, trans. Rosemary Sheed (1967; repr., New York: Herder & Herder, 2015); Henri de Lubac, *Augustinianism and Modern Theology*, trans. Lancelot Sheppard (London: Chapman, 1969). Since much of the debate involved the proper interpretation of Thomas Aquinas among Roman Catholic theologians (see esp. Feingold, *The Natural Desire to See God*), it could easily be dismissed by Protestant thinkers as a largely intramural discussion. Nonetheless, we have already seen the discussion involves more fundamental questions about what it means to be human.

65. Lubac, *Augustinianism and Modern Theology*, 75.

66. Lubac, *The Mystery of the Supernatural*, 55.

deepest in man's being."[67] The extrinsic view, on the other hand, not only undermines a right understanding of the human person but of creation itself. As Healy summarizes, the extrinsic view "precluded the idea that the mystery of Jesus Christ reveals the original purpose and meaning of creation itself—reveals, we might say, the nature of nature."[68]

To understand the concern, let's return for a moment to the hypothetical situation in which God creates humanity in the garden but does not call them to the supernatural finality we see in Christ. In this state, according to the extrinsic view, humanity would have its own set of natural capacities that could be utilized according to natural desires in pursuit of a purely natural telos. Such humans could have gone on to live perfectly normal and happy lives completely apart from any grace other than that of the common grace by which God creates and preserves the universe. We do not even have an intrinsic desire for grace because that belongs to the supernatural order and does not correspond to our natural capacities. In such a situation, the additional gift of grace by which God elevates humanity begins to sound extraneous and optional. Humanity does not actually *need* this additional grace in any strong sense of the word since he has a perfectly legitimate order in which to live out his natural existence.[69]

According to de Lubac, then, the great weakness of the extrinsic view is that it devalues grace. Rather than viewing grace as essential to humanity, it comes across as an extraneous add-on to an already complete nature. De Lubac argues instead that humanity has only a single, supernatural telos. Although we do have "natural" capacities and desires, they are themselves oriented toward this supernatural

---

67. Joseph Ratzinger, *Eschatology, Death, and Eternal Life*, trans. Johann Auer (Washington, DC: Catholic University of America Press, 1988), 154–55.

68. Nicholas J. Healy, "Henri de Lubac on Nature and Grace: A Note on Some Recent Contributions to the Debate," *Communio* 35 (2008): 545.

69. Bear in mind that this hypothetical scenario does not describe *fallen* humanity. So this does not suggest that fallen humans could somehow achieve a good telos independently of grace, only that *unfallen* humans in such a state could pursue their true telos without any additional grace.

telos such that there can be no true happiness or fulfillment for humanity apart from eschatological consummation. Consequently, since even prelapsarian humanity was oriented toward eschatological consummation and had an innate desire for this finality, de Lubac cannot countenance any suggestion that God could have left Adam and Eve in that state without offering them the grace necessary for their only true telos. Rather than envisioning a state of natural bliss, de Lubac argues that only suffering would have resulted in such a situation since it would leave humanity with a desire—indeed their deepest desire—that would never be fulfilled.[70] He also rejects the possibility of a hypothetical universe in which humanity exists without a supernatural telos at all, contending that such creatures would not be *human*.[71] For de Lubac, we cannot define humanity in abstraction from the supernatural telos to which God has actually called us. Consequently, no matter how similar some other creatures might be in this hypothetical scenario, they would not count as human.

Nonetheless, de Lubac agrees that we need to distinguish nature from grace if we are going to have any understanding of true gratuity, even recognizing the value of the *natura pura* concept to some degree.[72] According to him, though, the *natura pura* is an abstract postulate that is only necessary *retrospectively*. Once we see the reality of the human person in the light of grace, we postulate the *natura pura* as a concept necessary for understanding the gratuity of this supernatural state. Since it remains merely a concept, though, it does not require affirming a natural telos that remains in some way achievable by humans today.[73] Neither should it serve as the starting point for abstract speculations about the nature of humanity.

---

70. Lubac, *The Mystery of the Supernatural*, 69–70.

71. Ibid., 54.

72. According to Grumett, de Lubac affirms at least four benefits of continuing to affirm the *natura pura* (David Grumett, "De Lubac, Grace, and the Pure Nature Debate," *Modern Theology* 31, no. 1 [2015]: 132).

73. Susan Wood, "The Nature-Grace Problematic within Henri de Lubac's Christological Paradox," *Communio* 19 (1992): 394–95.

For de Lubac, then, we have to understand humanity in light of the fact that God actually calls us to a supernatural telos—namely, one that can only be received as a gift of grace—and that telos determines the essence of what it means to be human. But he contends that this remains a truly gratuitous gift because God was not obligated to create the particular universe he did, one in which eschatological consummation is the only true telos of the human person. Yet this relationship between grace and obligation leads us into the first major objection.

On Divine Obligations

Although de Lubac's argument offers a notably different perspective than the extrinsic account, critics worry that it suffers from at least two fatal flaws; the first of which is that it undermines the gratuity of grace. This issue arises from de Lubac's argument that human persons have only a single telos and, consequently, that they have an innate desire for that telos. To be human is to be oriented toward eschatological consummation. If humans are intrinsically oriented toward eschatological consummation, however, it begins to sound as though God would somehow be obligated to provide this telos for humanity. As I mentioned in the previous section, the only alternative is to imagine that God could create humans for the sole purpose of eschatological consummation and then withhold from them the grace necessary to achieve that telos. This would result in a humanity perpetually frustrated by its inability to fulfill its own finality, and it seems unfitting for a good and gracious God to leave his own creatures without even the possibility of attaining the telos for which he himself created them. God thus seems to have an obligation to his creatures (*debitum naturae*), one that he established by instilling in them a telos they cannot achieve through the exercise of their natural capacities. Yet if God is obligated to provide eschatological consummation, it no longer appears to be grace since people commonly maintain that grace cannot be obligated.

Thus, we end up with an argument that looks something like the following:

1. God has called humans to a supernatural telos.
2. This supernatural telos can only be reached as a gift of God's grace.
3. Humanity would be in a state of perpetual frustration if God called humans to only a single telos and then withheld the grace necessary to achieve that telos.
4. It is contrary to God's goodness to leave humanity in a state of perpetual frustration.
5. Consequently, if humanity has only a single telos, then God is obligated to provide the grace necessary to achieve that telos.
6. Grace cannot be obligated.
7. Therefore, the supernatural telos cannot be humanity's only telos.

The first proposition seems reasonably secure unless we are willing to reject either a teleological account of humanity or the idea that humans have a supernatural telos. However, although such a teleological account creates problems for those operating from more naturalistic perspectives, presupposing some form of teleology (i.e., created for and oriented toward some purpose) in a Christian view of the human person seems reasonably safe.

The second proposition seems likewise beyond dispute since the alternative is to envision eschatological consummation as something humans could achieve through the exercise of their natural capacities alone.

We could push back on the third proposition by arguing that no frustration would result from having a telos that cannot be achieved. Yet that would be a difficult contention to support. If humanity has a desire for this telos, then the perpetual frustration of that desire would result at least in the suffering of perpetually unfulfilled longing. Even if we reject the idea that humans innately desire their eschatological telos, they are still perpetually frustrated in achieving that telos. With or without the psychological dimension, then, the frustration remains. If that is the case, then the worry about God's goodness in the fourth proposition also remains. It runs contrary to the idea that God is good and wants the best for his creatures to think that he would create them for a particular telos and then make it impossible to achieve that telos.

The fifth proposition requires a bit more reflection since many will be inclined to reject the idea that God can in any way be obligated to his creatures. Even if God created humanity with an intrinsic orientation toward eschatological consummation, we might maintain that this does not mean he now owes it to his creatures to provide what is necessary for achieving that end. If he does, that is simply a gift of grace that goes beyond the gift of creation. Imagine, for example, that I create a robot for the sole purpose of carving pumpkins, and I instill into the robot all of the capacities necessary for carrying out that purpose and no other. Then, when the robot is ready, I decide not to provide any pumpkins, depriving the robot of the gracious gift necessary for it to carry out its purpose. Would this create some kind of injustice? It is difficult to see why it would. People might wonder why I would waste my time building the robot if I had no intention of allowing it to carry out its intended function, but there is no good reason to think that I am somehow obligated to do so. Even if I eventually discard the robot because it is not carrying out its pumpkin-carving purpose, it is still well within my rights to do so.

Although I think it is probably right to argue that God cannot be obligated to his creatures simply in virtue of having created them, the reference to God's goodness earlier suggests that there is another form of the obligation argument that may be more difficult to address. Maybe the relevant obligation is something that obtains between God and his own nature and purposes. If God created humans for a particular telos, it would seem to be part of his own plan that they (or at least some of them) achieve this telos. While this might not create an obligation between God and the *creature*, we might argue that God is obligated to *himself* to carry out his own plans. The only alternative seems to be that God could abandon his own purposes, which would open the door to all kinds of worries about God's faithfulness and reliability. Yet if God is in any way obligated to provide the supernatural telos, even if the obligation is to himself, we still seem to have the problem that the supernatural telos of the human person is no longer a gift of grace but the demand that comes from obligation.

Consequently, it would seem that the only viable option remaining is to critique the sixth proposition and affirm that grace can in fact be obligated in some sense. Instead, we might argue that it is at least conceivable for something to be both obligated and grace-based at the same time. De Lubac does this by describing the relationship between nature and grace as "singular and paradoxical."[74] Yet Jenson raises a legitimate concern here: "Moreover, to deal with the fundamental relation of nature and supernature, de Lubac finally takes refuge in 'paradox', always a danger sign."[75] Unless we want to avoid the suspicion that we are affirming nonsense, we need to provide at least some reason for thinking that the contradiction is only apparent.

Oakes addresses this concern by pointing out that the same paradox accompanies any expression of love, which lies at the heart of grace. "For if love is the essence of grace, then something peculiar enters the picture here: we all *need* love, but love is not love if it has been coerced out of the supposed lover. . . . What is the value of love if it is not freely given? Thus the paradox: we need love but cannot demand it. Love is love precisely because it is a gift freely—that is gratuitously—given."[76] Consider, for example, the relationship between a parent and a child. We all know that there is

74. Lubac, *The Mystery of the Supernatural*, 133.

75. Robert W. Jenson, *Systematic Theology* (New York: Oxford University Press, 1997), 2:67.

76. Oakes, *A Theology of Grace in Six Controversies*, 3.

an important sense in which the child needs love if she is to flourish as a human person. So, on the one hand, we want to say that the parent is in some way obligated to provide the love this child so desperately needs. Indeed, when we encounter situations in which the parent fails to provide the requisite love (e.g., situations involving child neglect), we rightly experience indignation. Something unjust has occurred when a parent withholds love from a child. At the same time, though, we also have a strong intuition that true love cannot be obligated. Although my children need love, I am fairly certain they would not want to hear that I love them because I feel I am obligated to do so. The same holds true for spousal love. Even though I made a vow on my wedding day to love my wife always, creating a form of obligation, I can only imagine how she would respond if I gathered her into my arms, gazed into her eyes, and told her that I loved her out of a deep sense of obligation. In various other circumstances, then, we have intuitions that lead us to conclude that the same act can be both obligated and grace-based at the same time.

It may be, however, that we can find an easier resolution in the covenantal idea that God can graciously obligate himself to perform some action. All God's covenants find their basis in grace since there is nothing that could obligate God to enter into those covenantal arrangements in the first place. Having done so, however, God takes to himself the obligation to carry out the terms of the covenant. Consequently, there is a sense in which we can say that God is obligated to provide the blessings of the covenant in response to the people's faithfulness. At the same time, though, we must also say that the blessings are an expression of grace since the covenant itself is grounded in grace. If we follow this path, we end up affirming that the obligation to provide the grace necessary for humanity's supernatural telos arose as part of the same eternal act in which God determined to create humanity for that telos. As Robert Jenson points out, the obligation worry only arises if we imagine that we must ascribe some kind of logical or chronological priority to the creation of humanity and view the supernatural telos as something subsequently added to that creational state.[77] If we maintain instead that the act of creation just is the ordination to eschatological consummation, then we leave no conceptual space for any kind of *debitum naturam* and, consequently, for the gratuity argument itself.

The Intelligibility of Human Nature

A second objection centers on the intelligibility of human nature.[78] Critiquing Balthasar in particular, Steven Long argues that the intrinsic approach robs nature of having any "significant ontological density and intelligibility in its own right."[79] In other words, by arguing that humanity is intrinsically oriented toward its supernatural telos, this view seems to deny that we can understand what it means to be human in any way apart from some kind of natural perspective. This not only undermines the legitimacy of nontheological perspectives on humanity (e.g., the sciences), impairing our ability to engage in interdisciplinary dialogue, public theology, and apologetics, but it renders the incarnation itself incoherent. According to Long, the logic of Nicaea depends on our ability to discern that the Son became human, which requires that we know at least something of what it means to be human *before* the incarnation. "To hold that human nature is not intelligible in its species in distinction from grace is to make the Nicene doctrine the doctrine that, in Christ, God assumes a 'who knows what?'"[80]

The extrinsic view, on the other hand, maintains that human

77. Jenson, *Systematic Theology*, 2:68. Lossky argues for something similar from the Eastern tradition, "knows nothing of pure nature to which grace is added as a supernatural gift. For it, there is no actual or 'normal' state, since grace is implied in the act of creation itself" (Vladimir Lossky, *The Mystical Theology of the Eastern Church* [Crestwood, NY: St. Vladimir's Seminary Press, 1976], 101).

78. Steven A. Long, *Natura Pura: On the Recovery of Nature in the Doctrine of Grace*, Moral Philosophy and Moral Theology (New York: Fordham University Press, 2010); Bernard Mulcahy, *Aquinas's Notion of Pure Nature and the Christian Integralism of Henri de Lubac: Not Everything Is Grace* (New York: Peter Lang, 2011).

79. Long, *Natura Pura*, 53.

80. Ibid., 74.

nature is fully intelligible in its own right. Although the existential condition of humanity changes from one mode of existence to another, *"pure nature* in the sense of *all that defines human nature as such*—is found in all who have the nature."[81] Even fallen humanity remains fully human with the requisite, albeit disordered, properties and capacities, and is thus available to study from nontheological perspectives. This does not mean, however, that Long envisions the natural order as some kind of "secular" realm entirely denuded of God's presence. Instead, he contends that human nature is still "essentially ordered to God" but only *"by its own character*—that is, as *naturally* ordered to God."[82] In other words, even in a state of pure nature, humans would still have desired to know God to the extent possible through the use of their natural capacities alone. They remain creatures made by the Creator for a purpose. Yet this retains the emphasis on the natural necessary to avoid the concerns raised by the intrinsic approach. Thus, Long commends de Lubac for understanding "the critical importance of teleology," but he faults him for "a deficient confidence in *natural* teleology."[83]

Suppose, for example, that I build a pergola in my backyard. That pergola would have certain properties that correspond to "natural" purposes like providing shade, adding beauty, and showing off my barely existent carpentry skills. Each of those is fully available to analysis from anyone who walks through the backyard. Yet none of them reveals the true telos of the pergola: the joy of my wife. I guarantee that the *only* reason I would spend time building a pergola in the backyard is as a gift for my wife; so you can only understand the true meaning of the pergola from this perspective. Nonetheless, it remains a *pergola*, which is a concept that is abstractly intelligible in its own right irrespective of this higher teleology. That is how we recognize it as a pergola. Additionally, I could discuss the pergola with someone who is an expert in pergola construction, and

---

81. Ibid., 81.
82. Ibid., 45.
83. Ibid., 203. Emphasis added.

I would certainly have much to learn from such an expert even if he knew nothing of the pergola's higher telos. So the pergola remains abstractly intelligible in its *natura pura* even if its true meaning is only seen in light of its higher telos.

Even if this is true, however, it is not clear that we need an extrinsic view to make this argument work. For the charge to stick, an intrinsic account would have to maintain that human persons cannot be understood *in any way* from natural perspectives. Yet such a conclusion is unwarranted. De Lubac does not reject the idea that we have natural properties and capacities that are oriented toward natural ends and can be understood as such, at least to an extent. Instead, he argues that these must be understood as *penultimate* realities meant to serve the higher telos of eschatological consummation.[84] For example, sight is a natural capacity of the human person, something that can be studied and largely understood in natural terms. Yet, it is entirely possible to maintain that the true telos of human vision is seeing God's glory in and through his creation, preeminently in his people. The capacity may have a penultimate finality (e.g., seeing beauty), but that does not change the fact that it is intrinsically oriented toward a higher finality (e.g., seeing God's beauty). Nontheological disciplines will never be able to study the latter since it involves a supernatural end that transcends their disciplinary reach, but that does not prevent them from having much to say about the utilization of that capacity to accomplish natural ends. Consequently, as we will see in chapter 5, the intrinsic view does not undermine the legitimacy of nontheological perspectives on the human person or the value of interdisciplinary dialogue, though it will shape that dialogue in particular ways.

More importantly, the intrinsic view challenges the presupposition that even the "natural" properties and capacities of the human person can be understood rightly in abstraction from the supernatural telos. Return again to the pergola analogy. Once someone knows the true telos of the pergola, she begins to see even the

---

84. See esp. Healy, "Henri de Lubac on Nature and Grace."

"natural" properties of the pergola differently, understanding why I designed it to shade certain areas of the garden and not others (the places where she likes to sit), and why it's probably not the most attractive pergola in the world (a gift from my own, unskilled hands). Properties of the pergola that seem available to analysis from a purely "natural" perspective turn out to be dependent on the higher telos in ways that are not immediately obvious. Keith Johnson argues that a similar dynamic is at work in the theology of Karl Barth. As we will see in chapter 5, Barth likewise affirms that the relationship between nature and grace "can be known only retrospectively in the light of knowledge of the saving work of Jesus Christ on the cross."[85] This retrospective movement allows for nature to be "abstractly intelligible" to a degree, but it insists that everything we think we know about humanity must be reinterpreted in light of the supernatural telos we see in Jesus.

This provides resources as well for responding to Steven Long's worries about the incarnation. No one denies that we can know at least some things about humanity independently of knowing humanity's supernatural telos. That would be absurd since it would mean that non-Christians have no concept of what it means to be human. D. Stephen Long thus acknowledges, "Certainly we cannot make sense of the incarnation if we cannot distinguish between the nature of a human being and that of a donkey."[86] Yet he goes on to note that Nicaea did not simply adopt preconceived ideas about humanity and then apply them to the humanity we see in Jesus. Instead, they allowed their understanding of humanity to be reshaped and transformed by this climactically new revelation of what it means to be human. The revelation was not only of "vere Deus," but also of "vere homo."[87]

85. Keith L. Johnson, "When Nature Presupposes Grace: A Response to Thomas Joseph White, O.P.," *Pro Ecclesia* 20, no. 3 (2011): 280.

86. D. Stephen Long, "Natura Pura: On the Recovery of Nature in the Doctrine of Grace," *Modern Theology* 27, no. 4 (2011): 697.

87. Ibid.

CONCLUSION

The Gospel of John offered the starting point for our first study of the biblical and theological issues involved in developing a christological anthropology. Beginning with Pilate's *ecce homo*, we surveyed the story of the *anthrо̄pos* in the gospel. On one level John's Gospel tells a story in which various people wrestle with the identity of the amazing individual. At a deeper level, though, John subtly directs our attention to the story of Adam, presenting Jesus as the new Adam who comes to fulfill God's creation purposes for humanity. That reading of John's narrative receives support from the many ways in which John uses creational imagery throughout the gospel, allowing his readers to discern echoes of creation in unlikely places. Finally, I argued as well that the outpouring of the Spirit in John 20:22 likewise connects Jesus and Adam, again portraying Jesus as the one in whom we see the inauguration of new creation realities.

Through all of this, a critical aspect of the story is the fact that the new creation we have in Jesus transcends the original creation in significant ways. In Jesus we see not just the *renewal* of creation but also its *consummation*. Consequently, this is the framework through which we need to understand the anthropological significance of the *ecce homo*. In Jesus we see the eschatological fulfillment of God's creational purposes for his people.

Yet our discussion of John's *anthrо̄pos* story quickly involved us in the complex debate about the proper way to understand the relationship between nature and grace. According to a prominent strand of modern Catholic theology, we must maintain a clear distinction between these two orders of being; otherwise we will inevitably undermine the gratuity of grace and the intelligibility of human nature. As important as these concerns might be, however, I have argued that the intrinsic account has the resources to address them. As we move into the following chapters, then, we will continue to explore the issues involved in thinking that the supernatural telos we see in Jesus simply *is* the definition of what it means to be truly human.

CHAPTER 2

First Adam, Last Adam, and the Necessity of the Incarnation

———•———

TWO FIGURES HAVE CONSISTENTLY dominated discussions about what it means to be human: Adam and Christ.[1] One stands at the beginning of humanity's story, made in the image of God and untainted by the corrupting power of sin. The other rises at the climax of redemption history, the "last Adam" who inaugurates new humanity. The first offers the possibility of glimpsing the intentions God had for humanity from the beginning; the second depicts humanity through the lens of God's own Son. One suggests that the best way to understand ourselves is by starting at the *beginning* of the story, focusing on what we learn about humanity before sin entered the picture. The other implies that some stories must be read with the *end* in mind, allowing that to inform how we understand what came earlier. To a considerable degree, then, every theological anthropology receives its decisive shape from the way it conceives of Adam and Christ's roles in our understanding of humanity. This is oversimplified, of course. Theologians understand the relationship between Adam and Christ in a variety of ways, each of which has the potential to nuance how we approach theological anthropology. Nonetheless, this remains a seminal issue in theological anthropology and one

---

1. Throughout this chapter, I will be presupposing the historicity of Adam, and I will not be addressing the complex debates surrounding the question or whether "Adam" can refer to a representative community of humans rather than just a single individual. Whether we would need to draw different conclusions in the chapter based on different presuppositions about the historicity of Adam is something I will leave to others to work out.

First Adam, Last Adam, and the Necessity of the Incarnation | 69

that must be addressed by anyone seeking to develop a christological anthropology.

This chapter will approach it through the lens of the Adam/Christ parallel that Paul develops in 1 Corinthians 15.[2] Although this is not the only place Paul addresses the relationship between these two pivotal figures,[3] it warrants particular attention for two reasons. First, this is the earliest instance in which Paul develops the parallel at length, giving us the opportunity to see how he first presented the issue. Second, unlike Paul's other extended discussion (Rom 5:12–21), which focuses entirely on understanding Adam and Christ in light of sin and redemption, we will see that 1 Corinthians 15 has a broader frame of reference, dealing with the parallel from the perspective of creation as well as sin. Consequently, Paul suggests in this passage that Jesus's status as the "second Adam" comes as the eschatological fulfillment of God's plans for creation and not just his response to the fall.

Yet this immediately raises an important question. If Jesus is the "second Adam" with respect to creation and not just redemption, does this not suggest that the Son would have become incarnate even if humans had not fallen into sin? This kind of *incarnation anyway* argument has generated increased attention in recent years, and it has clear implications for christological anthropology since it locates the incarnation at the heart of God's creational purposes for humanity. So we will focus our attention in the second half of the chapter on understanding the nature of these arguments and what bearing they have on theological anthropology.

With this debate, it might seem as though we are merely rehearsing issues addressed in the prior chapter. There too we encountered questions about the extent to which eschatological consummation is intrinsic to God's plans for creation. And indeed, there is some correlation between those who affirm that creation has a single telos

---

2. I will be using the generic term "parallel" to describe the relationship between Adam and Christ rather than a more specific term like "typology" to avoid biasing the discussion by presupposing a particular kind of relationship from the outset.

3. E.g., 2 Cor 5:14–15; Rom 1:18–32; Phil 2:5–11; Rom 7:7–8:3.

and those who maintain that the incarnation would have happened even if humanity had not fallen into sin (e.g., Duns Scotus and Barth). Yet we need to recognize that these are distinct questions. As we will see later in this chapter, it is entirely possible to affirm that eschatological consummation is intrinsic to God's purposes for creation and still deny that the incarnation would have happened irrespective of sin. Consequently, the conclusions drawn in the prior chapter do not necessarily determine the appropriate answer to the question of this chapter.

ESCHATOLOGICAL EMBODIMENT:
ADAM AND CHRIST IN 1 CORINTHIANS 15

Paul introduces the Adam/Christ parallel in one of his earliest letters, referring to it twice in 1 Corinthians 15 as part of his discussion of the resurrection (15:22, 45). In the broader argument of the chapter, Paul is responding to those who deny the reality of the resurrection, apparently stemming from their low view of the physical body. Convinced of the fully spiritual nature of salvation, they cannot believe that something as crass as the physical body could be central to the eschatological state of human persons.[4] Consequently, they may even have affirmed something like a spiritual resurrection which has already taken place, explaining the elements of an over-realized eschatology that crop up throughout the letter.[5] To all of this, Paul responds with a decisive, "No!" The resurrection of the body is central to the Christian faith as the outworking of God's purposes for his people.

When Paul introduces the Adam/Christ parallel in this passage, then, he is not merely speculating on the relationship of these two figures or on the broader questions of how anthropology relates to Christology or protology to eschatology; instead, he presents

---

4. James D. G. Dunn, "1 Corinthians 15:45—Last Adam, Life-Giving Spirit," in *Christ and Spirit in the New Testament: Studies in Honour of Charles Franscis Digby Moule*, ed. Barnabas Lindars and Stephen S. Smalley (Cambridge: Cambridge University Press, 1973), 127–41.

5. Anthony C. Thiselton, "Realized Eschatology at Corinth," *New Testament Studies* 24, no. 4 (1978): 510–26.

the Adam/Christ parallel as a framework for understanding the fundamental significance of the resurrection in the overall story of humanity and the gospel.[6] Nonetheless, the way Paul wields the Adam/Christ parallel in the context of this argument has broader implications. Although we cannot hope to address everything in this complex passage, we can try to understand how Paul applies the Adam/Christ framework to the resurrection issue, and what this suggests about the relationship between these two pivotal figures and their significance for anthropology as a whole.

The Man from Heaven

Before we dive into the particulars of the Adam/Christ parallel in this passage, we need to address an issue that arises toward the end of the chapter. Paul twice refers to Jesus as "the heavenly man" (15:48, 49), which many take as references to a prevailing myth in the broader culture about a primordial or archetypal being who exists eternally and serves as the template for humanity.[7] If this is the case, then Paul presents Jesus as the embodiment of this eternal archetype, making this a parallel between time (Adam) and eternity (heavenly man) more than a parallel between two historic individuals. Although this idea was popular in earlier scholarship, more recently scholars have questioned both the prevalence of the idea during Paul's time and the legitimacy of claiming that it shaped Paul's thinking in any meaningful way.[8] It also fits poorly with Paul's earlier argument that "the spiritual" must come *after* "the natural" (15:46–47), a parallel that directly informs the distinction between the heavenly and the earthly in the following verses. One could

---

6. Fee thus comments on "how narrowly focused" all of the Adam/Christ passages are in Paul (Gordon D. Fee, *Pauline Christology: An Exegetical-Theological Study* [Peabody, MA: Hendrickson, 2007], 517).

7. See esp. Oscar Cullmann, *The Christology of the New Testament* (Philadelphia: Westminster, 1959).

8. E.g., Robin Scroggs, *The Last Adam: A Study in Pauline Anthropology* (Philadelphia: Fortress, 1966); Dunn, "1 Corinthians 15"; Anthony C. Thiselton, *The First Epistle to the Corinthians: A Commentary on the Greek Text*, The New International Greek Testament Commentary (Grand Rapids: Eerdmans, 2000), 1280.

refute this by arguing that "after" here refers only to the sequence in which they appear in the historical order, contending that the heavenly man is actually *first* in the order of God's eternal plans. But a more important criticism comes from Fee's argument that "from heaven" should be understood as a *qualitative* claim rather than one about *origin*.[9] In verse 48, Paul refers to other Christians as having a heavenly mode of existence, which clearly suggests that the reference to heaven in this context denotes a *kind* of existence we live rather than the *origin* of particular persons; otherwise, he would be saying that we too originate eternally in heaven. For a variety of reasons, then, we should reject the idea that Paul is referring here to some kind of primordial man myth.[10]

Yet that leaves us with a lingering question about the background for Paul's Adam/Christ parallel. For those of us who have grown up hearing stories about Adam and Eve in the garden, Paul's appeal to Adam comes as no great surprise. It seems perfectly reasonable to us that he would be intrigued by this figure from the beginning of humanity and the obvious parallels between him and Jesus Christ, the two figures who demarcate pivotal moments of human history. For many, though, this reference to Adam comes as a bit of a surprise given that Adam plays a relatively small role in the Bible. After his big splash in the first five chapters of Genesis, Adam appears in the Old Testament only in a single genealogy (1 Chr 1:1), with a possible reference in one other text (Hos 6:7).[11] Even in the New Testament, the only explicit references to Adam outside of Paul's letters are genealogical (Luke 3:38; Jude 14). Throughout most of the Bible, then, Adam's only explicit role is as the first human.[12] Other

---

9. Gordon D. Fee, *The First Epistle to the Corinthians*, The New International Commentary on the New Testament (Grand Rapids: Eerdmans, 1987), 792.

10. See esp. G. Sevenster, "Remarks on the Humanity of Jesus in the Gospel and Letters of John," in *Studies in John: Presented to Professor Dr. J. N. Sevenster on the Occasion of His Seventieth Birthday* (Leiden: Brill, 1970), 185–93; Rudolf Schnackenburg, "Die Ecce-Homo-Szene und der Menschensohn," in *Jesus und der Menschensohn: Für Anton Vögtle* (Freiburg im Bresgau: Herder, 1975).

11. Interpreters debate whether "Adam" in this passage refers to a person or a location.

12. L. Joseph Kreitzer, "Christ and Second Adam in Paul," *Communio Viatorum* 32, no. 1–2 (1989): 55.

biblical authors show little interest in developing any theological significance beyond this basic fact.

Rather than appealing to myths about a primordial human, though, contemporary scholarship appeals more commonly to Paul's Jewish context. Many of the Jewish writings written around the time of Paul suggest a growing interest in Adam and his theological significance.[13] Some of those texts focus on the glorious status of Adam in creation, often portraying Adam as having superhuman qualities.[14] Others reflect on Adam's role in the fall, identifying him as the one responsible for the subsequent condition of humanity.[15] Both perspectives, of course, find support in the Genesis narratives, though it is only in this post–Old Testament period that thinkers began to reflect seriously on the implications of those narratives. As interesting as all of this is, we need to be careful with this material, much of which was written after Paul, and it is notoriously difficult to establish whether Paul was aware of the rest.[16] Nonetheless, as Scroggs comments, "Speculation about Adam covers the entire period."[17] Consequently, these parallels demonstrate that when Paul begins reflecting on the theological significance of Adam, he is probably not creating his ideas *de novo*. Instead, he is operating in a theological milieu in which it appears that a number of thinkers have had their attention grabbed by this figure who stands at the beginning of the story and whose actions had such ramifications for all who followed. Unlike these other thinkers, however, Paul

---

Fee notes that even Paul's letters do not prepare us for this move: "There is nothing earlier in this letter or in 1–2 Thessalonians that quite prepares us for the sudden mention of Adam in this passage" (Fee, *Pauline Christology*, 516).

13. Scroggs, *The Last Adam*, 16–58; Kreitzer, "Christ and Second Adam in Paul," 59–61.

14. See esp. John R. Levison, *Portraits of Adam in Early Judaism: From Sirach to 2 Baruch* (Sheffield: JSOT Press, 1988).

15. E.g., 4 Ezra 3:7; 2 Baruch 17:3; 19:8; 48:24; 54:15, 19; Sir 40:1–11. Sir 25:24 similarly emphasizes the consequences of the fall for the rest of humanity, though it focuses on Eve as the one responsible.

16. Thiselton, *The First Epistle to the Corinthians*, 1227.

17. Scroggs, *The Last Adam*, 17. Dunn thus concludes that even if we cannot establish direct connections, we should affirm that Paul was at least "aware" of such material (Dunn, "1 Corinthians 15," 135).

does not focus on *Adam* as the exemplar of humanity, directing our attention instead to the *second Adam*.

The Adams' Families (1 Cor 15:20–23)

In the first of two Adam/Christ discussions in 1 Corinthians 15, Paul focuses on the reality of death and the importance of the resurrection. In the process, Paul makes several important moves. First, he locates the parallel in the context of Adam as the head of *fallen* humanity. Second, he identifies Jesus as the "firstfruits" [*aparchē*] of the resurrection, a term that emphasizes both continuity and discontinuity with respect to Jesus and the rest of humanity. Finally, he introduces the question of universalism by using language that makes it sound as though all human persons are included in Christ in such a way that they will ultimately be saved. All three of these have important implications for christological anthropology, though the third is a question that we will not address fully until chapter 5.

The broader context of this passage comes from the question of whether Jesus has truly been raised from the dead (15:12–19). Paul responds by contending that only the resurrection of Jesus allows us to escape from the bondage of death and experience the freedom of life that has been God's plan from the beginning. If Jesus himself has not been raised into this new way of being, then there is no hope for the rest of humanity. Paul thus assumes the reality of death as a major obstacle to experiencing all that God intends for his people, identifying resurrection and life as the only possible solution. That prepares us to hear the core claim of the passage: "For as in Adam all die, so in Christ all will be made alive" (15:22).

Many simply assume from this that Paul must be talking about Adam as the head of *sinful* humanity. Paul tells us elsewhere that death comes as a consequence of sin (Rom 5:12), so the same principle applies here. Yet this does not necessarily follow. As we will see in chapter 8, many modern theologians argue that creaturely limitations, including death, are essential to being a creature. While the fall into sin changes the way we *experience* death (i.e., the "sting" of death in 1 Cor 15:56), death itself is intrinsic to our creaturely status. If this is the case, then when Paul says, "in Adam all die," he is simply identifying a creational reality rather than a fallen one. According to some exegetes, the problem is that we allow Romans 5 to determine our exegesis of 1 Corinthians 15.[18] Reading the latter passage on its own allows us to see the creational framework of the passage. Although we should be careful about assuming that Paul talks about death in precisely the same way in both passages, the fact that he describes death as an "enemy" to be defeated through Christ's resurrection (1 Cor 15:25–26) makes it difficult to think that he views death here as a purely creational reality. Therefore, even though there is no explicit reference to sin, we can conclude that here Paul identifies Adam as the head of the humanity, subject to the sphere of the "enemy," which includes sin and death.

Jesus, on the other hand, is "the firstfruits [*aparchē*] of those who have fallen asleep" (1 Cor 15:20). Drawn from its use in the Old Testament where it referred to the first portion of the harvest offered as a thanks offering to God,[19] the *aparchē* was thus part of the harvest, as the temporally first expression of the harvest, but it also played a unique role relative to the rest of the harvest, as the representative pledge that more would in fact follow.[20] To say that Jesus is the *aparchē* of the resurrection, then, is to claim that his humanity has both temporal and causal significance.[21] He is not only the first to participate in this new resurrection reality but also the one who serves as the pledge of more to come. Jesus is "the first installment of the crop which foreshadows and pledges the ultimate offering of the whole."[22]

---

18. E.g., C. K. Barrett, *The First Epistle to the Corinthians* (Peabody, MA: Hendrickson, 1968), 374.

19. Martinus C. de Boer, *The Defeat of Death: Apocalyptic Eschatology in 1 Corinthians 15 and Romans 5*, Journal for the Study of the New Testament 22 (Sheffield: JSOT Press, 1988), 109.

20. Joost Holleman, *Resurrection and Parousia: A Traditio-Historical Study of Paul's Eschatology in 1 Corinthians 15*, Supplements to Novum Testamentum, vol. 84 (New York: Brill, 1996), 49.

21. Fee, *The First Epistle to the Corinthians*, 751.

22. Barrett, *The First Epistle to the Corinthians*, 350–51; David E. Garland, *1 Corinthians*, Baker Exegetical Commentary on the New Testament (Grand Rapids: Baker Academic,

Paul then offers two parallel explanations for his claim that Jesus is the *aparchē* of the resurrection, the first of which emphasizes the centrality of Christ's humanity. Death came through a particular *anthrōpos*, introducing a problem that can only be solved by someone who is also an *anthrōpos* (15:21).[23] Here Paul reinforces both the idea that the *aparchē* must itself be a part of that which it represents and that it serves as a guarantee of that which follows. This establishes both continuity and discontinuity between Jesus and the rest of humanity. On the one hand, he is still part of the harvest. Like the rest of us, he experiences both death and resurrection, walking alongside us through both the darkest and brightest moments of human existence. Yet the *aparchē* also suggest discontinuity in that he is not only the first to walk the path, but he alone is the one who makes it possible for others to follow. The second explanatory clause (15:22) parallels the first with its emphasis on two individuals who introduce life and death into the world, yet it also sharpens Paul's argument in two ways. First, this clause emphasizes the *scope* of the representation exercised by these figures. The first says merely that death and resurrection came through the two *anthrōpoi*, but the second emphasizes that *all* (*pantes*) humans are somehow wrapped up in these two figures. Paul thus describes Jesus as the *aparchē* of the resurrection to emphasize that Jesus is fully human, that he is the first of a new humanity, and that he has created a new humanity in which others will in fact participate.

When you combine the first two issues we've discussed in this passage, you end up with the third: universalism. Given that all humans are subject to death, it seems reasonable to take the statement that "in Adam all die" as anthropologically universal. Consequently, some contend that it would be inconsistent to restrict the scope of the second claim, "in Christ all will be made alive." If so,

---

2003), 706. Thiselton points out, "There are clear parallels with the force of ἀρραβών, down payment in guarantee of more to come, applied to the Holy Spirit in 2 Cor 1:22 and 5:5" (Thiselton, *The First Epistle to the Corinthians*, 1224). We will also see that the same logic is at work in the use of the term "firstborn" (*prōtotokos*) in Rom 8:29; Col 1:15; and Heb 1:6 (see ch. 4).

23. Fee, *The First Epistle to the Corinthians*, 751.

according to this argument, this clause results in the conclusion that all humans will eventually be saved.[24] The totality of the harvest represented in Jesus as the *aparchē* includes all human persons. In an earlier book, I noted that a significant number of theologians who affirm a christological anthropology end up veering toward some kind of universalism, or at least an openness to such a conclusion.[25] So, although we will not address this question in full until chapter 5, we should not be surprised to find a similar issue arising here.

Nonetheless, making the argument from *this* passage seems unconvincing. For the argument to work, we would need to think that Paul is making statements about anthropology in general—"all die" and "all will be made alive"—simply identifying Adam and Christ as the instrumental means in virtue of which those anthropologically universal statements are true. In other words, we would need to read Paul's argument something like this: *"Just as everyone dies,* and the reason they die is because they are in Adam, *so also everyone will be made alive,* and the reason they will be made alive is because they are in Christ." So the focus of the argument would be on the anthropological statements, with the clauses about Adam and Christ playing a largely explanatory role. However, it is far more likely that Paul had the precise opposite in mind. Rather than making general statements about anthropology, Paul is specifically identifying what is true about the two spheres: *in Adam* and *in Christ*. Unlike the previous summary, then, Paul's actual argument works more like this: "Just as *in Adam* everyone dies, so also *in Christ* everyone will be made alive." The stress is on the two spheres with the rest coming as a description of the truths operative in those spheres. If that is the case, though, then Paul's argument entails nothing about *how many* people are included in each sphere. Now it does happen to be the case that *in Adam* was an anthropologically

---

24. E.g., Robert D. Culver, "A Neglected Millennial Passage from Saint Paul," *Bibliotheca Sacra* 113, no. 450 (1956): 141–52; Wilber B. Wallis, "Problem of an Intermediate Kingdom in I Corinthians 15:20–28," *Journal of the Evangelical Theological Society* 18, no. 4 (1975): 229–42.

25. Marc Cortez, *Christological Anthropology in Historical Perspective: Ancient and Contemporary Approaches to Theological Anthropology* (Grand Rapids: Zondervan, 2016), 229–31.

universal status prior to the advent of Christ, but that does not change the fact that Paul's focus here is not on whether this claim is anthropologically universal but on whether it applies to all of those who are *in Adam*, which it does. The parallel in the second half of the verse follows the same logic. Paul does not claim that life comes to all humans by means of Christ; instead, he contends that all of those who are *in Christ* receive life.[26] Technically, it would be possible to argue on other grounds that Paul's *in Christ* category includes all human persons, but this would be difficult to square with claims Paul makes elsewhere that suggest the opposite.[27] Regardless, the logic that "all" in this verse requires some form of universalism fails without substantial additional support.

In the first of our two key passages, then, Paul establishes that Adam and Christ stand at the head of two very different kinds of humanity: one that is characterized by sin and death and the other by resurrection and life. Importantly, Paul identifies Jesus as the *aparchē* of the resurrection, emphasizing both continuity with the rest of humanity and also his representative uniqueness. Though he is fully *anthrōpos*, he is also the unique *anthrōpos* who inaugurates a new way of being *anthrōpos*. Yet this does not necessarily mean that the scope of the harvest will include all human persons. Resurrection and life apply only to those who are truly *in Christ*.

In this passage, then, Paul associates Adam with fallen humanity, discussing the Adam/Christ parallel in the context of sin and redemption. If that is the only way Paul understood the parallel, we would end up with a story in which Christ is primarily viewed as the one who restores humanity to its creational state. What we lost in Adam, we regain in Christ. However, our next passage

---

26. W. V. Crockett, "Ultimate Restoration of All Mankind: 1 Corinthians 15:22," in *Studia Biblica 1978: Papers on Paul and Other New Testament Authors*, ed. E. A. Livingstone (Sheffield: JSOT Press, 1980), 83–87; Garland, *1 Corinthians*, 707–9; Gordon D. Fee, "Praying and Prophesying in the Assemblies: 1 Corinthians 11:2–16," in *Discovering Biblical Equality: Complementarity without Hierarchy*, ed. Ronald W. Pierce, Rebecca Merrill Groothuis, and Gordon D. Fee, 2nd ed. (Downers Grove, IL: InterVarsity, 2005), 740–50.

27. Barrett, *The First Epistle to the Corinthians*, 352; Kreitzer, "Christ and Second Adam in Paul," 72.

hints at something else, a way of understanding the parallel that stretches back to creation itself, suggesting that Jesus comes as the fulfillment of God's creational plans for humanity and not just as a way of redeeming us from sin.

To Each Its Own Body (1 Cor 15:35–49)

In this section, Paul's focus shifts to viewing Adam as the representative of *creational* humanity and not simply *fallen* humanity. The shift comes in verse 35 when Paul moves from discussing *whether* the resurrection will happen to *how* the resurrection will happen. That brings with it a corresponding shift from the necessity of the resurrection in light of the sin/death problem to the idea that the resurrection is necessary for the transformation of our human bodies, regardless of whether they are fallen, into a state suited for eschatological consummation.[28] Paul's interlocutors find it absurd to think that any kind of body would be suitable for such an eschatological condition.[29] If they are right, we would have to view the eschatological state as fundamentally opposed to the bodily state that we find in the creation of humanity. In contrast, Paul argues that we should affirm a kind of bodily existence that is both appropriate to the resurrection state and in some way continuous with what we have in creation. Consequently, the question driving this section is: "With what kind of body will they come?" In other words, Paul is now dealing with a question about the nature of embodiment, which is clearly a creational reality. Unlike the earlier passage which focused more narrowly on death and resurrection, Paul here presents the Adam/Christ relationship as one that spans everything from creation to glorification.

The creational context of Paul's argument comes out in verses 36–41. There Paul develops the idea that there are different kinds of bodies in the world and that each is appropriate to a given form of life.

---

28. Others disagree that Paul has creational humanity in mind here. Scroggs thus claims, "Nowhere in the Epistles is Adam the perfect man before his sin. Paul knows only the Adam of sin and death" (Scroggs, *The Last Adam*, 100).

29. Fee, *The First Epistle to the Corinthians*, 776.

He thus uses the diversity of the created world to prepare his readers to consider that there may be yet another kind of body, the resurrected body, that is similarly suited for its particular form of life. Some might object that the reference to death at the beginning of the passage still locates this entire discussion within the context of the fall (15:36). Yet he uses this language of death to draw an entirely natural analogy. The fact that a seed must "die" to produce a plant is part of the creational order, not a consequence of the fall. Paul then moves seamlessly from that creational analogy to the idea that a similar process is at work with the various states of human embodiment, at least raising the question of whether the death of our current bodies can be viewed as part of the creation order and not simply a consequence of the fall.[30] He even emphasizes that each body has its unique form of "splendor" (*doxa*; 15:40), a term that Paul does not associate with sinful states of being. In this context, then, the word conveys the idea that each of these various states of embodiment is part of God's creational design and not a consequence of the fall. To have a particular kind of body is to have the kind of *doxa* that God intended.[31]

The second key reason for viewing this passage in the context of creation comes from the fact that when Paul quotes the creation narrative to support his argument, he appeals to Genesis 2:7 rather than anything in Genesis 3. "So it is written: 'The first man Adam became a living being'; the last Adam, a life-giving spirit" (15:45).[32] Indeed, by calling Adam a "living being," a phrase associated with other creatures before the fall (Gen 1:20, 21, 24), Paul confirms that

---

30. See ch. 8.

31. We will not be discussing the nature of the resurrection body beyond the mere fact that it is a *body*. Although people sometimes claim that since Paul describes it as a "spiritual body," we should conclude that the resurrection body will be incorporeal (e.g., Scroggs, *The Last Adam*, 65). Yet most now recognize that "spiritual" in Paul's letters denotes that which is properly "fitted for the new age" of the Spirit (Fee, *The First Epistle to the Corinthians*, 786). Consequently, the term focuses on the quality of the body rather than its underlying ontology.

32. The first part of this verse is almost a direct quotation of Gen 2:7 in the LXX, though Paul inserts "first" and "Adam" into the quotation, probably as a way of setting up the parallel with Christ in the second part of the verse. Since some LXX manuscripts read "Adam man" at this point, however, Paul may be drawing from one of those sources (Roy E. Ciampa and Brian S. Rosner, *The First Letter to the Corinthians*, The Pillar New Testament Commentary [Grand Rapids: Eerdmans, 2010], 819).

he is presenting Adam as representative of a condition viewed as a creational good.[33] So when Paul describes the two forms of human embodiment as "spiritual" [*pneumatikos*] and "natural" [*psychikos*] (15:44, 46), we should not take this as referring to the same dynamic as expressed with the fallen/unfallen distinction. These are the same terms Paul uses in 2:14 to distinguish the natural person, who cannot understand the things of the Spirit, from the spiritual person, who can. Even there, though, it is not clear that such a distinction parallels fallen/unfallen since it is entirely possible that even an unfallen human person would still need the Spirit to understand the things of God. Regardless, Paul almost certainly does not intend us to hear *psychikos* in a pejorative way since the cognate noun occurs in the quotation of Genesis 2:7, which we have already established is a reference to the creational state of the human body.[34]

An important challenge arises in this latter part of the passage as well. For many, the specific terms used to describe the natural body in verses 42–43 clearly suggest that Paul has the fallen state of the body in mind. The natural body is perishable, dishonorable, and weak, unlike the spiritual body which is imperishable, glorious, and powerful. Yet this would be an odd conclusion given that the previous stage in the argument affirmed the essential goodness of various kinds of embodiment. Why would Paul suddenly switch without explanation into an entirely different framework in which one form of embodiment is viewed as sinful and fallen? Instead, it is more likely that Paul is continuing his previous line of thought, focusing not on the ways in which human bodies have been reshaped as a consequence of the fall, but on the fact that God created humans as embodied beings from the beginning. Additionally, each of the specific terms used can be understood as describing the state of the

---

33. Thiselton, *The First Epistle to the Corinthians*, 1283.

34. Andrew T. Lincoln, *Paradise Now and Not Yet: Studies in the Role of the Heavenly Dimension in Paul's Thought with Special Reference to His Eschatology*, Society for New Testament Studies Monograph Series 43 (New York: Cambridge University Press, 2004), 43. Fee thus concludes, "The transformed body, therefore, is not composed of 'spirit'; it is a body adapted to the eschatological existence that is under the ultimate domination of the Spirit" (Fee, *The First Epistle to the Corinthians*, 786; Thiselton, *The First Epistle to the Corinthians*, 1276).

body at creation. The Bible routinely refers to perishability as a part of the created order (1 Pet 1:22–25; 1 Cor 15:50; Rom 1:23). Unlike God who has life in himself, we are mortal creatures who were brought into existence and would easily slip back into nonexistence if it were not for the sustaining power of God. Thus, many have argued that even before the fall humans were only conditionally immortal.[35] We can say much the same thing about the distinction Paul draws between weakness and power. Even if we want to affirm the inherent goodness of Adam and Eve in the garden, the very fact that they fell from that good state suggests some kind of weakness, one that did not come as a consequence of the fall. Paul contrasts this with the "power" of the resurrected state in which we will accomplish the purposes God established for us.[36] The third contrast appears at first glance to be of a different kind. Here Paul refers to the natural body as "dishonorable" (atimia) in contrast to the doxa of the spiritual body. Yet, although Paul does occasionally use atimia in a negative sense (Rom 1:26; 1 Cor 11:14; 2 Cor 6:8), he also uses it to denote things that have more mundane purposes in distinction from those that are more directly dedicated to God (Rom 9:21; 2 Tim 2:20). That may well be the distinction Paul has in mind here, identifying the natural body as having more mundane purposes than the spiritual body, without the additional implication that such mundane purposes should be viewed through the lens of the fall. Consequently, it is entirely possible to take all of this language as a description of the creational state of the human body, which would fit the overall thrust of Paul's argument.[37]

It may seem as though we have strayed a bit far from our topic with this discussion of the resurrection body. However, we need to appreciate that Paul has creational humanity in mind in this passage if we are going to understand the broader implications

---

35. See, for example, Victor P. Hamilton, *The Book of Genesis: Chapters 1–17* (Grand Rapids: Eerdmans, 1990), 173; Kenneth Mathews, *Genesis 1–11:26*, vol. 1, The New American Commentary (Nashville: Holman Reference, 1996), 211–12.

36. Thiselton, *The First Epistle to the Corinthians*, 1274.

37. See esp. Garland, *1 Corinthians*, 733.

of his Adam/Christ parallel. According to this framework, Jesus comes not just as the one who addresses what went wrong in the fall (15:20–23), but also as the one who advances creation toward its intended telos (15:35–49).[38] Paul thus uses the language of "first" and "last" to introduce a temporal order in the relationship between these two forms of humanity in which Adamic humanity must precede christological humanity. That was already a part of the seed analogy since that which is planted must come before that which grows out of the planted seed (15:36). But Paul makes this logic explicit in verse 46: "The spiritual did not come first, but the natural, and after that the spiritual." Historically, this is rather obvious. Of course Adam came before Jesus. Yet Paul's argument runs deeper. At creation, Adam became the first of an earthly form of humanity (15:47–49), which Paul has already described as being perishable, mundane, and weak. Paul goes on to argue that this earthly form of humanity cannot inherit the kingdom of heaven (15:50), not because it is inherently sinful, but because it has not yet been transformed into the "heavenly" humanity that we see in Jesus.

Thus, although Paul does not go into hypothetical discussions about what would have happened if humans had not fallen into sin, his argument implies that some kind of transformation from the earthly humanity of the first Adam to the heavenly humanity of the second would have been required nonetheless. This passage thus relates directly to our discussion in the prior chapter about the relationship between nature and grace. If the argument of that chapter is correct, then here Paul is outlining the only true telos of the human person: eschatological consummation.[39] Yet there is an additional question we have not yet asked. If Jesus is so central to the meaning and actualization of true humanity, then must we

---

38. Lincoln, *Paradise Now and Not Yet*, 43.

39. Notice, though, that you could still affirm most, if not all, of the argument in this chapter even if you disagree with the conclusions of the last chapter. Even if you think there is a distinctively natural telos for humanity in addition to the supernatural telos of eschatological consummation, creating the hypothetical possibility that God could have allowed humans to remain in their natural condition, most still affirm that in the concrete order actually established by God eschatological consummation is the only true telos for humanity.

affirm that the incarnation would have happened even if humanity had never fallen into sin? Or should we maintain instead that the incarnation has redemption from sin as its exclusive focus and argue that God could have brought humans to eschatological consummation in some other way? If the former is true, then we have another reason for maintaining the fundamental significance of Christology for understanding anthropology. If we affirm the latter, however, that would at least raise some challenging questions since it seems to affirm the possibility that humans could have accomplished their true telos even if the incarnation had never happened. In that case, the humanity of Christ is not fundamentally necessary for being or understanding humanity.

INCARNATION WITHOUT THE FALL

According to the argument presented above, the "new humanity" inaugurated by Jesus is the eschatological outworking of God's plans for humanity from the beginning. This leads naturally to the question, if the incarnation is fundamentally oriented toward creation rather than redemption, should we not conclude that the incarnation would have taken place even if humanity had never sinned? If so, what difference does this make for theological anthropology? Such a conclusion clearly emphasizes the anthropological centrality of Jesus Christ since it maintains that the incarnation is fundamental to God's creational purposes. However, if the incarnation is fully contingent upon sin, there should be a way of understanding what it means to be human apart from the incarnation. So it would seem that if we answer "no" to this question, we must also say "no" to christological anthropology. Nonetheless, after considering the various arguments for and against this approach, we will see that this conclusion does not necessarily follow. Although I will argue that there are good reasons for thinking that the incarnation would have taken place irrespective of sin, I will also suggest ways in which someone could develop a robustly christological anthropology even if they remain unconvinced on this point.

Various versions of this *incarnation anyway* (IA) argument have received increased attention in recent years,[40] though the position has also garnered support from earlier theologians as well.[41] However, many respond to questions like this with a derisive, "Who cares?" By phrasing the question as a hypothetical—Would *X* have happened if *Y* had not happened?—IA sounds like the kind of counterfactual speculation that drives much of the science fiction industry. What would the world be like if Germany had won WWII? How would America be different if someone went back in time and stopped the assassination of John F. Kennedy? Questions like that might be a fun basis for fiction, but do they really belong in theology? Many worry that any such discussions are frivolous at best. Even worse, they threaten to lead theology astray as we replace revealed truths about what God actually has done with our own intuitions about what he *would* have done, which may just as well be shorthand for what we think God *should* have done.

Nonetheless, as Oliver Crisp points out, not all speculation is equally problematic. Crisp acknowledges that IA is speculative, but he contends that it may well be the kind of speculation that is "theologically productive" rather than the kind that is "idle or useless."[42] In other words, we can and should distinguish between a kind of fruitful theological speculation that presses toward greater clarity about what is assumed, implied, or even merely allowed

---

40. See esp. Richard J. Mouw, "Another Look at the Infra/Supralapsarian Debate," *Calvin Theological Journal* 35, no. 1 (2000): 136–51; Marilyn McCord Adams, *Christ and Horrors: The Coherence of Christology* (Cambridge: Cambridge University Press, 2006), 170–204; Edwin Chr. van Driel, *Incarnation Anyway: Arguments for Supralapsarian Christology* (New York: Oxford University Press, 2008); Oliver D. Crisp, "Incarnation without the Fall," *Journal of Reformed Theology* 10, no. 3 (2016): 215–33; Stefan Lindholm, "Would Christ Have Become Incarnate Had Adam Not Fallen? Jerome Zanchi (1516–1590) on Christ as Mediator," *Journal of Reformed Theology* 9, no. 1 (2015): 19–36.

41. E.g., Rupert of Deutz, Robert Grosseteste, John Duns Scotus, Friedrich Schleiermacher, Isaac Dorner, and Karl Barth (see esp. van Driel, *Incarnation Anyway* and Daniel P. Horan, "How Original Was Scotus on the Incarnation? Reconsidering the History of the Absolute Predestination of Christ in Light of Robert Grosseteste," *Heythrop Journal* 52, no. 3 [2011]: 374–91). Even some of the theologians who ultimately rejected incarnation anyway affirmed the validity and importance of this approach (e.g., Aquinas, *Summa Theologica* IIIa, Q.1, A.3; Bonaventure, *Sententiae* III, D.20, A.1, QQ. 2, 5, 6).

42. Crisp, "Incarnation without the Fall," 216.

by the biblical texts, and a more frivolous kind of speculation that wanders off into debates about issues with no clear import for the life, ministry, and doctrine of the church. One could argue that the doctrine of the Trinity and the hypostatic union themselves developed out of the first kind of speculative endeavor. We should thus be careful about dismissing a theological argument as "speculative" unless we are willing to explain why we think it is the latter kind of speculation rather than the former.

Additionally, regardless of whether you agree with IA as a theological position, a closer look at the arguments for it offer good reasons for thinking that this is an example of fruitful speculation. If nothing else, as I mentioned in the introduction, IA has a direct bearing on how we understand the relationship between Christology and anthropology. More fundamentally, though, the discussion involves the question about the end(s) for which God created the universe. According to IA advocates, if we take seriously the claim that God made everything "for Christ" (Col 1:16), we must not shy away from claiming that the incarnation is fundamental to God's plans for creation. In other words, the key question is not about what God *might have done* in some hypothetical alternate universe, but what God *has done* in this one. Why did God create the world and what is the role of the incarnation in God's plans for the universe? As we will see in the next section, these questions point toward the heart of the matter.

Three Versions of Incarnation Anyway

To understand the logic of IA, let's take a closer look at three recent forms of the argument, each of which offers a different way of affirming that the incarnation is central to God's creational design plan for the universe. Marilyn McCord Adams develops her position in dialogue with the medieval theologian Robert Grosseteste.[43] In her version of the argument, the Son is central to creation because of God's plan to unite everything in the Son. We see this preeminently

---

43. Adams, *Christ and Horrors*, 174–81.

in the church. According to this argument, *"whether or not humans and angels had sinned, and hence even if we hadn't, Divine cosmic purposes would include adopting us as God's children, making us not to be isolated atoms but members of the Church, that mystical body of which Christ is the head."*[44] Yet such a union is more than merely notional (just saying that we are part of Christ's body) or even volitional (simply ensuring that our wills align with God's). "Willing what God wills us to will, nilling what God wills us to nill, might make us friends of God or obedient servants. But to be God's *adopted* children and Christ's siblings, we have to share a nature with Christ, the natural Son. Since we cannot take on the Divine nature, God the Son would have assumed our human nature, even if Adam had never sinned."[45] Consequently, the incarnation was necessary for accomplishing a purpose that was central to God's plans for his people: adoption through Christ.

The argument continues, though, so that we come to see the incarnation as having significance for the entire universe. Here she addresses *"whether or not, even if we hadn't sinned, God would want to make Christ the One in Whom the cosmos holds together."*[46] One of God's fundamental purposes in creation, on this view, was to bring all parts of the universe together under a single "head" (e.g., Eph 1:10). As with the first stage in the argument, though, this kind of headship requires the Son both to be part of the universe (just as a head must be part of the body) and yet also chief over the universe. "Thus, unifying any universe containing material and spiritual creatures under a single head calls for a God-man in Whom Divinity and humanity are joined in unity of person."[47]

Edwin Christian van Driel offers a second form of the IA argument, one that begins with the idea of "eschatological superabundance."[48]

---

44. Ibid., 176–77. Emphasis original.

45. Ibid., 177.

46. Ibid., 178. Emphasis original.

47. Ibid., 179.

48. Van Driel, *Incarnation Anyway*, 150–55.

He contends that there is some good in the eschatological state that transcends the goodness we had in creation. We have already seen good reasons for thinking this is the case. Although people often speak of the eschatological state as a "return" to Eden, few mean this literally. At the very least, most affirm that humans will no longer be able to sin (*non posse peccare*), in contrast to Adam and Eve who were able to sin (*posse peccare*). If this is the case, then we can agree that there is a movement from good (being without sin) to greater good (being firmly established in sinlessness) between these two states of being. We could say more about what makes the eschatological state a greater good than that of creation, but all we need at this point is the idea that the eschaton involves some kind of superior state.

The second part of his argument revolves around "the centrality of Christ to eschatological consummation."[49] This too seems non-controversial given that the biblical authors routinely present Jesus as the one in whom the eschatological kingdom is inaugurated and ultimately realized, as well as the one who transforms God's people so we might be able to enjoy this eschatological goodness. Indeed, "The gifts of the eschaton are intimately bound up with his person: they are modeled after, brought about by, and directed at him."[50] Thus, it is at least reasonable to conclude that the incarnation is essential to bringing about the eschatologically greater state that is the culmination of God's plans for creation.[51]

Oliver Crisp's argument has similarities with both of the above, though his approach builds more explicitly on the idea of "christological union."[52] To explain what he has in mind, he offers

---

49. Ibid., 152.

50. Ibid.

51. Van Driel contends further that IA does a better job accounting for the fact that the incarnation continues in the eschaton. According to him, if the incarnation was only necessary for the purposes of the atonement, there would seem to be no reason for the incarnation to continue once atonement had been made. The fact that Hebrews affirms the necessity of an eternal incarnation suggests that the incarnation has an additional, and probably more fundamental, function.

52. Crisp, "Incarnation without the Fall."

the following as a possible way of understanding the relationship between the creation of humans and the incarnation:

> God desires to create a world in which there are creatures with whom he may be united, so that they may participate in his divine life. Indeed, participation of creatures in the divine life is a final goal of creation, perhaps even the ultimate goal (though we need not commit ourselves to that claim for present purposes). To that end, God conceives of human beings as creatures ideally suited to such a relationship. They are ideally suited because they are metaphysically amphibian, being composed of bodies (thereby rooted in the physical world God creates), as well as souls (thereby having a part that belongs to the immaterial world of spirits). Such metaphysical composition means that humans have a foot in both the physical world of creation and the spiritual world that includes the angels and God. To enable these human creatures to participate in the divine life God must take the initiative and unite himself with one of these creaturely natures, assuming it, and thereby generating an interface between divinity and humanity so that human beings may have a conduit by means of which they may be united to God.[53]

On his account, one of the fundamental purposes of creation is the "participation of creatures in the divine life."[54] God thus made humans as creatures that would be particularly suited for union with God, yet not in such a way that humans could produce this divine union on their own. Instead, God has to initiate the process by uniting himself to a particular human, thus creating a "link" between himself and the rest of humanity. This does not make the incarnation "necessary" in the sense that it is the only possible way God could have achieved this outcome.[55] But given the goal of having

---

53. Ibid., 219.

54. Ibid.

55. Crisp points out that his argument is quite similar to Aquinas's position. Although Aquinas did not affirm IA himself, viewing it as overly speculative, he still argued that such a position is entirely consistent with what we know about God. Since God is perfectly good,

creatures participate in the divine life through union with God, the incarnation seems a perfectly fitting way of bringing this about.[56]

This argument parallels what we saw in Adams above, though Crisp focuses more specifically on the incarnation as the "conduit" that allows humans to be united with God. Similarly, the argument overlaps with van Driel in focusing on the incarnation as that which brings about the eschatological blessing, differing primarily in the aspect of the blessing addressed. Yet all three arguments take a similar approach. God desires to bring about some great thing in creation, and the incarnation is central to the manner in which God chooses to make this happen. Importantly, none of these arguments requires the existence of sin for the generation of this greater good. Instead, this great goodness is something God intended for his creation from the beginning, which would in turn suggest that the incarnation has also been a part of God's plans for creation irrespective of sin. Consequently, the key issue involved in the discussion is not the kind of counterfactual speculation that worries so many. These arguments focus instead on the nature of creation, God's purposes for creation, and the role of the incarnation in bringing about those purposes. They do eventually arrive at the counterfactual question of whether the incarnation would have happened even if there had been no sin, but they do so only as the outworking of the argument rather than its speculative starting point.

Rejecting Incarnation Anyway

I do not want to imply that the only reason people have for rejecting IA is the speculation concern. Before we consider the implications of this argument for christological anthropology, then, we need to address at least four ways in which people might respond to the above arguments.

---

and since "it belongs to the essence of goodness to communicate itself to others," it is "fitting that God should become incarnate" in order to join the created nature to himself (*Summa Theologica* III, Q. 1, A. 1).

56. We might further say that it was contingently necessary. God could have done it other ways, but having determined to do it this way, it became necessary.

1. But the Bible. The most common response to IA is that it simply runs counter to the way the Bible actually talks about the incarnation. As Crisp admits, "Scripture speaks of Christ coming into the world to save sinners (1 Tim 1:15), not of Christ coming into the world irrespective of human sin in order to unite us to God."[57] We could say something similar about any of the various IA arguments. Each of them results in a way of understanding the incarnation that cuts against the grain of the biblical presentation. If the biblical authors consistently describe the incarnation as something that happens as a consequence of sin, why would we conclude differently?

Yet we can certainly ask if the biblical picture is quite as straightforward as such a claim suggests. I have already argued that 1 Corinthians 15 offers at least some support for this position. Additionally, Romans 8:29 talks about our conformity to the image of the Son as something that has been ordained from the beginning. Although Paul introduces justification in the next verse, the basic idea of being conformed to the image of the Son does not seem to require the fall. In other words, this verse at least suggests the possibility that even the biblical authors may have had some notion of the centrality of the incarnation irrespective of sin. Similarly, as I've already mentioned, Colossians 1:16 describes Christ as the one *"for whom* all things are created."[58] And we could make similar arguments from other New Testament texts that emphasize the centrality of the incarnation in God's eternal plans (e.g., Eph 1:4; 2 Pet 1:4).

As we saw in the discussion of Adams's argument, an additional set of texts that must be included in the discussion are those that present the church as fundamental to God's eschatological purposes for creation. Ephesians places a particularly strong emphasis on the cosmic significance of the church. In the first chapter alone, Paul describes the church as essential for bringing "unity to all things in heaven and on earth under Christ" (1:10), the body of Christ that is

---

57. Crisp, "Incarnation without the Fall," 229.

58. Ibid., 230, emphasis his. Although some might dismiss this as a reference to the eternal Son rather than the incarnate Christ, we will see in the next chapter that there are good reasons for rejecting any facile separation of the two in this verse.

"the fullness of him who fills everything in every way" (1:23). Later in the book, Paul draws a parallel between the "one flesh" of Genesis 2:24 and the church, suggesting that he thinks the centrality of the church in God's plans is a creational reality and not just something God introduced as a consequence of sin.[59] Throughout Ephesians, we have a clear picture in which God's eschatological plans for creation are not complete until the Son has been exalted *and* the church has received the full measure of what God has planned for his people. Thus, the church is central to God's plans for the eschaton. Yet the New Testament is equally clear about the centrality of Jesus for the church. The church is the body of Christ that has its being in union with Christ through the power of the Spirit. Consequently, the church is necessary for God's eschatological purposes, and if Jesus is necessary for the church, then we must affirm that Jesus is necessary for God to accomplish those purposes. The only alternative here is to suggest that God might have had purposes for creation that involved *neither* Jesus *nor* the church, which is the option we will consider next.

I am not claiming in this section that IA is the only legitimate way to read these texts. The point remains that the majority of the biblical texts still discuss the incarnation in relation to sin. That is unavoidable given that the Bible as a whole focuses primarily on the story of humanity after its fall into sin. Yet it would be too much to say that IA lacks a biblical basis entirely. Although most of the arguments used to support IA are more specifically theological, advocates can point to an important set of texts that suggest we should not restrict the meaning of the incarnation to this purpose alone.

2. Consummation Anyway. A second way that critics of IA might respond to our example arguments is to contend that God could have brought about the desired benefit without the incarnation. Suppose, for example, that we grant the surpassing goodness of the eschatological state and that this was part of God's purposes for creation from the beginning. Is it not entirely possible that God designed creation in such a way that had sin not intervened it would

59. Adams, *Christ and Horrors*, 177–78.

have proceeded from its initially good state to the greater good of the final state without any need for incarnation? We would thus be able to affirm many of the key aspects of the above arguments without granting that the incarnation would have happened even if creation had never fallen.

We should notice, however, that any such response is every bit as speculative as the IA argument it seeks to reject. Indeed, it seems even *more* speculative. The IA argument as described above proceeds on the basis of the eschatological end as we actually have it in Christ. In other words, it takes as its starting point the eschatological plan that God has in fact revealed to us as well as the centrality of the incarnate Christ for accomplishing those purposes. Rather than being a speculative attempt to pry into counterfactual realities about what might be, this argument focuses on that which is (or will be) and contends that this should provide the ground for making theological judgments in other areas. The proposed counterargument, on the other hand, must speculate about the possibility of achieving the same eschatological goal (or at least some comparably great eschatological goal) independently of Jesus. So we should note at the very least that this argument also qualifies as speculative, requiring some discussion of whether it falls into the "frivolous" or the "fruitful" categories.

At the same time, though, we should notice that, as it is formulated, this response risks sounding as if humans could simply move from their natural state into the supernatural state of eschatological consummation without intervening grace. Yet this is something even those who affirm a dual-telos approach to the nature/grace discussion would reject. According to proponents of the dual-position position, prelapsarian humans could have accomplished their *natural* telos without any additional grace beyond that of creation and God's providential governance of the universe. Yet they also reject any suggestion that humans can bring about their *supernatural* end without an act of God's grace that goes beyond their natural condition. Consequently, the dual-telos position does *not* entail the idea that humans can somehow bring about this supernatural end through the use of natural capacities alone.

So the real question is not about whether it is possible that human persons could have brought about the state of eschatological consummation independently of grace. Instead, the real question is about the nature of the gracious act God needed to perform in order to elevate humanity from its creational to its eschatological condition. Advocates of IA contend that the incarnation simply *is* this act of elevation. Even though this elevation came after the fall into sin in the actual unfolding of history, that does not change the fact that the incarnation is the sole instance of this elevating grace that we see in the Bible. Thus, the burden of proof is on anyone who wants to speculate about the possibility that God could have elevated humanity in some other way despite strong biblical statements about the centrality of Jesus for bringing about eschatological consummation.

3. No Consummation. We can deal with a third possible response more quickly since it rehearses arguments we addressed in the previous chapter. This third response would be to reject the idea that an eschatologically superior state was part of God's designs for creation from the beginning. Instead, the "natural" state of creation before the fall might have its own telos that needed no further perfection. Such an argument would not entail that God could not bring about a higher perfection if he wanted to, only that no additional telos is necessary to creation. On this account, if the fall had not occurred, everything would have remained essentially the way it was. We would still need to "be fruitful and multiply" and to "exercise dominion" over creation, but we could accomplish both tasks utilizing the capacities of our natural condition.

To make this argument work, of course, we would have to go back and revise (or reject) the arguments of the previous chapter. Instead of identifying a single telos for humanity (eschatological consummation), we would have to maintain that humans have a distinctively natural telos and that it is at least conceivable that God could have left human persons in this natural state. But there is an even steeper price to pay.

If we are really going to say that there is no consummation of any kind and that God's original plans for creation involved no essential change in the human condition, we have to conclude, at the very least, that on such an account humans would have remained *posse peccare* forever. Irrespective of what we might think about the likelihood of humans remaining in a sinless condition forever despite the fact that each human person would remain entirely capable of committing sin, this would also involve a significant departure from an idea that "has become standard in all Western traditions."[60]

4. Sin Anyway. A final response maintains the connection between the incarnation and sin as well as the inevitability of the incarnation by concluding that sin itself was in some way inevitable. This would be a form of the *felix culpa* argument in which sin, while remaining an evil in itself, becomes the means by which God produces some greater good. On such an account, we do not have to wrestle with the question of whether the incarnation would have happened without the fall because the fall itself is intrinsic to God's plans for humanity. The eschatological blessing produced by means of the incarnation comes only as a consequence of the fall.

We should note here that one common form of the *felix culpa* argument is actually a form of the *no consummation* argument above. The argument contends that God had an original plan for creation that did not require any eschatological consummation which involves an essential change to that created condition. Once sin enters the equation, though, God determines to use sin and the ensuing story of redemption as the means by which he would introduce an even greater good. On this account, the fall is not a part of God's original plans for creation, but it is still a "happy" fault in that it becomes the occasion for greater goodness. Such an account, though, requires a *no consummation* position with respect to the created order since it views the created state as complete in itself. Although this version of the argument contends that there is a subsequent development in the story in which God brings creation to a higher state, this

---

60. Driel, *Incarnation Anyway*, 151.

development is not intrinsic to God's original plans for creation. Thus, this version of the *felix culpa* argument will still be subject to the concerns raised above about the *no consummation* argument.

To distinguish *no consummation* from the form of the *felix culpa* argument I have in mind here, we need to suppose instead that the fall itself was a part of God's plans from the beginning. In other words, the creation state was *not* complete in itself, and the fall was always part of the divinely intended means by which God would raise creation to eschatological consummation. Let's call this the *sin anyway* position since it would maintain that sin was always intended to be a part of the story of humanity. The greatest difficulty faced by such a position is that it appears to make God responsible for sin in a rather direct way. God made the world in such a way that sin was inevitable. That he did so because of some higher good merely results in an "ends justifies the means" kind of argument, which is inevitably unsatisfying. Adams points out that this comes with the "metaphysically preposterous" implication that the highest good available to a created being, union with God through the Son, comes only as a consequence of sin.[61] Additionally, although this kind of *sin anyway* argument would technically not qualify as an IA argument, since it does not envision the possibility of the incarnation *apart from* humanity's fall into sin, it still contends that the incarnation is a necessary part of God's plans for humanity. In other words, since it maintains that sin is essential for eschatological consummation and that the incarnation is the necessary response to sin, it affirms the inevitability of the incarnation in God's plans for humanity. Consequently, although it might qualify as a critique of IA, it does so without serious implications for a christological anthropology.

Is Incarnation Anyway Necessary?

Before we conclude this section, we need to consider the implications of all this for developing a christological anthropology. It seems evident that IA supports the idea that the humanity of Jesus Christ

---

61. Adams, *Christ and Horrors*, 176.

is paradigmatic for humanity in general since it contends that the incarnation was essential to God's plans for humanity irrespective of humanity's fall into sin. But what about the alternative? Is the IA position necessary for affirming a christological approach to theological anthropology? Not necessarily. We have already seen that if you are willing to affirm the version of the *sin anyway* argument offered above, you have at least some reason for thinking that IA is not necessary for developing a christological anthropology. Even if you do not find the *sin anyway* approach convincing, the fact that there is at least one way of developing a christological anthropology without appeal to IA arguments demonstrates that the former is possible without the latter.

There is another approach we have not yet considered. Instead of focusing on the incarnation as the necessary ground for understanding humanity, maybe we could appeal instead to something inherent in the eternal Son. In other words, instead of affirming that the incarnate Jesus is the revelation of what it means to be truly human, maybe we should affirm that the archetype of humanity somehow resides in the essence of the eternal Son. This would mean that the humanity of Jesus is truly human insofar as it is a true manifestation of this eternal ideal, but it is not the actual archetype of true humanity. The incarnate Christ would thus be a true fulfillment of the archetype rather than the archetype itself. This would still seem to be a robustly christological approach to anthropology since it would ground our understanding of humanity in the second person of the Trinity, but it would not require that we affirm the IA approach since there is nothing in this argument that would require us to affirm that the eternal Son would eventually become incarnate in a particular human nature. Instead, it remains entirely possible to argue that the incarnation itself might have come only as a response to sin even while contending that the archetype of humanity is truly christological. That leads us to the next stage of our discussion (chapter 3), which will focus on the *imago Dei* and the relationship between the identity of the eternal Son and the incarnate Christ.

CONCLUSION

In the first half of the chapter, we looked at the Adam/Christ parallel as Paul develops it in 1 Corinthians 15. Although Paul's discussion focuses on specific issues regarding the resurrection rather than our more general questions about the relationship between Christology and anthropology, he nonetheless develops that parallel in ways that have significance for our discussion. Most importantly, although the earlier part of the chapter focused on the Adam/Christ parallel in the context of the fall, that does not seem to be the case in the second half of the chapter. There he compares Christ to the Adam we see in Genesis 2, suggesting that Paul views Christ as the eschatological consummation of his creational plans for humanity. Christ is the "second" Adam not merely in historical sequence but as the teleological completion of what God began in the "first" Adam.

In the second half of the chapter, we shifted to another related question. If Jesus is the "second Adam" in the sense of fulfilling God's purposes for humanity at creation, it sounds as though the incarnation would have taken place irrespective of humanity's fall into sin. Such *incarnation anyway* arguments have grown increasingly common in contemporary theology, and despite concerns about an overemphasis on hypothetical speculations, we saw that these arguments take seriously the concrete order of history that we see in the biblical narratives. Most importantly, they contend that these narratives reveal two important facts: (1) eschatological consummation is the telos that God has chosen for his people, and (2) this eschatological consummation only comes about through Jesus Christ. There are other ways of making sense of these two basic affirmations, but it does not appear that IA is any more speculative or ill-founded than any of these other approaches. On the contrary, the arguments in favor of IA should be taken quite seriously, and they offer strong support for developing a christological understanding of the human person.

CHAPTER 3

Divine Presence

The *Imago Dei* and the Divine Identity of the Son

THE *IMAGO DEI* is an obvious locus for our third study reflecting on the relationship between Christology and anthropology. As Wolfhart Pannenberg notes, the *imago Dei* has long served as one of two "central themes" in theological anthropology, alongside the doctrine of sin.[1] Indeed, John Paul II referred to it as "the immutable basis of all Christian anthropology,"[2] and Louis Berkhof calls it "the essence of man."[3] Although we will see that some have raised important questions about the centrality of the image, it remains vitally important in modern theological anthropology.[4] Additionally, the New Testament authors clearly view the *imago Dei* as a robustly christological concept. With few exceptions, references to the *imago* in the New

---

1. Wolfhart Pannenberg, *Anthropology in Theological Perspective* (Edinburgh: T&T Clark, 1985), 20.

2. John Paul II, *Apostolic Letter Mulieris Dignitatem* (Vatican City: Libreria Editrice Vaticana, 1988), no. 6.

3. Louis Berkhof, *Systematic Theology* (London: Banner of Truth, 1984), 205.

4. For important recent examples, see Stanley J. Grenz, *The Social God and the Relational Self: A Trinitarian Theology of the Imago Dei* (Philadelphia: Westminster, 2001); Hans-Georg Ziebertz, *The Human Image of God* (Leiden: Brill, 2001); J. Richard Middleton, *The Liberating Image: The Imago Dei in Genesis 1* (Grand Rapids: Brazos, 2005); Ian A. McFarland, *The Divine Image: Envisioning the Invisible God* (Minneapolis: Fortress, 2005); J. P. Moreland, *The Recalcitrant Imago Dei* (London: Hymns Ancient & Modern Ltd, 2009); John Kilner, *Dignity and Destiny: Humanity in the Image of God* (Grand Rapids: Eerdmans, 2014); Richard Lints, *Identity and Idolatry: The Image of God and Its Inversion*, New Studies in Biblical Theology 36 (Downers Grove, IL: InterVarsity, 2015).

Testament are explicitly christological.[5] Consequently, if the image of God is central to theological anthropology, and if Jesus is central to understanding the *imago Dei*, we have good reasons for affirming the centrality of Jesus for understanding what it means to be human.

Nonetheless, a number of dangerous pitfalls await the unwary traveler journeying down this christological path. Some question whether the image should be this central to theological anthropology given that it only occurs in a handful of biblical passages. As Claus Westermann contends, "Gen 1:26f. is not making a general and universally valid statement about the nature of humankind; if it were, then the Old Testament would have much more to say about this image and likeness. The fact is that it does not, and this has been noted on a number of occasions."[6] If this is correct, then even the christological reorientation of the concept in the New Testament would not necessarily warrant using it as a central feature of a christological anthropology.

A second issue introduces even more significant challenges. The *imago Dei* is one of the most notoriously debated topics in theological anthropology, raising the question of whether it is even possible for this to serve as a central concept in a christological anthropology. According to David Kelsey, "Exegetical debates about Genesis 1:26–28 are simply too inconclusive to warrant giving 'image of God' the central, anchorlike role it has traditionally played in theological anthropology's accounts of what human being is."[7] If we cannot determine the meaning of the *imago*, though, we would still have a difficult time using this idea to ground a christological vision of humanity. At best, we would be left with a claim that looks something like this: "The *imago Dei*, whatever that is, finds its ultimate meaning in Jesus." This is roughly similar to claiming, "Jesus is schlumphfy, and schlumphfy is really important for understanding

5. See 1 Cor 11:7; Jas 3:9.

6. Claus Westermann, *Genesis 1–11: A Commentary* (Minneapolis: Augsburg, 1984), 155.

7. David H. Kelsey, *Eccentric Existence: A Theological Anthropology*, 2 vols. (Louisville: Westminster John Knox, 2009), 900.

humanity." Although this would succeed in establishing that Jesus is central to the meaning of humanity, such a claim cannot provide any meaningful content to our knowledge of humanity given that, as far as I am aware, schlumphfy doesn't actually mean anything. The *imago* will not prove terribly helpful for developing a christological understanding of humanity if it has no meaningful content.

Finally, when we look closely at the New Testament texts that relate the *imago Dei* to Christology, we run into the difficult question of discerning whether these texts refer to the Son in eternity or in the incarnation. In other words, when Paul says that the Son is "the image of the invisible God" (Col 1:15), is this a statement about the Trinity (the Son's eternal relationship to the Father) or about anthropology (the Son as the paradigmatic instance of a human living as a true image bearer in creation)? How we answer this question has consequences for utilizing the *imago Dei* when developing a christological account of humanity, so we will need to spend some time exploring this issue. In the end, I will suggest that the best approach is to conclude, without rejecting the idea that the Son is consubstantial with the Father from all eternity, (1) that the *imago Dei* refers specifically to the humanity of the Son in the incarnation and (2) that the *imago Dei* is still an eternal truth about what it means to be human.

THE IMAGE OF GOD AS DIVINE PRESENCE

The *imago Dei* might inform theological anthropology in several ways. It could play a largely *formal* role, providing a way of structuring claims about what it means to be human, but offering little, if any, material content for that anthropology. For example, some have argued that the *imago Dei* is impossible to define because it is inherently mysterious. If human beings are supposed to image an infinite and transcendent God who is himself inherently mysterious, we need to define the image in similar terms.[8] Such an account

8. E.g., Elizabeth A. Johnson, "The Incomprehensibility of God and the Image of God Male and Female," *Theological Studies* 45, no. 3 (1984): 441–65; Kathryn Tanner, "In the Image

of the image means that the *imago Dei* itself says little about the content of what it means to be human, but it requires anthropology to take a particular shape, one oriented around transcendence and mystery. Or we might contend that the image plays a largely *material* role in anthropology. This would be the case for anyone who thinks the image has some discernible content, but does *not* view the image as formally central such that it shapes anthropology as a whole.[9] As we will see, though, limiting the image to its formal centrality alone fails to appreciate that the concept has real meaning in the biblical texts. The *imago Dei* is more than a mere cipher that we can infuse with whatever meaning we find most appropriate. Similarly, restricting the image to its material significance fails to appreciate the strategic role the *imago Dei* plays in the biblical account of humanity. Consequently, the dominant position traditionally has been to affirm that the image is both formally and materially significant for anthropology.

The Formal Centrality of the *Imago Dei*

In his monumental *Eccentric Existence: A Theological Anthropology*, David Kelsey registers two concerns about those who try to make the image of God "the conceptual center" of our view of humanity.[10] His primary concern has to do with viewing the Bible as "a single canonical narrative that has a single plot or narrative logic."[11] Instead, Kelsey argues throughout that there are three different kinds of narratives in the Bible—those about God relating to the world to create, to redeem, and to bring to eschatological consummation—and that each has its own narrative logic. For example, narratives about God

---

of the Invisible," in *Apophatic Bodies: Negative Theology, Incarnation, and Relationality*, ed. Chris Boesel and Catherine Keller (New York: Fordham University Press, 2009), 117–34.

9. This seems to be the case, for example, in Hans Schwarz, *The Human Being: A Theological Anthropology* (Grand Rapids: Eerdmans, 2013). Schwarz offers a definition of the image that contributes to the content of his anthropology, but he does not structure the work around the *imago Dei*, and many of the particular discussions in the book unfold without particular connection to the image.

10. Kelsey, *Eccentric Existence*, 895.

11. Ibid., 897.

creating do not logically require any concept of redemption. In other words, nothing in the logic of a creation story requires that such a creation would eventually fall. Neither would such a story require God to redeem creation if it did in fact fall. When we read the creation narratives in ways that are shaped by redemption and consummation narratives, we end up twisting the logic of creation and missing the point of those stories. This does not mean we need to keep these three kinds of stories entirely separate, only that we guard against the temptation to allow one to shape the others.

Applied to the *imago Dei*, then, this argument suggests that it is illegitimate to take a concept from one of these narratives and use it as a formal principle that shapes everything we say about the human person, including anthropological truths derived from other kinds of narratives. At most we might conclude that the *imago Dei* is central for one set of narratives, making it a valuable piece of a theological anthropology, but not its formal center. Additionally, Kelsey also argues that since Genesis 1–3 comes as the introduction to the Pentateuch, which is a story driven by the logic of *redemption*, we should not use these narratives when developing a creational perspective on humanity. Instead, he privileges the wisdom literature, contending that only here do we get a perspective on humanity that is not already shaped by the logic of redemption and/or consummation.[12]

Kelsey's approach should be valued for its strong emphasis on the often underappreciated creation theology of the wisdom literature, and for its cautionary words on not allowing certain aspects of the biblical narrative to dominate in such a way that the others lose their distinctive voices. At the same time, though, I find myself less satisfied with Kelsey's argument for three distinct narratives with their own inner logics. Catherine Pickstock helpfully contends that although there is nothing inherent in the *concepts* of creation, redemption, and consummation that requires them to be interrelated, we have to deal with the story that we actually

---

12. See esp. ibid., 176–89.

find in the Bible, not the logical possibility of some other story (or set of stories).[13] She thus points out that many view creation in the Bible (whether in Genesis or elsewhere) as involving a good gift that requires a reciprocal response and "was inseparable from the issuing of final gratitude."[14] In other words, even without an eschatological perspective, it is possible to view the creation story as involving a movement from gift to reciprocal response that results in an anthropological telos at the heart of the story. Indeed, she rightly asks whether Kelsey's attempt to understand the creation narrative entirely on its own requires a problematic bifurcation between nature and grace, an issue that we addressed in the previous chapter. Moving to the New Testament, she argues that we must view redemption as a "pivot" in a single story.[15] In Jesus we have not just a story about redemption, but "a re-narration of the story of creation" that requires us to understand creation through the lens of redemption, not because the logic of creation requires it but because that is the story that has actually been given to us.

We might also question Kelsey's argument for more canonical reasons. To some extent, Kelsey's argument only holds if we find no significance in the fact that Genesis 1–3 comes at the beginning of the *Bible* and not just at the beginning of the *Pentateuch*. If we take this canonical perspective seriously, we cannot skip over these texts in favor of the wisdom literature when developing a theology of creation, nor can we fail to understand these chapters without taking into account the rest of the story in which they are firmly embedded.[16] Indeed, I find it problematic to argue that even the wisdom literature should be interpreted as if it had a creational logic that was entirely separate from the overall narrative in which those books find their location and meaning.

---

13. Catherine Pickstock, "The One Story: A Critique of David Kelsey's Theological Robotics," *Modern Theology* 27, no. 1 (2011): 26–40.

14. Ibid., 28.

15. Ibid., 30.

16. For a similar concern, see David Fergusson, "Humans Created according to the Imago Dei: An Alternative Proposal," *Zygon* 48, no. 2 (2013): 449.

In addition to this narratival concern, Kelsey also lodges a critique on the formal centrality of the *imago Dei* given the scarcity of the concept in the Old Testament. Since the *imago Dei* "is put to no theological use in the Old Testament outside of Genesis,"[17] and since the interpretation of Genesis 1:26–28 "is so problematic and controversial that the most careful and influential exegeses seem to cancel out each other,"[18] the Old Testament simply does not warrant affirming the centrality of the image. Although he thinks the New Testament offers greater resources for developing a view of the image, he still located his treatment of the image in the appendices of his two-volume work.

The question Kelsey raises is perfectly legitimate. If the image is central to a biblical view of humanity, why does it occur so infrequently and with such great ambiguity?[19] Yet John Kilner points out that "the particular places where references to God's image appear are unusually significant in the Bible."[20] The earliest references comes with the creation of humanity (Gen 1:26–28), which "is not an incidental matter but something that readers of the Bible are to notice and remember."[21] The strategic location of this reference has long attracted the interest of interpreters, but Kilner argues that the second and third uses are equally decisive. Coming at the beginning of Genesis 5, the second occurrence comes immediately after the fall and right before the first of many genealogies in Genesis. To Kilner, this suggests that even after the radical changes that took place with the fall, the *imago* continues to be constitutive of God's purposes

---

17. Kelsey, *Eccentric Existence*, 900.

18. Ibid.

19. If we limit ourselves only to those texts that explicitly use the Hebrew terms *tselem* (image) or *demut* (likeness) with clear reference to the image of God, then the concept only occurs three times in the OT, all of them in Genesis (Gen 1:6–27; 5:3; 9:6). There is some debate about whether particular New Testament texts refer explicitly to the image, but regardless we are still dealing with only a handful of texts (Rom 8:29; 1 Cor 11:7; 15:49; 2 Cor 3:18; 4:4; Col 1:15; 3:10; Jas 3:9).

20. Kilner, *Dignity and Destiny*, 37. G. C. Berkouwer similarly argues that biblical references to the *imago* "have a special urgency and importance" (*Man: The Image of God* [Grand Rapids: Eerdmans, 1962], 67).

21. Kilner, *Dignity and Destiny*, 38. Richard Lints suggests that just as the creation narratives themselves "echo" across the rest of scripture, we shouldn't be surprised to find that the same is true for the *imago* (Lints, *Identity and Idolatry*, 59).

for humanity. The third use carries a similar emphasis, appearing right after the flood as part of the Noahic restatement of God's plan for creation (Gen 9:6). Thus, Kilner concludes that "humanity's image-of-God status yet again appears in order to reiterate what is irremovable from who human beings are."[22] We do not find any direct references to the image in the rest of the Old Testament,[23] though we could perhaps speculate that nothing more is needed given the foundational significance of the creational and postlapsarian references noted already. The fourth "pivotal point" in the story comes with the incarnation: "Not only does the New Testament identify Christ as God's image, but humanity's dignity and destiny are also freshly defined in terms of that image."[24] According to Kilner, then, although the vast majority of scripture lacks explicit reference to the image, we can identify its significance by noting the references we do have occur at particularly important points in the narrative of creation, fall, and redemption.

A second common argument for establishing the significance of the *imago*, though, is "the possibility that Scripture often deals with the concept of the image of God without using those exact words."[25] Discerning whether the concept is operating in the "background" of a text requires, of course, that we first determine its meaning. So we will not be able to assess the validity of this argument until later. Yet I think we will see that there is much to be said for the idea that the *imago Dei* is a concept that drives much of the biblical narrative even when it is not explicitly present.

Finally, there is a third possibility for how the *imago* might still be intimately related to the rest of the biblical narrative despite its scarcity. Suppose that I am writing a story in which I introduce the main character in the first paragraph as "an exploding star" without

---

22. Kilner, *Dignity and Destiny*, 38.

23. However, many see Psalm 8 as a clear allusion to the image of God, particularly with its reference to the creation of humanity in a context that emphasizes motifs like glory and dominion.

24. Kilner, *Dignity and Destiny*, 38.

25. Berkouwer, *Man: The Image of God*, 67.

explaining precisely what that means. As the reader, you already have some notion of what an exploding star is—and we will see that ancient readers would likewise have already had some knowledge of what it means for a creature to be an "image" of a divine being—but you do not yet know precisely how I intend for this metaphor to serve as a description of the main character. You can guess, but no more than that. Suppose further that I never come out and state the meaning of the metaphor, simply allowing the narrative to unfold. Even if I never used that metaphor again, you might still be able to see how it anticipated what followed. Its defining significance lies not in its number of uses but in the extent to which it is integrated into and shapes the overall story.

Although we cannot assess the strength of these final two arguments until we get a clearer picture of the *imago* itself, we can at least see that it is entirely possible for a concept to be biblically central despite a scarcity of explicit reference. If we were to stop with just affirming the centrality of the image, we would still have enough to support a christological anthropology, though in a merely formal way. The fundamental ambiguity in the actual meaning of the image would prevent it from making any real contribution to the actual content of our anthropology. We need to press on to discover if we can say anything more about the meaning of the image.

The Material Content of the Image: Idols, Images, and Divine Presence

We should begin with the terms used in Genesis 1:26–28 to describe the *imago Dei*: "image" (*tselem*) and "likeness" (*demut*). Although this will seem obvious to many, some might be surprised by the decision to start our discussion in the Old Testament. Given the christological reorientation of the *imago Dei* we will address in the next section, and the fact that the majority of the image texts are in the New Testament, it might seem reasonable to begin by looking first at Jesus himself.[26] Yet even Paul, who makes some of the strongest

26. Kilner, *Dignity and Destiny*, 52.

claims about Jesus as the true image of God, uses the language of the image in a way that assumes some prior knowledge about how that language functioned in the Old Testament. So we will need to wrestle with that material before we turn our attention to the *imago Dei* in the New Testament.

We first need to recognize that *tselem* and *demut* fit within a broader constellation of terms the Bible uses to refer to idols and idolatry.[27] Although *tselem* can be used metaphorically, it most often "designates three-dimensional cult statues of various false gods."[28] *Demut* occurs less frequently in the context of idols, but it too functions within that same general domain.[29] It thus seems likely that however we understand *tselem* and *demut* in Genesis, our interpretation should at least be informed by the conceptual background of what idols were and how they functioned in the ancient world. As James Barr concludes, "There is an antecedent probability that the term 'image of God' might suggest, and might therefore require some delimitation against, the then familiar use of images or idols of the divine."[30]

We sometimes misunderstand the nature of idols, however, partly because of the biblical texts themselves. In several places, the biblical authors offer some effective rhetoric against idols, emphasizing the futility of worshiping objects made by human hands (e.g., Deut 4:28; 2 Kgs 19:18; Isa 37:19; 40:18–19; 44:9–20; Ezek 20:32). In each of these passages, the author presents an idol as something made by humans and therefore unworthy of worship. The problem for our purposes, however, is that such rhetoric can lead us to misconstrue

---

27. James Barr, "The Image of God in the Book of Genesis—A Study of Terminology," *Bulletin of the John Rylands Library* 51, no. 1 (1968): 11–26; David J. A. Clines, "The Image of God in Man," *Tyndale Bulletin* 19 (1968): 73; Edward Mason Curtis, "Man as the Image of God in Genesis in the Light of Ancient Near Eastern Parallels" (Ph.D., University of Pennsylvania, 1984); Middleton, *The Liberating Image*, 25.

28. Middleton, *The Liberating Image*, 25.

29. Barr, "The Image of God"; Curtis, "Man as the Image of God in Genesis in the Light of Ancient Near Eastern Parallels."

30. Barr, "The Image of God," 15. See also John F. Kutsko, *Between Heaven and Earth: Divine Presence and Absence in the Book of Ezekiel* (Winona Lake, Ind: Eisenbrauns, 2000); Lints, *Identity and Idolatry*, 31–42.

the way idols were actually viewed in the ancient Near East. More than just wood and stone, an idol was a manifestation of divine presence in the world.[31] Although the idol would certainly have been crafted by a human, it also would have gone through a cultic ritual during which some divine being was understood to infuse its divine presence into the idol, thereby making the idol a living thing.[32] That is why it was considered blasphemous to desecrate or even disrespect an idol in any way. Thus, according to José Faur, the "fundamental principle" for any understanding of idols in the ancient world "was the identification of a god with his idol."[33] This identification was the pervasive framework for understanding idols in the biblical world. We do not need to think the biblical authors were unaware of this framework or that they completely rejected it to understand their rhetoric. They do not criticize the pagans for their failure to understand what an idol really is, but because the idols they worship represent false gods!

If that is the background against which we need to understand the image of God,[34] we need to view the *imago Dei* as a declaration that God intended to create human persons to be the physical means through which he would manifest his own divine presence in the world.[35] Indeed, some have argued that certain details from the

---

31. For a good discussion of this, see José Faur, "The Biblical Idea of Idolatry," *The Jewish Quarterly Review* 69, no. 1 (1978): 1–15.

32. Michael B. Dick, *Born in Heaven, Made on Earth : The Making of the Cult Image in the Ancient Near East* (Winona Lake, IN: Eisenbrauns, 1999); Catherine L. McDowell, *The Image of God in the Garden of Eden: The Creation of Humankind in Genesis 2:5–3:24 in Light of the mīs pî pīt pî and wpt-r Rituals of Mesopotamia and Ancient Egypt* (Winona Lake, IN: Eisenbrauns, 2015).

33. Faur, "The Biblical Idea of Idolatry," 7.

34. Middleton rightly warns about the inherently tenuous nature of any attempt to reconstruct the historical/cultural setting of an ancient text like this (Middleton, *The Liberating Image*, 93), and there is considerable debate about whether to understand the *imago Dei* against a Mesopotamian or Egyptian background (for overviews, see Curtis, "Man as the Image of God in Genesis in the Light of Ancient Near Eastern Parallels"; W. Randall Garr, *In His Own Image and Likeness: Humanity, Divinity, and Monotheism* (Leiden: Brill, 2003); Middleton, *The Liberating Image*). Despite differences of detail, though, the concept of an idol as a physical totem through which a divine being manifests presence seems relatively stable across the various cultures.

35. Since idols were often understood to resemble the deities, some might wonder if this requires us to think that humans resemble God in some physical way. We will consider the body's role in the *imago Dei* a bit later, but for now it is worth noting that nothing in the concept of an idol requires similarity, and some idols were mere lumps of rock (Kilner, *Dignity and Destiny*, 57).

creation narrative in Genesis 2 mirror the washing/opening of the mouth ceremony used to consecrate idols. According to Andreas Schüle, we should notice at least the following:

> Similarities occur in the general pattern—the material shaping of a body, its being brought to life, the change of environment from some desert place to the garden—but also in details like the furnishing of the garden with plants and animals and the fact that God himself is present there and joins with Adam and Eve in the early evening hours when there is a nice breeze coming in from the Mediterranean sea.[36]

If this is the case, it provides additional confirmation that we need to hear the language of "image" against the background of ancient Near Eastern views on the nature and function of idols, viewing the creation of the *adam* in Genesis 2:7 as God fashioning his own idol in the world.[37]

Some have described views like this under the heading of *representational* views of the image.[38] The drawback to such a label is that it is not clear that the language of representation suffices to capture the robust emphasis on real *presence* at work here. Consider for example the statues that a king might erect throughout his kingdom to represent his own kingly presence.[39] Although there is a sense in which the king is understood to be "present" in the statue, even warranting the special care and treatment of such regal tokens, the "presence" in view here is entirely symbolic. The king is

---

36. Andreas Schüle, "Made in the 'image of God': The Concepts of Divine Images in Gen 1–3," *Zeitschrift für die Alttestamentliche Wissenschaft* 117, no. 1 (2005): 13; see also Catherine L. McDowell, *The Image of God in the Garden of Eden*.

37. Of course, this also needs to be understood in light of the Bible's clear prohibitions against idolatry. For a good discussion of this, see Lints, *Identity and Idolatry*.

38. E.g., Grenz, *The Social God and the Relational Self*, 197–99.

39. For example, in Daniel 3:1–7 Nebuchadnezzar erects statues (*tselem*) of himself throughout the land to represent him when he is not there. Such representational uses of statues were common throughout the ancient Near East (see esp. ibid., 189–99; Middleton, *The Liberating Image*, 104–7).

not actually present in the statue; indeed, the king's personal *absence* is precisely why he needs the statue to perform the function that it does. In an earlier work I addressed this challenge with the idea of "representational presence,"[40] a phrase I used to identify things that were so closely identified with the reality they represented that we could say the reality was in some way really present in and with the symbol. So, for example, although a national flag clearly has a symbolic function, it represents a nation in such a way that wherever you fly the flag that nation is understood to be present in some real sense. In such cases, the symbol does not indicate the *absence* of the reality but its *representational presence*. Although I still find that distinction helpful, particularly for developing a more robust understanding of the nature and function of symbols, I wonder if even this is adequate to the conceptual framework of image/idol in the ancient Near East. Despite moving beyond the *merely* symbolic, this representational presence still seems more notional than real. I could be wrong, but I suspect that most of us see the representational power of the flag as entirely wrapped up in certain epistemic commitments. If I imagined a universe in which no one thought that flags had any real significance, they would no longer have the power to manifest any kind of representational presence. In the framework of image/idols, however, we are operating with something much more ontological than epistemological. On this account, suppose that we took an idol and buried it in a time capsule until everyone had forgotten that it was the idol of a particular deity. When our grandchildren opened the time capsule, they would have no notion that this small statue was in any way related to the presence of a divine being. Yet that would not change the nature of the idol or the reality of divine presence. (Although, presumably, they would now be faced with a rather annoyed deity who will seek revenge for locking her in a box like that.) Consequently, the idea of divine presence associated with idols must press beyond even a

---

40. Marc Cortez, *Theological Anthropology: A Guide for the Perplexed* (New York: T&T Clark, 2009), 31–32.

robustly symbolic understanding of presence and toward something more concrete.

This more robust notion of divine presence prepares us to appreciate the fundamental significance of the Spirit for biblical anthropology.[41] If the *imago Dei* denotes the idea that humans are a primary means through which God manifests his own presence in the world, then the *imago* is inherently pneumatological because of the intimate link between God's presence and the Spirit throughout the Old Testament (e.g., Pss 51:11; 104:30; 139:7; and Hag 2:5). Some have even argued that the creation narratives themselves offer a clear basis for affirming a pneumatological view of the image. Though there is considerable debate about how to understand the *ruach* "hovering over the waters" in Genesis 1:2, many view this as a reference to God's Spirit, which is elsewhere associated with God's creative activity. Indeed, Middleton identifies the Spirit in Genesis 1:2 simply as "God's creative presence."[42] And we have already seen reasons for thinking that Genesis 2:7 might be an allusion to the cultic ritual in which a divine being infuses his spirit into some material object. If that is the case, then even though the second creation account does not use the explicit language of the *imago Dei*, the concept continues to shape the narrative even there.

This approach also gives us resources for incorporating at least some of the insights of other approaches to the image. Many scholars today prefer to view the image as something humans are called to *do* rather than something they *are*. Such functional views typically appeal to the emphasis on dominion in Genesis 1:26–28 and parallel texts in the ancient Near East that describe kings as "images" of some divine being, by which they mean that he is the divinely

---

41. For a more extensive discussion, see Marc Cortez, "Idols, Images, and a Spirit-ed Anthropology: A Pneumatological Account of the *imago Dei*," in *Third Article Theology: A Pneumatological Dogmatics*, ed. Myk Habets (Minneapolis: Fortress, 2016), 267–82.

42. Middleton, *The Liberating Image*, 86. This theme carries over strongly into the New Testament. In his extensive study of the Spirit in the Pauline literature, Gordon Fee concludes that we can define the Spirit there as "God's Empowering Presence" (Gordon D. Fee, *God's Empowering Presence: The Holy Spirit in the Letters of Paul* [Peabody, MA: Hendrickson, 1994]).

authorized representative who rules in the deity's place.[43] Yet many contend that the best way to understand the grammar of Genesis 1:26 is to view dominion as something that comes *as a consequence of* being made in the image.[44] If this is the case, then the *imago Dei* was always intended to be closely associated with the function(s) that humans carry out in the world, but this function remains distinct from the meaning of the image itself.[45] We would thus end up with an essence/function distinction that may also help us relate the *imago Dei* to the various capacities of the human person. Traditionally, people have associated the image with one or more human capacities (e.g., rationality). On the divine presence view, however, such capacities cannot *define* the image since a divine being does not depend on the capacities of the idol to manifest its presence. Indeed, some of the idols in the ancient world were mere lumps of rock.[46] We would thus need to say that the basic meaning of the *imago Dei* has nothing to do with any particular capacities of the human person, even though capacities remain necessary for the ways in which we live in response (function) to the reality of being made in the image of God (essence). We are called to use whatever capacities we do have to carry out the divinely intended functions as a consequence of the truth that we are images of the living God.

The Christological Reorientation of the *Imago Dei*

As I mentioned earlier, the *imago Dei* is an intriguing resource for christological anthropology because of the startling shift that takes

43. For a good overview of these arguments, see Middleton, *The Liberating Image*, 93–146.

44. Mathews, *Genesis: 1–11:26*, vol. 1, The New American Commentary (Nashville: Holman Reference, 1996), 211–12; Victor P. Hamilton, *The Book of Genesis: Chapters 1–17* (Grand Rapids: Eerdmans, 1990); Henri Blocher, *In The Beginning: The Opening Chapters of Genesis* (Downers Grove, IL: InterVarsity, 1984); Gerhard von Rad, *Genesis: A Commentary* (Philadelphia: Westminster, 1961); Franz Delitzsch, *A New Commentary on Genesis*, trans. Sophia Taylor (Edinburgh: T&T Clark, 1899).

45. This in turn allows us to affirm that even humans who do not seem able to participate in the respective function are still *imago Dei* beings.

46. Clines, "The Image of God in Man," 92.

place in the New Testament. Unlike the Old Testament, which focuses on the idea that all humans are made in the image of God, the New Testament views the image almost exclusively through the lens of Christology. Jesus alone is "the image of the invisible God" (Col 1:15; cf. 2 Cor 4:4), the "exact representation" of God's nature (Heb 1:3). We thus find that the focus of the *imago Dei* has constricted to such an extent that only *one* person actually qualifies! However, other passages make it clear that Jesus's unique status as *the* image of God does not preclude others from participating in that reality. Thus, the good news is that we can be "transformed into his image" (2 Cor 3:18) as we "put on the new self" that is being "renewed in knowledge in the image of its Creator" (Col 3:10; cf. Eph 4:22–24). Although this latter verse might sound as though it were shifting away from the exclusively christological focus of these other passages, the "new self" in Paul is a thoroughly christological concept, and even this passage quickly directs our attention to the unity that we all experience in Christ as a consequence of being included in this new self (Col 3:11). Throughout, then, the focus remains on the image as a christological reality in which we have been invited to participate. Indeed, this is precisely what we have been destined for since before the creation of the world (Rom 8:29).

Nonetheless, the interpretation of the image offered in the last section coheres nicely with what we see in Christ. The New Testament authors consistently identify Jesus as the one through whom God truly manifests his divine presence in the world. Jesus is "God with us" (Matt 1:23), the eternal Word dwelling with us (John 1:14), and the one in whom "God was pleased to have all his fullness dwell" (Col 1:19). This also explains the connection between the *imago Dei* and "glory" in the New Testament (e.g., 2 Cor 3:18; 11:7; Heb 1:3). Throughout the Bible, God's glory is closely related to his divine presence,[47] and in the previous chapter we

---

47. Sverre Aalen, "Δόξα," in *New International Dictionary of New Testament Theology*, ed. Colin Brown (Grand Rapids: Zondervan, 1986), 2:44–52.

discussed the fundamental significance of the Spirit for the person and work of Jesus, noting John's emphasis on Jesus as the one who inaugurates true humanity specifically by pouring the Spirit into God's people. This fits with what we noted in the prior section about the relationship between the Spirit and God's presence, both of which lie at the heart of the *imago Dei*. Paul demonstrates the interconnection of Jesus, the Spirit, and the *imago Dei* in a single intriguing statement: "And we all, with unveiled faces reflecting the glory of the Lord, are being transformed into the same image from one degree of glory to another, which is from the Lord, who is the Spirit" (2 Cor 3:18 NET). Rather than downplaying the significance of pneumatology in theological anthropology, as some might fear, the christological reorientation of the *imago Dei* asserts the central importance of the Spirit for understanding what it means to be fully human.

Indeed, if we locate divine presence at the heart of what it means to be the image of God, then the full reality of the image simply is the incarnation: the fullness of God's presence in bodily form. That does not imply, however, a merely quantitative difference between the divine presence in the incarnation and that which is experienced by other humans who are made in God's image. Rather, this is the significance of saying that Jesus alone is the true *imago Dei*, the only instance of a hypostatic union in which both divine and human natures unite in a single person. Nonetheless, in Jesus we see that being human fundamentally involves manifesting God's own glorious presence through the indwelling power of the Spirit. In the incarnation, we have the singular instance of the *imago Dei* in all its fullness, yet other humans are called to participate in the reality of the image by being united with the Son through the power of the Spirit.[48]

---

48. Kilner thus makes a distinction between two different kinds of images at work in the New Testament. Christ is an "imprint-image," which denotes that Christ is an exact copy of the original (i.e., he is divine). Every other human person is a "likeness-image," which emphasizes a close connection with the original, but not an identity relationship (Kilner, *Dignity and Destiny*, 59).

THE IDENTITY OF THE IMAGE:
THE ETERNAL SON OR THE INCARNATE CHRIST?

At this point, though, some difficulties arise: What exactly are the biblical authors referring to when they say that the Son is the image of God? Do they understand this as a claim about the eternal Son who is consubstantial with the Father and thus the eternally perfect image of the Father? Or are they talking instead about the incarnate Jesus who comes as the perfect expression of what it means to be a human person made in the image of God? In other words, is this claim primarily about the *Trinity* (the Son's eternal relationship to the Father) or *anthropology* (humanity's role as God's image bearers)?

Rather than trying to answer this question by surveying all the relevant texts, however, I think it will be more profitable to dig into two specific texts: one in which Paul famously presents the Son as the true image (Col 1:15) and another that has generated considerable discussion about whether this refers to the eternal Son or the incarnate Christ (Heb 1:3). In the process, I will contend that we should understand the *imago Dei* in the New Testament as *primarily an anthropological claim* identifying Jesus as the perfect expression of what it means to be human, rather than a Trinitarian claim about the relationship between the Father and the Son in eternity. This does not in any way mean that we should reject the idea that the Son is consubstantial with the Father, or that he is in some way the perfect reflection of the Father, but only that the primary focus of the image texts in the New Testament is on the manifestation of God's presence *in creation* through the *humanity* of Jesus.

The Image of the Invisible God

In our first text, Paul identifies the Son as the true image of God in no uncertain terms: "The Son is the image [*eikōn*] of the invisible God, the firstborn overall all creation" (Col 1:15). There was some debate among early theologians about whether this text referred to the eternal Son in his divine nature or to the incarnate Christ, but many of those theologians contended that the first was clearly the correct option because only one who is consubstantial with the Father could possibly be the perfect image of the Father.[49] Paul seems to make this even clearer by emphasizing the *invisibility* of the Father, which suggested to many of these theologians that the perfect *eikōn* of the Father must also be essentially invisible, focusing their attention on the eternal Son rather than the incarnate Christ. They also noted that Paul immediately relates the Son's status as the *eikōn* of God to his involvement in the creation of the universe (1:16), which suggests that imaging God is also something that the Son does from all eternity and not just by means of the incarnation. Such an interpretation also maintains the parallel that many identify in this passage between the eternal Son in creation (1:15–17) and the incarnate Christ in redemption (1:18–20).

Despite these compelling arguments, however, we have a number of reasons for thinking that the picture may not be as simple as this approach suggests. First, the argument from the invisibility of God runs into at least one substantial problem: the New Testament repeatedly affirms that we see the invisible God in the incarnate Jesus. As John states most clearly, "Anyone who has seen me has seen the Father" (John 14:9). This resonates with what we said earlier about the incarnate Son as the manifestation of the divine presence, which Paul affirms by saying that Jesus is the one in whom "the fullness of God was pleased to dwell" (Col 1:19 ESV). Just in case we might mistake this last phrase as referring to the eternal Son, Paul makes his point even more clear in the following chapter, describing Christ as the one in whom "all the fullness of Deity lives in *bodily* form" (2:9).[50] So the New Testament emphasizes that it is precisely through the material body of Jesus that God makes himself visible in the world. Indeed, the very nature of an idol entails that

---

49. See esp. J. B. Lightfoot, *Saint Paul's Epistles to the Colossians and to Philemon* (Grand Rapids: Zondervan, 1968), 148–50.

50. Emphasis added.

the *imago Dei* is an inherently material concept.[51] Consequently, the fact that the Son is said to be the image of the *invisible* God does not constitute any real problem for the incarnational view.

At first glance, the consubstantiality argument runs into the problem that only the Son is said to be the image of God, yet the Spirit is also consubstantial with the Father. If consubstantiality is the basis of the Son's *imago* status, should we not attribute the *imago* to the Spirit as well? Yet the argument could easily be adjusted to maintain that consubstantiality is *necessary* but not *sufficient* for being a perfect image of the Father. Consequently, it would seem that consubstantiality alone cannot ground the unique relationship between the Son and the image. In addition to consubstantiality, maybe some particular relationship to the Father is required, one that characterizes the Father-Son relationship and not the Father-Spirit relationship. Thus, the Son is the *imago* in virtue of consubstantiality *and* his unique relationship to the Father. If so, then we still have the argument that only someone who is consubstantial with the Father could be the perfect image of the Father.

A more important problem with the consubstantiality argument derives from the assumption that a true image must be nearly identical to the reality that it seeks to image. Yet nothing about the nature of the *imago Dei* suggests that even a true *eikōn* involves perfect replication. Indeed, insofar as an *eikōn* involves the union of divine and creaturely realities, there must always be a fundamental difference between the *eikōn* and the reality that manifests itself through the *eikōn*. No matter how intimate the relationship might be, the fundamental difference remains. Thus, the consubstantiality argument only works on the presumption of an entirely different view of the image—one that requires perfect replication—which does not cohere with the basic nature of the *imago Dei* argued for above.

---

51. We have already seen that materiality is inherent to the meaning of an image/ idol, which lies behind the meaning of *eikōn* as well (see Otto Flender, "Εικων," in *The New International Dictionary of New Testament Theology*, ed. Colin Brown [Grand Rapids: Zondervan, 1986], 2:286–88). Not only is *eikōn* the preferred term for translating *tselem* in the LXX, but it is also a common term for idols in the NT (e.g., Rom 1:23; Rev 13:14).

The argument from creation in verse 16 is a stronger argument, but it too has problems. As I will argue in the next section, the biblical authors do not follow modern theological conventions about distinguishing clearly between propositions that belong properly to the Son in his preincarnate state and those that apply to the Son in the incarnation. Like many early theologians, Paul views both sets of propositions as being true of the same *person*, and thus has no problem moving seamlessly from statements about redemption (1:13–14) to statements about creation (1:16–17) and then back to redemption (1:18–20), attributing all of these claims to the "Son."[52] If this is the case, then the mere fact that Paul refers to the Son's role in creation is inadequate to support the conclusion that the *eikōn* must also refer to the Son in eternity.

A number of biblical scholars have more recently raised an objection about viewing Paul's statement as a reference to the *imago Dei* at all. Instead, they contend that the language in this verse refers not to Genesis 1 but to the wisdom/word tradition that had become prominent in Hellenistic Judaism, in which wisdom is viewed as the intermediary principle that bridged the gap between the otherwise unknowable, invisible God of the universe and the creaturely, visible realm of the world.[53] Wisdom thus played an active role in creation, but she also entered creation in the Torah as the embodiment of God's instruction to his people (Wis 9; Sir 24:3–17). They find additional support for this interpretation in the reference to Christ as "firstborn" and his role as the mediator of creation, both of which are concepts associated with Wisdom. Such an interpretation would not only require us to associate the *eikōn* more clearly with the preincarnate Christ, but it would also

---

52. M. C. Steenberg, *Of God and Man: Theology as Anthropology from Irenaeus to Athanasius* (London: T&T Clark, 2009), 3.

53. E.g., James D. G. Dunn, *The Epistles to the Colossians and to Philemon: A Commentary on the Greek Text*, The New International Greek Testament Commentary (Grand Rapids: Eerdmans, 1996), 87–90; Jeffrey S. Lamp, "Wisdom in Col 1:15–20: Contribution and Significance," *Journal of the Evangelical Theological Society* 41, no. 1 (1998): 45–53; Christopher A. Beetham, *Echoes of Scripture in the Letter of Paul to the Colossians* (Boston: Brill, 2008), 175–77.

mean that this text is entirely irrelevant for understanding the *imago Dei*.[54]

Although this approach constitutes an important development in Pauline studies, we need to be careful about taking these conclusions too far. Indeed, some have rejected this approach entirely, arguing that we have no good basis for thinking that Paul was influenced by this wisdom framework.[55] Yet others have reasonably suggested a mediating approach. For example, Moo argues that since both the *imago Dei* and wisdom traditions take Genesis 1 as their starting point, it would be quite easy for someone like Paul to use language in such a way as to draw on aspects of both at the same time.[56] If this is the case, Paul is using *eikōn* to point in two directions at once. On the one hand, the Son is the incarnate one who has come as the perfect *imago Dei* through whom God will truly manifest his presence in the world, and, at the same time, the Son is the eternal Wisdom through whom God created the universe and who entered the world to enlighten God's people. The former is a more purely anthropological frame of reference, locating the Son in the story of God's image bearers; the latter more properly emphasizes the eternal relationship between the Son and the Father, which is then worked out in creation. If Moo is correct, the language of the *eikōn* is sufficiently evocative to allow readers to hear echoes of both ideas in the same passage.

In light of all this, we have good reasons for thinking that Colossians 1:15 refers (at least partly) to the image of God and that it does so in reference to the Son's incarnate state. Not only does this cohere better with the understanding of the image presented in

---

54. Dunn thus rejects *imago Dei* interpretations, stating simply, "none of this seems to be in mind here" (Dunn, *The Epistles to the Colossians and to Philemon*, 88).

55. See esp. Gordon D. Fee, *Pauline Christology: An Exegetical-Theological Study* (Peabody, MA: Hendrickson, 2007), 317–25. While remaining open to the Wisdom background, O'Brien also suggests caution, noting several important differences as well (Peter O'Brien, *Colossians, Philemon* [Waco, TX: Word, 1982], 39–40).

56. Douglas J. Moo, *The Letters to the Colossians and to Philemon*, The Pillar New Testament Commentary (Grand Rapids: Eerdmans, 2008), 118. See also O'Brien, *Colossians, Philemon*, 42–44; Marianne Meye Thompson, *Colossians and Philemon*, The Two Horizons New Testament Commentary (Grand Rapids: Eerdmans, 2005), 29.

the first half of the chapter, but we have not seen any good reason for thinking that the *eikōn* must refer to the eternal Son. To repeat what I said above, though, this in no way suggests that we should reject what theologians have traditionally meant when affirming that the eternal Son is the perfect image of the Father. We can still maintain that the Son is consubstantial with the Father such that he alone is the perfect reflection of the Father. Yet it remains the case that the language of the *imago Dei* in the Bible is anthropological language. So when Paul claims that the Son is the image of the invisible God, he is saying something that is true of the Son in virtue of the incarnation, which makes this a statement with specifically anthropological implications.

The Identity of the Eternal Son

In Hebrews 1:1–4, we encounter many of the same questions, but with an even clearer focus on those surrounding the referent of the *imago Dei*. Although this text does not use the explicit language of the *imago Dei*, most agree that the same basic ideas are in view when the author says that the Son is "the radiance of God's glory and the exact representation of his being."[57] Yet here the connection with the divine nature of the Son seems even clearer than in Colossians 1. Who besides the eternal Son could radiate God's own glory, and what human could be the "exact representation" of the divine being?[58] Indeed, David Allen remarks that each word in this verse "pulsates with deity."[59] Taken in conjunction with statements about the Son's role in the creation and preservation of the universe (Heb 1:2–3),

---

57. We have already seen the close relationship between image and glory, which is similarly emphasized here. And most interpreters see *charactēr* here as denoting the same basic idea of *eikōn* (e.g., Paul Ellingworth, *The Epistle to the Hebrews: A Commentary on the Greek Text* [Grand Rapids: Eerdmans, 1993], 99; David Lewis Allen, *Hebrews* [Nashville: B&H, 2010], 127; F. F. Bruce, *The Epistle to the Hebrews*, rev. ed., The New International Commentary on the New Testament [Grand Rapids: Eerdmans, 1990], 48). Indeed, O'Brien contends that *charactēr* carries this notion even more emphatically than *eikōn* (Peter O'Brien, *The Letter to the Hebrews*, The Pillar New Testament Commentary [Grand Rapids: Eerdmans, 2010], 55).

58. This verse thus became one of the dominant texts in pro-Nicene arguments during the fourth century (see Frances M. Young, "God's Image: The 'Elephant in the Room' in the Fourth Century?," in *Studia Patristica* [Leuven: Peeters, 2011], 57–71).

59. Allen, *Hebrews*, 116.

as well his status as "heir of all things" (1:2b), a title that would be eminently suited to the one who has eternally been the Son of the Father,[60] and in a broader context that focuses on the Son's superiority over the angels (1:5–14), it seems difficult to avoid the conclusion that the *imago Dei* is here applied to the Son in virtue of his divine nature.

Nonetheless, the passage also emphasizes the humanity of Christ in important ways. Indeed, rather than focusing our attention immediately on the eternal reality of the Son, the author locates this discussion in the context of the Son's revelatory work in the incarnation (1:1–2a). He then concludes the passage with a reflection on the Son's redemptive work and glorification (1:3b-4), which similarly requires an incarnational frame of reference. Regardless of how we understand the intervening claims, then, we should recognize that the passage focuses primarily on the Son in his incarnate state, which fits with the Christology of Hebrews as a whole.[61] Many have argued that although the language of being "appointed" heir refers to an eternal decree of God, the specific focus of the appointment is that which is enacted in history: the coming of the Son in the incarnation to redeem God's people and inherit the "name" that is greater than any other name (1:4). In chapter 4, I will even argue that the title "heir" itself should be understood at least partially as a reference to the Son's humanity rather than his eternal relationship to the Father. Consequently, in a passage that clearly emphasizes the eternal, divine nature of the Son, we actually have what appears to be a mixed set of statements that refer to both the eternal and the incarnate states at the same time.[62] However we understand

---

60. Although the latter part of the passage focuses on things that are true of Jesus's incarnate person and work (1:3b-4), that simply means we need to recognize that the structure of the passage moves from eternity to history in a manner that many find quite similar to the logic of John 1:1–14. All of this would seem to support the conclusion that the author of Hebrews associates the *imago Dei* primarily with the eternal Son rather than the incarnate Jesus.

61. Eric Farrel Mason, *"You Are a Priest Forever": Second Temple Jewish Messianism and the Priestly Christology of the Epistle to the Hebrews* (Leiden; Boston: Brill, 2008); Kevin B. McCruden, *Solidarity Perfected: Beneficent Christology in the Epistle to the Hebrews* (New York: de Gruyter, 2008); Brian C. Small, *The Characterization of Jesus in the Book of Hebrews* (Leiden; Boston: Brill, 2014).

62. Dunn refers to this as an "odd juxtaposition" of claims that results from the author of Hebrews trying to combine two different worldviews (James D. G. Dunn, *Christology in the*

the relationship between these various claims, then, we should be careful about assuming that verse 3 must refer only to the Son in his divine nature. Instead, since we have already identified a number of good reasons for thinking that *imago Dei* language refers to the embodied humanity of the Son in the incarnation, it would be reasonable to think that something similar is at work here as well.

However, this cannot mean that the *imago Dei* only comes into being at the moment of the incarnation, as though it had no significance before this. We have already seen that according to Paul we have been "predestined to be conformed to the image of his Son" (Rom 8:29). And Genesis 1:26–28 clearly views the *imago Dei* as having anthropological significance prior to the historical moment of the incarnation. However we understand the interesting mix of eternal and temporal claims in this passage, it certainly sounds like the author of Hebrews thinks it appropriate to associate the *imago Dei* with eternal truths about the creation and preservation of the universe. From this perspective, then, there must be some sense in which the Son has been eternally associated with the *imago Dei* such that it can serve as the predestined telos of God's people. But how can that be if the *imago Dei* language of the New Testament focuses primarily on the embodied humanity of the Son?

We could probably identify a number of ways to answer this question, but I would like to focus on three proposals that have been particularly influential in recent discussions. The most traditional approach is the one we have been discussing throughout. On this account, it is really the eternal Son who is the true *imago Dei*, and the incarnate Christ is a particularly apt reflection of that true image—an image of the image. John Webster thus contends that all of the christological predicates in this passage refer primarily to the eternal Son, based largely on the contention that "Son" is an inherently divine title in Hebrews. Rejecting Käsemann's argument that the motif of sonship in Hebrews inherently locates the Son

Making: A New Testament Inquiry into the Origins of the Doctrine of the Incarnation [Philadelphia: Westminster, 1980], 52).

in relation to the other sons, Webster contends that this approach "is vitiated by failure to see that both the relation of the Son to the many sons as first-born and also his function as pioneer require that his Sonship be determined first and foremost by his relation to the Father."[63] In other words, although there is an important sense in which the title "Son" applies to the incarnate state, it does so derivatively. He is Son in virtue of his eternal nature, and this is what grounds the fact that he is Son in the incarnation.

As we have seen, such an approach has considerable support from the tradition, and it succeeds in grounding the eternal significance of the *imago Dei* by locating it in the divine nature of the Son. Nonetheless, I have already argued that the language of the *imago Dei* is anthropological and embodied, making it difficult if not impossible to understand from this perspective.[64] Consequently, we will need to look elsewhere to find a way of maintaining that the image of God is about Christ's embodied humanity and that it is eternally paradigmatic for all of humanity.

One way of doing this is to argue that the Son himself is God's eternal *idea* of what a true human should be. Thus, for Friedrich Schleiermacher the Son is the one in whom God eternally determined to fulfill his plans for humanity.[65] In the Son, we see God's blueprint for a true human, and this blueprint has existed eternally in the mind of God. Indeed, Schleiermacher contends that the true humanity of the Son is the ultimate telos of creation itself.[66] James Dunn offers a similar argument, concluding that we should reject

---

63. John Webster, "One Who Is Son: Theological Reflections on the Exordium to the Epistle to the Hebrews," in *Epistle to the Hebrews and Christian Theology*, ed. Richard Bauckham et al. (Grand Rapids: Eerdmans, 2009), 79.

64. Once again, though, I want to emphasize that this is not because I reject the idea that the Son is the perfect image of the Father. It simply remains the case that I do not find the language of the *imago Dei* as the most apt language for expressing this important truth.

65. Friedrich Schleiermacher, *The Christian Faith*, ed. H. R. Mackintosh and J. S. Stewart (Berkeley: Apocryphile, 2011), §89.3. See also Marc Cortez, *Christological Anthropology in Historical Perspective: Ancient and Contemporary Approaches to Theological Anthropology* (Grand Rapids: Zondervan, 2016), 124–26.

66. See esp. Friedrich Schleiermacher, "On Colossians 1:15–20 (1832)," trans. Esther D. Reed and Alan Braley, *Neues Athenaeum* 5 (1998): 48–80.

any idea of a "real personal pre-existence" of the Son, arguing instead that the Son only preexists in the eternal plan of God.[67] When the text talks about the Son as the one "through whom" God made the universe, then, we should take this as a description of the Son's purposive role in creation rather than as indicating that he operated as a personal agent in the act of creation.[68] On this view, the *imago Dei* is both eternally paradigmatic for humanity and something that is primarily true in virtue of Christ's humanity because the former is the blueprint that came to its truest expression in the latter.

Obviously, though, this conclusion comes at a rather high price. In order to ground the paradigmatic significance of the *imago Dei* in this way, we have to accept at least the possibility that the Son provides the intrinsic meaning of creation but does not himself transcend creation in any meaningful sense. This approach also does not seem to deal adequately with the fact that according to the biblical texts the Son is not only the one *for whom* but also as the one *in whom* and *through whom* creation took place (Col 1:16; Heb 1:2). This implies a far more active role for the Son, which in turn suggests that the Son's eternal identity is in view in these texts. Indeed, quite a number of scholars have recently argued in support of the Son's personal preexistence from a wide range of New Testament texts, calling into question the legitimacy of this approach.[69]

An alternative would be to emphasize the eternal significance of the Son's humanity by identifying it as that which grounds the eternal identity of the Son.[70] Most commonly associated with the

---

67. Dunn, *Christology in the Making*, 54–56.

68. See, for example, G. B. Caird, "Son by Appointment," in *New Testament Age: Essays in Honor of Bo Reicke*, ed. William C. Weinrich (Macon, GA: Mercer University Press, 1984), 73–81. Kenneth Schenck draws a more cautious conclusion, arguing only that Hebrews does not provide any real explanation for the kind of existence the Son might have before the incarnation and that "one should not draw particular conclusions from them concerning the exact nature of that existence" (Kenneth Schenck, "Keeping His Appointment: Creation and Enthronement in Hebrews," *Journal for the Study of the New Testament* 66 [1997]: 113).

69. Douglas McCready, *He Came Down from Heaven: The Preexistence of Christ and Christian Faith* (Downers Grove, IL: InterVarsity, 2005); Simon J Gathercole, *The Preexistent Son: Recovering the Christologies of Matthew, Mark, and Luke* (Grand Rapids: Eerdmans, 2006).

70. See esp. Bruce L. McCormack, "'With Loud Cries and Tears': The Humanity of the Son in the Epistle to the Hebrews," in *Epistle to the Hebrews and Christian Theology*, ed. Richard

theology of Karl Barth, this approach contends that although the Son has a real, personal existence from all eternity, the *identity* of the Son is determined by the concrete particularities of his historic existence.[71] To understand this argument, we need to appreciate the challenges created whenever we try to understand the relationship between time and eternity. On the one hand, the incarnation is a temporal event, something enacted in history. On the other hand, though, the incarnation is something that God determined to do from all eternity. If that is the case, although from a historical perspective we might distinguish between a time when the Son was incarnate (*logos ensarkos*) and a time when he was not (*logos asarkos*), from God's perspective there is no such distinction. The Son's identity has been shaped eternally by the reality of the incarnation. As McCormack says, "The being of the Son is given in election."[72] In this way, we can say both that the *imago Dei* is something true of the Son in virtue of the incarnation *and* that it is eternally true of the Son in virtue of God's decree of election because the identity of the eternal Son is shaped by the reality of the incarnation.

Different versions of this approach exist on a spectrum from stronger to weaker. Stronger versions emphasize the strict identity between the incarnate Christ and the eternal Son, rejecting any role for the *logos asarkos* in theology.[73] The eternal Son simply is the incarnate Jesus. Others contend that although the incarnation constitutes the identity of the eternal Son in such a way that we

---

Bauckham et al. (Grand Rapids: Eerdmans, 2009), 37–68; Bruce L. McCormack, "The Identity of the Son: Karl Barth's Exegesis of Hebrews 1.1–4 (and Similar Passages)," in *Christology, Hermeneutics, and Hebrews: Profiles from the History of Interpretation* (London: T&T Clark, 2012), 155–72.

71. See esp. Barth's discussion of election in *CD* II/2. For further discussions of this point, see Cortez, *Christological Anthropology in Historical Perspective*, 141–46 and esp. Marc Cortez, *Embodied Souls, Ensouled Bodies: An Exercise in Christological Anthropology and Its Significance for the Mind/Body Debate* (London: T&T Clark, 2008), chs. 1–3.

72. McCormack, "With Loud Cries and Tears," 59. Kelsey similarly concludes, "In Hebrews, it is the preexistent Christ who is identified with the 'exact imprint of God's very being', not Jesus in his humanity. However, it is also the case that in Hebrews it is Christ in his particular concrete humanity who defines the identity of the preexistent Christ" (Kelsey, *Eccentric Existence*, 905).

73. E.g., Robert W. Jenson, "Once More the *Logos asarkos*," *International Journal of Systematic Theology* 13, no. 2 (2011): 130–33.

should not talk about any *real* difference between them, the *logos asarkos* retains some conceptual value.[74] Thus, for example, the concept of the *logos asarkos* is necessary if we are going to say that God *freely* elected to become incarnate in Christ. Here the *logos asarkos* functions much like the *natura pura* did in the previous chapter. Even if we do not think the *logos asarkos* ever actually existed, it is an abstraction that we must affirm if we are going to acknowledge that the incarnation was a gift of God's grace. In a weaker sense yet, some contend that the *logos asarkos* is ontologically and not just logically prior to God's decree of election.[75] Here as well, we would not need to identify some "time" in which the Son existed in abstraction from the reality of the incarnation, only that there is a sense in which we must retain the ontological priority of the *logos asarkos* over the *logos ensarkos*. Proponents of this approach are generally concerned that the conceptual form of the argument fails to guard sufficiently the transcendence of the Son and, ultimately, makes the very nature of God ontologically dependent upon creation.[76]

For our purposes, it is important to notice that all three versions of the argument succeed in establishing that the *imago Dei* is true of the Son in virtue of the incarnation *and* that the *imago Dei* is eternally true in virtue of God's eternal decree to become incarnate in Christ. To use Barth's words, the "ontological determination of man is grounded in the fact that one man among all others is the

---

74. McCormack, "The Identity of the Son," 167–68.

75. Although to the best of my knowledge George Hunsinger has not addressed Heb 1:1–4 at length, he has responded to McCormack's arguments, and this seems the best place to locate the basic position he is defending. For the most complete summary of his arguments, see George Hunsinger, *Reading Barth with Charity: A Hermeneutical Proposal* (Grand Rapids: Baker Academic, 2015).

76. For a good introduction to the debate, see the following: Bruce L. McCormack, "Grace and Being: The Role of God's Gracious Election in Karl Barth's Theological Ontology," in *The Cambridge Companion to Karl Barth*, ed. John B. Webster (Cambridge: Cambridge University Press, 2000), 92–110; Paul D. Molnar, *Divine Freedom and the Doctrine of the Immanent Trinity: In Dialogue with Karl Barth and Contemporary Theology* (Edinburgh: T&T Clark, 2002); Kevin W. Hector, "God's Triunity and Self-Determination: A Conversation with Karl Barth, Bruce McCormack and Paul Molnar," *International Journal of Systematic Theology* 7, no. 3 (2005): 246–61; George Hunsinger, "Election and the Trinity: Twenty-Five Theses on the Theology of Karl Barth," *Modern Theology* 24, no. 2 (2008): 179–98.

man Jesus,"[77] and this is true specifically because "the man Jesus" is the focus of God's eternal decree of election. Before creation, the essence of what it means to be human has been eternally grounded in the humanity of Christ. Despite the fact that all three of these approaches succeed in establishing the eternal significance of the *imago Dei* in the humanity of Christ, the first two do so at some cost. As already noted, the first raises real questions about whether we can maintain the true freedom of God if we must affirm the strict identity between the eternal Son and the incarnate Christ. If that is the case, it seems that creation itself is necessary to the nature of God. The second approach softens the argument somewhat, yet many still worry that although it may succeed in establishing God's freedom, it does not defend similar worries about the *triunity* of God. In other words, since the *logos asarkos* is merely a conceptual abstraction, some worry about the implication that the Trinity itself only comes into existence with the decree of election. This is precisely what the third approach seeks to defend against, establishing the ontological priority of the Son and the corresponding priority of the triune nature of God. This third approach thus raises the fewest concerns and has the most potential for establishing the idea that it is specifically in the concrete humanity of Christ that the *imago Dei* has paradigmatic significance for all human persons from all eternity.

CONCLUSION

In this chapter, then, I have argued for both the formal and the material centrality of the *imago Dei*. Formally, the image is central because of the way it shapes the biblical narrative about humans from the beginning, but even more so because of its identification of Jesus as the true *eikōn* of God. Consequently, theological claims about the human person will need to be shaped in some way by this christological view of the image. Materially, I have argued that the image is best understood against the background of the ancient Near Eastern concept of an *idol*, leading to an emphasis on divine

---

77. *CD* III/2, 132.

presence as the heart of the *imago Dei*, a conclusion that also requires us to recognize the fundamental importance of pneumatology and human embodiment for theological anthropology.[78]

When we turn from the Old Testament background of the *imago Dei* to the christological orientation of the New Testament, however, we immediately face two challenging questions with significant implications for christological anthropology. On the one hand, we need to determine whether the New Testament texts attribute the true *imago* to the Son in virtue of his eternal divine nature or in virtue of his incarnate humanity. Although I have no intention of undermining the fundamental truth that the eternal Son is consubstantial with the Father and thus the perfect reflection of the divine being, I have argued that the specific language of the *imago Dei* is fundamentally anthropological language. The claim that the Son is the true image of God is thus primarily a claim about the concrete humanity we see in the gospels, even if we continue to maintain an inseparable relationship between the Son in the incarnation and the Son who preexists in eternity.

That latter point introduces the third issue we had to address in this chapter. If we are going to say that the *imago Dei* is an anthropological truth focused on Jesus's embodied humanity *and* that it has paradigmatic significance for all other humans, we need to find some way of explaining the eternal significance of Jesus's humanity. We considered three options for explaining this move, and I argued that the best option is to affirm that the humanity of Christ is eternally significant in virtue of God's eternal decision for the Son to become incarnate. I also noted that this option further subdivides into three further positions, arguing that the weakest form of this argument has the greatest potential for grounding a christological anthropology. We will return to these conclusions in chapter 5 when we discuss the methodological implications of these various biblical and theological decisions.

---

78. I realize that this leaves many unanswered questions about the nature of this divine presence in humans, how it relates to God's presence elsewhere (e.g., creation, sacraments), and how sin affects this view of the image. Unfortunately, complex questions like that lie beyond the scope of this chapter and will have to wait for my forthcoming volume on divine presence.

CHAPTER 4

"He Has Spoken"

Revelation, Fallenness, and the Humanity of Christ

IN THE FIRST THREE CHAPTERS, we explored the biblical basis for a christological anthropology in the gospels (Jesus as the true *anthrōpos*) and Paul (Jesus as the true *imago Dei* and the second Adam). Now we turn our attention to a third New Testament voice, the book of Hebrews. Although we have already encountered Hebrews to an extent in chapters two and three, we have not yet looked closely at what this important book has to contribute to a christological anthropology. Specifically, Hebrews will provide us with an opportunity to focus on two significant issues we have not yet engaged deeply. The first has to do with the claim that Jesus *reveals* truths about humanity. I have already argued that Jesus should be materially and not just formally central to theological anthropology, but we have not yet addressed the question of revelation directly. As we will see, Hebrews begins with a revelatory claim that has implications for understanding the relationship between Christology and anthropology.

However, after arguing that Jesus reveals true humanity, we run into an even more challenging issue. From one perspective, Hebrews sounds as though it envisions Jesus as the most perfect possible expression of humanity. He is "without sin" (4:15 ESV), the "unblemished" sacrifice (9:14), and the high priest who is "holy, blameless, pure, set apart from sinners, exalted above the heavens" (7:26). It would be difficult to imagine stronger language for emphasizing the radical perfection and purity of the incarnate Christ. From another angle, though, Hebrews describes Jesus's humanity in ways that make it sound more like our own: weak, fallen, and in need of perfecting (e.g., 4:15; 5:8–9). Indeed, the reason he is able to sympathize with our weakness as our great High Priest is because he experienced such weakness himself.

The tension between these two perspectives has produced a debate in contemporary theology about whether Jesus assumed an *unfallen* or a *fallen* human nature in the incarnation. Although most view the former as the traditional position, many theologians now question whether it adequately accounts for the language of Hebrews and the soteriological necessity that Christ fully enter into our fallen condition. However, the *fallen* position raises questions about how such a fallen human can serve as our unblemished sacrifice and perfect high priest. Additionally, the way we answer such questions has implications for christological anthropology. If Jesus assumed a perfect and unfallen human nature, we risk ending up with a christological anthropology that is overly idealized and abstract, with little significance for understanding the humanity that we experience every day. And if Jesus himself had a fallen nature, it would seem that we need to revise our conclusions about Jesus being the paradigm of *true* humanity. On this account, we risk being able to claim only that he offers the preeminent example of living faithfully as a fallen human.

As with the first three chapters, we will begin by looking at the book of Hebrews itself, focusing here on a number of key texts that present the Son's incarnate life as having revelatory significance for humanity as a whole. The second half of the chapter will shift to the *fallenness* debate and its significance for understanding the nature of the humanity we see revealed in Christ.

THE REVELATION OF TRUE HUMANITY IN HEBREWS

The book of Hebrews offers fertile soil for reflecting on the nature of the relationship between Christology and anthropology. Few would question that Hebrews is one of the most christologically rich books in the

New Testament with its extensive reflections on Jesus's exalted status, his relationship to God's redemptive work in the Old Testament, and his priestly work on behalf of his people. At the same time, Hebrews also has a keen interest in humanity, and particularly the humanity of Christ. Indeed, Bauckham contends that all three of Hebrews's key christological motifs—*son, lord,* and *high priest*—emphasize both Christ's deity and his humanity.[1] For Hebrews, the fact that Jesus was made "fully human in every way" (2:17) is central for understanding his identity and work (see esp. 2:5–18; 4:14–5:10). Indeed, as Hagner comments, "It is remarkable that the two New Testament writings that most stress the deity of Christ, the Fourth Gospel and the Epistle to the Hebrews, are at the same time the most emphatic about his full humanity."[2] Thus, the author of Hebrews locates the claim that Jesus comes as a true *anthrōpos* at the center of his theological argument.

"He Has Spoken to Us by His Son"

Hebrews begins with a claim about the uniqueness and supremacy of the revelation that comes through the Son: "In the past God spoke to our ancestors through the prophets at many times and in various ways, but in these last days he has spoken to us by his Son" (1:1–2a). With greater emphasis on the verbs that drive this opening sentence, Amy Peeler translates it thus: "God, after speaking, spoke."[3] This anticipates a key motif in Hebrews: divine speech. The author of Hebrews consistently portrays God as one who speaks to his people, a God who "is not distant, but involves himself with humanity by speaking to them."[4] Indeed, many have argued that divine speech lies at the center of the book.[5]

---

1. Richard Bauckham, "The Divinity of Jesus Christ in the Epistle to the Hebrews," in *Epistle to the Hebrews and Christian Theology* (Grand Rapids: Eerdmans, 2009), 15–36.

2. Donald A. Hagner, "The Son of God as Unique High Priest: The Christology of the Epistle to the Hebrews," in *Contours of Christology in the New Testament*, ed. Richard L. Longenecker (Grand Rapids: Eerdmans, 2005), 252.

3. Amy L. B. Peeler, *You Are My Son: The Family of God in the Epistle to the Hebrews*, repr. ed. (New York: Bloomsbury, 2015), 1.

4. Ibid., 3.

5. James Thompson, *Hebrews* (Grand Rapids: Baker Academic, 2008), 20; cf. William L.

I suspect that many of us hear these opening lines and assume they focus on the Son's role in revealing the Father, especially in light of the fact that the author goes on to emphasize the Son's unique relationship to the Father (1:3).[6] Yet these words and the verses that follow constitute the famous exordium of Hebrews, an introduction that anticipates many of the fundamental motifs that will be developed in what follows.[7] And, as we will see, humanity is indisputably one of the central themes of the book, focusing most of its attention on the amazing "Son" who became our faithful High Priest by joining himself to humanity, and his relationship to the "sons" who move toward what God intended through the work of the Son.[8] Indeed, one could argue that the revelation of humanity in Christ is a more fundamental theme in Hebrews than the revelation of God, though it would probably be more accurate to say that the revelation of humanity in Hebrews is inseparable from the revelation of God. So we can reasonably conclude that what "God has spoken to us by his Son" includes at least truths, perhaps fundamental truths, about what it means to be human.[9]

Importantly, this divine speaking through the Son comes as the *ultimate* expression of divine communication. God has spoken through the Son "in these last days," a phrase used throughout the

Lane, *Hebrews 1–8* (Waco, TX: Word, 1991), 1; William L Vander Beek, "Hebrews: A 'Doxology' of the Word," *Mid-America Journal of Theology* 16 (2005): 13; Peter T. O'Brien, *God Has Spoken in His Son: A Biblical Theology of Hebrews* (Downers Grove, IL: IVP Academic, 2016).

6. Many commentators suggest as much when they focus exclusively on God's self-revelation as the main point of this divine speech (e.g., O'Brien, *God Has Spoken in His Son*, 41; David Lewis Allen, *Hebrews* [Nashville: B&H, 2010], 152; Jonathan Griffiths, *Hebrews and Divine Speech* [London: Bloomsbury, 2014], 42–48).

7. Lane thus refers to it as "The majestic opening statement is programmatic for the entire discourse" (Lane, *Hebrews 1–8*, 17).

8. See esp. Peeler, *You Are My Son*.

9. Throughout Hebrews, though, this divine speech does more than convey information. Instead, Hebrews views God's speech as active. Rather than merely describing that which is, God's word brings new realities into being. Thus, divine speech both describes and creates new ways of being in the world. If this is the case, while not diminishing the revelation of God, we need to press further and consider what this divine speech might be saying and doing in other areas as well. Kenneth L. Schenck, "God Has Spoken: Hebrews' Theology of the Scriptures," in *Epistle to the Hebrews and Christian Theology*, ed. Daniel R. Driver et al. (Grand Rapids: Eerdmans, 2009), 323.

Old Testament to describe a time of eschatological fulfillment.[10] The phrase thus emphasizes both "the singularity and the finality of God's eschatological speech in the Son."[11] On this basis, O'Brien cautions against any attempt to identify a "third stage" of revelation, one that surpasses the revelation already given in the Son,[12] as though this was just one instance of revelation among many. Instead, regardless of what we might think about whether God continues to provide new revelation after the time of Christ, Hebrews presents the revelation given through the Son as qualitatively distinct from any other. Consequently, insofar as God speaks to us about the meaning of humanity in and through the Son, he does so with climactic significance.

"The Son Is the Radiance of God's Glory"

The author of Hebrews follows up this initial hint about the revelatory significance of the Son's humanity by presenting the Son as the paradigmatic human in the exordium itself. After introducing the Son at the beginning of verse 2, however, the author goes on to make seven claims about the identity of this revelatory figure, many of which allude to the paradigmatic status of Christ's humanity. That is clearly the case in verses 3–4 where the author addresses the Son's redemptive work, which necessarily involves his humanity. Since we wrestled with the complex issues surrounding the relationship between the eternal Son and the incarnate Christ in our chapter on the *imago Dei*, we do not need to rehearse those arguments here. Yet it is worth remembering that, according to the argument of that chapter, when the author declares the Son to be the "radiance of God's glory and the exact representation of his being" (1:3), he identifies him as the true image of God, thus placing an important anthropological claim at the heart of the exordium. Even if we

10. Allen, *Hebrews*, 102.

11. Harold W. Attridge, *The Epistle to the Hebrews: A Commentary on the Epistle to the Hebrews* (Philadelphia: Fortress, 1989), 36.

12. O'Brien, *God Has Spoken in His Son*, 27.

conclude that this phrase somehow refers to the Son in virtue of his divine nature as well as his human nature, it remains the case that we have a statement that at least *includes* anthropological truths as central to the identity of the one who is Son.

In addition, we should also consider the first of the seven claims, which indicates that the Son was "appointed heir [*klēronomon*] of all things" (1:2b). This has often been taken as a statement about the eternal Son since being the heir of the Father seems like a necessary implication of his eternal sonship. But the idea that Christ has been designated as the *klēronomos* also locates him within the story of humanity. Throughout Hebrews the term *klēronomos* and its cognates are used frequently to denote that which has been promised to God's people if they believe and persevere (1:14; 6:12, 17; 9:15). Noah and Abraham stand as exemplars of those who became heirs through faith (11:7–8), with Esau serving as the counter-example of someone who foolishly sold his birthright and forfeited his inheritance (12:17). Indeed, Lane points out that the language of being appointed heir probably hearkens back to Genesis 17:5 where Abraham is also appointed as heir of the promise.[13] Others have noted the similarity between the language in this verse and that of Psalm 2:8, where the royal son receives the promise of the nations as an inheritance.[14] Lane thus concludes that Hebrews is using the Old Testament motif of the heir "to connect the beginning of redemptive history with its accomplishment in the Son."[15] Indeed, we can reach even further back, noting that the Abrahamic promises themselves are grounded in the Adamic blessings of fruitfulness and dominion. To declare that the Son has been appointed as the "heir" identifies him as the one who will fulfill God's purposes for his people, the intentions he has had for humanity since the beginning of creation.[16] This does

13. Lane, *Hebrews 1–8*, 12.

14. Paul Ellingworth, *The Epistle to the Hebrews: A Commentary on the Greek Text* (Grand Rapids: Eerdmans, 1993), 94.

15. Lane, *Hebrews 1–8*, 12.

16. Kenneth Schenck, "Keeping His Appointment: Creation and Enthronement in Hebrews," *Journal for the Study of the New Testament* 66 (1997): 102.

not require us to reject the idea that the Son is also in some way the eternal heir of the Father. We only need to argue that in the context of Hebrews's broader argument it is likely that the phrase refers at least as much to the Son's status as the true human.

The exordium thus presents Jesus as the true image-heir, identifying him with the story of humanity, though marking him out as radically distinct within that story. He is not just another human, not even one who carries out the vocation of humanity in a quantitatively distinct way. Instead, Hebrews identifies the Son as the one through whom God uniquely speaks in the world because he is the true image and heir, the perfect representation of all that it means to be human.

"When God Brings His Firstborn into the World"

Reading through the rest of the first chapter of Hebrews, it would be easy to conclude that the author focuses largely on the eternal Son in his divine nature, arguing throughout that he is even more glorious than the angels, not turning his attention fully to the humanity of the Son until the second chapter.[17] Yet we need to be careful here. Notice first that the author introduces the Son's superiority to the angels in verse 4, which clearly focuses on the ascension of the Son. Yet the author of Hebrews also makes it clear that the ascended one is the *incarnate* Christ. The Son does not stop being human at the ascension, but he serves as our faithful High Priest forever because he continues to be fully human and thus able to represent us (7:17). Consequently, the exordium has already turned our attention to Christ's ascended state as the incarnate one.

This focus on the incarnate Son's superiority over the angels in the ascension continues throughout the first chapter. The key comes in verse 6, which declares the Son's superiority over the angels "when God brings his firstborn [*prōtotokos*] into the world

---

17. O'Brien more rightly notes that with chapter two the author shifts attention from the ascension to Jesus's earthly ministry. But note that O'Brien says most scholars take the catena of OT quotations as referring to the ascension, which is all about humanity (O'Brien, *God Has Spoken in His Son*, 61).

[*oikoumenēn*]" (1:6). Although many interpret *oikoumenēn* as referring to the world in which we currently live, reading the verse as a reference to the time when the Son became incarnate, others have rightfully argued that the term is better understood as a reference to the coming world to which Jesus ascends after the ascension.[18] This makes good sense in light of the claim that the Son is the *prōtotokos*, a term the author of Hebrews uses again to describe "the church of the firstborn" (12:23). This should remind us in turn of Paul's similar declaration that the Son is the "head of the body, the church" and the "firstborn [*prōtotokos*] from among the dead" (Col 1:18; cf. Rev 1:5). Interestingly, then, both of these authors use *prōtotokos* in the discussions of the *imago Dei* to describe the Son's role in bringing about God's eschatological purposes for his people. Similarly, though explicitly about the church, Paul claims that believers are "predestined to be conformed to the image of his Son" for the specific purpose that the Son might be "the firstborn [*prōtotokos*] among many brothers and sisters" (Rom 8:29). Although it is possible to understand *prōtotokos* as referring simply to temporal primacy—seeing Jesus as the first to experience this new creation reality—to do so would not do full justice to the language of primacy that consistently accompanies these claims. Jesus is not merely the first resurrected human, but he is also the one who establishes through the resurrection a new order of being in which others can now participate. Both in Paul and Hebrews, then, we have the idea that as the *prōtotokos* the Son inaugurates a way of being in which he both participates alongside others—his "brothers"—and yet remains radically unique as the eternal paradigm and telos.[19]

---

18. David Moffit offers the most extensive, recent treatment of this argument (*Atonement and the Logic of Resurrection in the Epistle to the Hebrews* [Leiden: Brill, 2011], 45–144). See also Lane, *Hebrews 1–8*, 27; Ellingworth, *The Epistle to the Hebrews*, 117–18; Kenneth L. Schenck, "A Celebration of the Enthroned Son: The Catena of Hebrews 1," *Journal of Biblical Literature* 120, no. 3 (2001): 469–85; Allen, *Hebrews*, 174; Ardel B. Caneday, "The Eschatological World Already Subjected to the Son: The Οἰκουμένη of Hebrews 1.6 and the Son's Enthronement," in *A Cloud of Witnesses: The Theology of Hebrews in Its Ancient Contexts*, ed. Richard Bauckham et al. (London: T&T Clark, 2008), 28–39.

19. Beyond the Pauline literature, we have one other instance where *prōtotokos* is used in close proximity to image-language (Heb 1:7). The connections are more tenuous here since

Throughout, the author of Hebrews directs our attention to the Son's ascension as the time when the Son both enters into the reality of the new creation and prepares the way for others to follow. Hebrews later declares that this is what makes him "the pioneer [*archēgon*] of their salvation" (cf. 12:2). Although it is possible that *archēgon* means no more than "hero" or "champion," drawing our attention to Jesus as a truly human individual who endured suffering so he could lead God's people to glory,[20] most take the word as indicating something closer to "pioneer," someone who goes before the people and prepares the way so that they can follow.[21]

The catena of Old Testament quotations that comprise the majority of the first chapter thus continue the emphasis of the exordium on the Son's paradigmatic humanity. Once again, though, this does not mean we have to reject the eternality that many find in the "today" of verse 5, and we could emphasize the eternal perspective again in the "beginning" of verse 10. As with the exordium, then, the author of Hebrews describes the Son with a complex set of claims that refers simultaneously to the Son's eternal and incarnate identities.

"But We Do See Jesus"

Moving into the second chapter, the author of Hebrews offers another argument for the paradigmatic status of Christ's humanity in the context of arguing for the redemptive significance of Christ's *full* humanity. The Son entered our human state so that he might save us from death (2:9, 14), becoming part of the "same family" as humanity (2:11), so that he might bring "many sons and daughters to glory" (2:10). The passage culminates with the powerful statement that "he had to be made like them, fully human in every way" (2:17).

---

the reference to the image is more removed (1:3) and the reference to Jesus as the *prōtotokos* more clearly emphasizes his uniqueness (as superior to the angels) than to his commonality with other humans. Yet that latter motif is clearly important in the argument of Hebrews and is part of the broader context of the passage (2:5–18). So it is at least conceivable that a similar dynamic may be at work here as well.

20. Lane, *Hebrews 1–8*, 56–57.

21. Ellingworth, *The Epistle to the Hebrews*, 160–61.

Yet this alone is not adequate for establishing the idea that Jesus somehow reveals what it means to be truly human. After all, I too qualify as fully human,[22] yet I am fairly certain that no sane person would want to identify me as some kind of anthropological norm. Rather than just claiming the *full* humanity of Christ, this passage goes further and suggests that his humanity is paradigmatic of true humanity.

We see this first in verses 2–9, which begins by quoting a psalm famous for its reflections on the question, "What is mankind [*anthrōpos*]?" According to the psalmist, the answer lies in the unique creation of the human person. We are creatures who were made to be a little lower than the angels but who were nonetheless crowned with glory and honor and placed in authority over all creation. Consequently, Psalm 8 is typically viewed as offering a definitive statement about what it means to be human in the light of creation. Yet many contend that the author of Hebrews interprets the psalm as referring directly to Jesus rather than to humanity as a whole.[23] Hebrews has been emphasizing the importance of Jesus throughout, even warning its readers about the hazards of neglecting the salvation made possible through him. So it would only make sense for the author to identify Jesus as the *anthrōpos* we are to be mindful of (2:6). This christological focus finds further support from the reference to the "Son of Man" in the following clause.[24] Although Hebrews does not refer to the Son of Man tradition elsewhere, some argue that it would have been sufficiently prominent by this time that the author would naturally have heard this phrase as having

---

22. As far as I know, at least.

23. E.g., Geoffrey W. Grogan, "Christ and His People: An Exegetical and Theological Study of Hebrews 2.5–18," *Vox Evangelica* 6 (1969): 245–76; David Peterson, *Hebrews and Perfection: An Examination of the Concept of Perfection in the "Epistle to the Hebrews"* (Cambridge: Cambridge University Press, 1982), 51–55; David A. deSilva, *Perseverance in Gratitude: A Social-Rhetorical Commentary on the Epistle "to the Hebrews"* (Grand Rapids: Eerdmans, 2000), 109–10; George H. Guthrie and Russell D. Quinn, "A Discourse Analysis of the Use of Psalm 8:4–6 in Hebrews 2:5–9," *Journal of the Evangelical Theological Society* 49, no. 2 (2006): 235–46.

24. E.g., F. F. Bruce, *The Epistle to the Hebrews*, rev. ed., New International Commentary on the New Testament (Grand Rapids: Eerdmans, 1990), 73; Hagner, "The Son of God as Unique High Priest: The Christology of the Epistle to the Hebrews," 252–54.

christological implications.[25] The passage continues by focusing on the troubling fact that God has already subjected everything to the Son, but the Son's dominion is obscured by the condition of the world around us (2:7–8). Nonetheless, the vision of the ascended Jesus sitting at the right hand of the Father assures us that God's plans will be accomplished (2:9). If this is the correct reading of the psalm, then the author of Hebrews directly identifies Jesus with a psalm that was originally intended as a statement about what it means to be human. Consequently, for the author of Hebrews, Jesus just is the *anthrōpos* of Psalm 8.

Yet others find this interpretation troubling.[26] According to them, the author intends that the quotation of Psalm 8 refer to humanity as a whole, with the christological shift coming later in Hebrews 2:9. They contend that this makes more sense of the fact that the author has already told us that everything has *not* yet been made subject to the Son (1:13), suggesting that 2:7 should be taken as a reference to the dominion given to all of humanity at creation. In addition, not only would this be the only place in Hebrews where the author uses *anthrōpos* to refer to Jesus as the paradigmatic human,[27] but they also find the "son of man" reference unconvincing because the author does not refer to it elsewhere,[28] and because the construction does not match the way the phrase is used in other son of man sayings.[29] On this view, the author contrasts the human condition (2:8) with the ultimate truth we see in Jesus (2:9).[30] We should notice, however,

---

25. E.g., Barnabas Lindars, *The Theology of the Letter to the Hebrews* (Cambridge: Cambridge University Press, 2010), 39–40.

26. See esp. Lincoln D. Hurst, "The Christology of Hebrews 1 and 2," in *The Glory of Christ in the New Testament: Studies in Christology*, ed. Lincoln D. Hurst and N. T. Wright (Oxford: Clarendon, 1987), 151–64; Grant R. Osborne, "The Christ of Hebrews and Other Religions," *Journal of the Evangelical Theological Society* 46 (2003): 249–67; Craig L. Blomberg, " 'But We See Jesus': The Relationship between the Son of Man in Hebrews 2.6 and 2.9 and the Implications for English Translations," in *A Cloud of Witnesses: The Theology of Hebrews in Its Ancient Context*, ed. Richard Bauckham et al. (London: T&T Clark, 2008), 28–39.

27. Blomberg, " 'But We See Jesus,' " 93.

28. Attridge, *The Epistle to the Hebrews*, 73–74.

29. Lane, *Hebrews 1–8*, 47.

30. Schenck thus concludes, "A proper understanding of Hebrews' argument requires

that this interpretation also presents Jesus as the true expression of what it means to be human. While the author might not attribute Psalm 8 directly to Jesus, this reading still presents Jesus as the one in whom the psalm finds its true fulfillment. Consequently, although I find the former interpretation more convincing, the outcome for the purposes of understanding the paradigmatic significance of Christ's humanity remains the same: "Jesus is the representative man of Psalm 8,"[31] the *anthrōpos* who uniquely fulfills the creational design for humanity.[32]

In chapter 2, we are also introduced to the importance of faith/faithfulness in the christological anthropology of Hebrews.[33] The redemptive significance of the Son rests in the fact that he suffered even to the extent of sharing our death (2:9–10, 14). Indeed, he can only serve as our merciful High Priest because of his own struggles and temptations (2:18). Later in Hebrews, we hear that Jesus can "empathize with our weaknesses" (4:15) and that he "learned obedience from what he suffered" (5:8). Despite all of this struggle and suffering, however, Jesus "did not sin" (4:15). Throughout Hebrews, Jesus is presented as the one who perfectly exemplifies the condition of "faith." More than that which we believe about God, faith in Hebrews is that by which humans persevere in living out their calling before God despite the difficulties of existence in a

---

us to read the psalm first in reference to humankind and only secondarily in reference to Christ (Schenck, "A Celebration of the Enthroned Son," 473).

31. O'Brien, *The Letter to the Hebrews*, 61.

32. Although Blomberg argues for a fundamental difference between these two interpretations (Blomberg, "'But We See Jesus,'" 91), Robert Gordon correctly notes that the anthropological significance of the passage is the same on either reading (*Hebrews* [Sheffield: Sheffield Academic, 2000], 50). And David Moffitt argues on exegetical grounds that we should affirm *both* interpretations as the likeliest reading (Moffitt, *Atonement and the Logic of Resurrection in the Epistle to the Hebrews*, 120–29).

33. See esp. Dennis Hamm, "Faith in the Epistle to the Hebrews: The Jesus Factor," *The Catholic Biblical Quarterly* 52, no. 2 (1990): 270–91; Victor Rhee, *Faith in Hebrews: Analysis within the Context of Christology, Eschatology and Ethics* (New York: Peter Lang, 2001); Dennis R. Lindsay, "*Pistis* and *'Emunah*: The Nature of Faith in the Epistle to the Hebrews," in *A Cloud of Witnesses: The Theology of Hebrews in Its Ancient Contexts*, ed. Richard Bauckham et al. (London: T&T Clark, 2008), 158–69; Todd D. Still, "*Christos as Pistos*: The Faith(fulness) of Jesus in the Epistle to the Hebrews," in *A Cloud of Witnesses: The Theology of Hebrews in Its Ancient Contexts*, ed. Richard Bauckham et al. (London: T&T Clark, 2008), 40–50.

broken world (e.g., 4:2; 6:12; 10:38).[34] It is the true mode of human existence. However, no one besides Jesus has truly exemplified the life of faith. Thus, when Hebrews describes the heroes of the faith in chapter eleven, the goal is not simply to provide an example that we might emulate, though this may certainly be included. Instead, Hebrews presents these individuals as faithful yet flawed glimpses of true humanity. When we turn to chapter twelve, though, we see Jesus, who is not placed *among* those faithful examples, as though he were merely the last/best in a long line of faithful humans. Instead, he is again referred to as the *archēgos* of our faith, but now with the addition that he is also its "perfecter."[35] If faith is fundamental to the anthropology of Hebrews, then the author is clearly claiming here that Jesus is both the paradigmatic instantiation of true humanity but also the one who prepares the way for others to participate in this new way of being.[36]

Even having focused primarily on just the first two chapters of Hebrews, we can see how consistently the author has portrayed Jesus as the one who reveals what it means to be truly human. Most interestingly, he does this by focusing on Jesus in at least three different "stages" of his existence: his eternal identity, his earthly life, and the ascension. However, the nature of the humanity we see revealed in that second stage, Jesus's life between Christmas and Easter, raises questions that will occupy us in the next section.

THE REVELATION OF HUMANITY AND THE PROBLEM OF THE SIN NATURE

All Chalcedonian theologians agree that the Son of God became fully human in the incarnation. That is what grounds the most basic claim of a christological anthropology: Jesus is human. Yet recent years have seen considerable disagreement about whether we

---

34. Lindsay, "*Pistis* and *'Emunah.*"

35. Christopher A. Richardson, *Pioneer and Perfecter of Faith: Jesus' Faith as the Climax of Israel's History in the Epistle to the Hebrews*, Wissenschaftliche Untersuchungen zum Neuen Testament 2. Reihe 338 (Tübingen: Mohr Siebeck, 2012).

36. O'Brien, *God Has Spoken in His Son*, 93.

should understand Jesus's humanity to be *fallen* or *unfallen*.[37] In other words, did the Son have to unite himself to our fallen humanity in order to redeem us from our sinful condition, or did he simply have to become fully human and thereby instantiate God's purposes for humanity. The former position finds considerable support in Hebrews. According to the author, Jesus can serve as our true High Priest because he became part of the human "family" (2:11) such that he experienced the same temptations we do (4:15), going so far as enduring the same death (2:9). Indeed, rather than presenting Jesus as one who was perfect from the very beginning, Hebrews portrays him as someone who needed to learn and grow, even having to be "made perfect" through his life experiences (5:8–9; cf. 2:8). Although he never sinned personally (4:15), he fully entered our fallen condition such that he "functioned from within the confines of a humanity altered by sin and the Fall."[38] According to many, all of this requires that we view the incarnation as the event in which the eternal Son assumed a fallen human nature to himself.[39] Many remain equally convinced that such an approach is inconsistent

---

37. Some of the more important recent discussions include Thomas G. Weinandy, *In the Likeness of Sinful Flesh: An Essay on the Humanity of Christ* (New York: T&T Clark, 2000); Kelly M. Kapic, "The Son's Assumption of a Human Nature: A Call for Clarity," *International Journal of Systematic Theology* 3, no. 2 (2001): 154–66; Oliver Crisp, "Did Christ Have a Fallen Human Nature?," *International Journal of Systematic Theology* 6, no. 3 (2004): 270–88; R. Michael Allen, "Calvin's Christ: A Dogmatic Matrix for Discussion of Christ's Human Nature," *International Journal of Systematic Theology* 9, no. 4 (2007): 382–97; Ian A. McFarland, "Fallen or Unfallen? Christ's Human Nature and the Ontology of Human Sinfulness," *International Journal of Systematic Theology* 10, no. 4 (2008): 399–415; Kornél Zathureczky, "Jesus' Impeccability: Beyond Ontological Sinlessness," *Science et Esprit* 60, no. 1 (2008): 55–71; Demetrios Bathrellos, "The Patristic Tradition on the Sinlessness of Jesus," in *Studia Patristica* (Leuven: Peeters, 2013), 235–41; Darren O. Sumner, "Fallenness and Anhypostasis: A Way Forward in the Debate over Christ's Humanity," *Scottish Journal of Theology* 67, no. 2 (2014): 195–212; Daniel J. Cameron, *Flesh and Blood: A Dogmatic Sketch Concerning the Fallen Nature View of Christ's Human Nature* (Eugene, OR: Wipf & Stock, 2016).

38. Weinandy, *In the Likeness of Sinful Flesh*, 160. Weinandy actually offers this as a definition of the fallenness position, though it works better as a statement about what everyone affirms.

39. For some of the more notable theologians who affirmed the fallenness position, see Edward Irving, *The Collected Writings of Edward Irving*, ed. G. Carlyle, vol. 5 (London: Alexander Strahan, 1865); Barth, *CD* II/1, 151; Hans Urs von Balthasar, *Mysterium Pachale: The Mystery of Easter*, trans. Adrian Nichols (Edinburgh: T&T Clark, 1990), 22; Wolfhart Pannenberg, *Jesus—God and Man*, trans. Lewis L. Wilkins and Duane A. Priebe, Second (Philadelphia: Westminster John Knox, 1977), 354–64; Thomas F. Torrance, *The Trinitarian Faith: The Evangelical Theology* (Edinburgh: T&T Clark, 1988), 161–63.

with other important emphases in Hebrews, namely that Jesus was our "unblemished" sacrifice (9:14) who is our perfect High Priest specifically because he does not need to offer sacrifice for his own sins (4:15–5:10). Although we will see that some of these theologians likewise emphasize the importance of saying that Jesus entered fully into our broken condition such that he could experience real temptation and suffering, they nonetheless reject the conclusion that this required him to assume a fallen human nature, arguing instead that Jesus's human nature was entirely free both from the effects of original sin and from personal sin.[40]

For many, dealing with an issue like this will seem like an exercise in rampant theological speculation. As Ian McFarland notes, "At first glance, the question of whether or not the incarnation involved the Word's assumption of a fallen or an unfallen human nature can seem like the epitome of theological hairsplitting: an example of doctrinal minutiae with little bearing on the life and teaching of the church."[41] Yet others contend that the issue has vital implications for understanding the gospel. As Barth wondered, if Jesus is not truly one of us, how can he serve as our mediator and High Priest?[42] Or, from the other perspective, if he is tainted by the same sin as our own, how can he be the perfect sacrifice who saves us? As McFarland summarizes, "The dilemma can be cast as follows: is the assumption of a fallen human nature necessary in order to affirm that Christ became like us 'in every respect', sin excepted; or does the assumption of a fallen human nature imply sinfulness?"[43]

The issue has theological significance in its own right, but it has special pertinence for our discussion because of its implications for christological anthropology. We cannot say that Jesus is paradigmatic for understanding humanity without asking about the

---

40. For a recent example, see Stephen J. Wellum, *God the Son Incarnate: The Doctrine of Christ* (Wheaton, IL: Crossway, 2016), 230–35.

41. McFarland, "Fallen or Unfallen?," 399.

42. *CD* II/1, 151. Similarly, Weinandy argues, "This is rightly a soteriological emphasis" (Weinandy, *In the Likeness of Sinful Flesh*, 5).

43. McFarland, "Fallen or Unfallen?," 400.

nature of the humanity we see revealed in him. This is particularly important given that the vast majority of what we know about Jesus's humanity comes from the period in question. Understanding the basic framework of christological anthropology and developing an appropriate methodology will thus require that we spend at least some time working through the question of whether the incarnate Christ had a *fallen* or an *unfallen* human nature. Consequently, the goal of this section will be to navigate the various issues involved in the fallenness debate and determine the best way forward. In the process I will argue for three points. First, we will see that the debate actually involves a broad range of positions and that several of them do not fare well under closer inspection. This will at least narrow the number of options we need to consider. Second, I will contend that several of the remaining options can support a robustly christological anthropology. Third, and most tentatively, I will suggest that the arguments in favor of the fallenness position are somewhat more convincing than the others.

Flavors of Fallenness

Before we can begin identifying the major positions involved in the discussion, we need further clarity about what is at stake. Many involved in this debate lament the unclarity about what it means to have a "fallen" nature. Does this simply mean that Jesus could get hungry and tired, that he could feel the pain of a stubbed toe, the anguish of a lonely night, the pang of a temptation, or even the crushing reality of death? If so, none will disagree. As we will see, most of the people involved in the discussion affirm two basic principles.[44] First, Jesus experienced many of the things we associate with the fall (e.g., suffering, temptation, death). While some view Christ's humanity as already glorified in the incarnation or as a kind of prelapsarian humanity unaffected by the consequences of the fall, most reject this as inadequate to what we see in the

---

44. For a nice summary of other important areas of agreement, see Kapic, "The Son's Assumption of a Human Nature."

gospels. Second, Jesus was not personally sinful (i.e., guilty). Here as well, some have been willing to draw this conclusion, but the vast majority contend that even if the Son assumed a fallen human nature, this does not result in him being guilty of sin. Since both sides are willing to affirm these two basic propositions, much of the debate focuses on the extent to which they can do so coherently.

The discussion also lacks clarity at times about the key issue. People often frame the discussion around the following question: "Did the Son assume a fallen nature at the incarnation?" So we differentiate the fallen and unfallen positions based on whether they answer that question affirmatively or negatively. But this way of framing the issue misses the fact that you can answer the question affirmatively but do so in a way that would not be satisfying to most advocates of fallenness. According to one common view, the Son assumed a fallen human nature at the incarnation, but it was immediately transformed into a redeemed nature, either because of its union with the divine nature or through the sanctifying work of the Spirit. On this account, then, the Son does *assume* a fallen nature, but since the transformation was immediate and instantaneous, there was never an actual time in which the Son *had* a fallen nature. Although such an approach answers the framing question affirmatively, this position would be entirely unacceptable to someone like Karl Barth, who maintained,

> There must be no weakening or obscuring of the saving truth that the nature which God assumed in Christ is identical with our nature as we see it in the light of the Fall. If it were otherwise, how could Christ be really like us? What concern would we have with him? We stand before God characterised by the Fall. God's Son not only assumed our nature but he entered the concrete form of our nature, under which we stand before God as men damned and lost.[45]

---

45. *CD* II/1, 153.

Barth's emphasis on Jesus entering "the concrete form of our nature" directs our attention not just to the moment of the incarnation but the shape and character of Jesus's historic existence. For advocates of fallenness, it is not just a matter of asking whether the Son assumed a fallen nature but whether that fallenness was part of his ongoing life and ministry. They contend that the fallen nature was sanctified and redeemed through Jesus's life and ministry, maintaining that this took place through the course of his entire life and was not just a consequence of the incarnation itself. Consequently, we would do better to frame the core question this way: "Did Jesus *have* a fallen nature?"

We thus end up with two distinct positions—*unfallen* and *fallen*—based on whether Jesus had a fallen human nature during his earthly life. Yet these basic positions both subdivide into two further positions. On the *unfallen* side, consider again the question of whether the Son assumed a fallen nature at the incarnation. Many proponents of the *unfallen* view say no, affirming instead that the Son assumed a prelapsarian human nature like that of Adam and Eve. Yet I have already mentioned another kind of *unfallen* position, in which the Son assumes a fallen nature that is instantaneously transformed and redeemed. Both deny that Jesus had a fallen nature during his earthly life, but they differ on whether he assumed a fallen nature at the incarnation. Similarly, *fallen* views agree that Jesus had a fallen nature during his earthly life, but they differ on whether that includes the "evil desire" (Jas 1:14) experienced by other fallen humans. We thus end up with something like the following as a summary of the basic positions involved in the discussion:

Unfallen A (creational): The Son assumed a creational (prelapsarian) human nature, but the Son also chose freely to experience at least some of the consequences of the fall (e.g., pain, temptation, death).

Unfallen B (redeemed): The Son assumed a fallen nature, but it was immediately transformed into a redeemed nature through union with the divine nature or the sanctifying work of the Spirit. Yet the Son still chooses freely to experience at least some of the consequences of the fall (e.g., pain, temptation, death).

Fallen A (no sinful desires): The Son assumed a fallen nature that is being progressively transformed into a redeemed nature through the Son's faithfulness and the sanctifying work of the Spirit. In virtue of having a fallen nature, the Son experiences some of the consequences of the fall (e.g., pain, temptation, death), but the Son does not experience sinful desires.

Fallen B (sinful desires): The Son assumed a fallen nature that is being progressively transformed into a redeemed nature through the Son's faithfulness and the sanctifying work of the Spirit. In virtue of having a fallen nature, the Son experiences all of the consequences of the fall, including sinful desires.

In the following sections, then, we will apply these four categories to a variety of issues as we attempt to understand the nature of Christ's humanity.

The Incarnation and the Healing of Humanity

Advocates of fallenness often contend that the Son had to assume a fallen human nature because only in this way could humanity itself be healed from the effects of the fall. Without denying the importance of the crucifixion and resurrection, such theologians maintain that the incarnation itself was part of the Son's atoning work, often appealing to Gregory of Nazianzus's famous maxim, "For that which he has not assumed he has not healed."[46] If we have fallen human natures, and if Jesus came to heal our broken humanity and redeem us from sin, then it would seem necessary

---

46. Gregory of Nazianzus, Ep. 101, in *A Select Library of the Nicene and Post-Nicene Fathers*, ed. Philip Schaff, vol. 7, series 2 (Grand Rapids: Eerdmans, 1978), 861.

for Jesus to assume that same human nature *in its fallenness*. That is why Paul declares that the Son came "in the likeness of sinful flesh" (Rom 8:3) and that "God made him who had no sin to be sin for us" (2 Cor 5:21).[47] Torrance states it boldly:

> It was certainly into a state of enmity that the Word penetrated in becoming flesh, into darkness and blindness, that is, into the situation where light and darkness are in conflict and where his own receive him not. There can be no doubt that the New Testament speaks of the flesh of Jesus as the concrete form of our human nature marked by Adam's fall, the human nature which seen from the cross is at enmity with God and needs to be reconciled to God. In becoming flesh the Word penetrated into hostile territory, into our human alienation and estrangement from God. When the Word became flesh, he became all that we are in our opposition to God.[48]

Otherwise we might be able to say that Jesus became fully human, but we would not be able to say that he healed our broken humanity because that is not what he assumed in the incarnation.

As McFarland rightly points out, however, Gregory's maxim does not entail that the Son had to assume a fallen nature.[49] Gregory's point was that Jesus had to assume human nature in its wholeness—in contrast to the Apollinarian view that Jesus did not have a human mind—and not that he had to assume human nature in its brokenness. Gregory goes on to say, "If only half Adam fell, then that which Christ assumes and saves must be half also; but if

---

47. Interpreters have devoted considerable attention to Rom 8:3 in particular, debating whether Paul's claim that the Son came "in the likeness of sinful flesh" entails some form of fallenness. See esp. Martin H. Scharlemann, "'In the Likeness of Sinful Flesh,'" *Concordia Theological Monthly* 32, no. 3 (1961): 133–38; Vincent P. Branick, "The Sinful Flesh of the Son of God (Rom 8:3): A Key Image of Pauline Theology," *The Catholic Biblical Quarterly* 47, no. 2 (1985): 246–62; Florence M. Gillman, "Another Look at Romans 8:3: 'In the Likeness of Sinful Flesh,'" *The Catholic Biblical Quarterly* 49, no. 4 (1987): 597–604.

48. Thomas F. Torrance, *Incarnation: The Person and Life of Christ*, ed. Robert T. Walter (Wilton Keynes, UK: Paternoster, 2008), 61.

49. McFarland, "Fallen or Unfallen?," 406.

the whole of his nature fell, it must be united to the whole nature of him that was begotten, and so be saved as a whole."[50] In other words, Gregory was not making a point about the *quality* of Jesus's humanity but about its *completeness*.

Here it is important to understand how sin relates to human nature. As many have pointed out, we must affirm that sin is not an *essential* property of a human nature since you can have a fully human person who is not characterized by sin (e.g., Adam, Eve, and glorified humanity). Instead, sin is a *contingent* property, something that may come to characterize a human nature in particular circumstances (post-fall humanity) but not others (eschatological humanity).[51] With this distinction in mind, it becomes easy to see why Gregory's axiom does not apply directly to the matter at hand. Gregory's argument hinges on the idea that the Son assumed the same nature as ours and that this included assuming every property essential to being human. Yet this does not entail that the Son had to assume a contingent property like fallenness any more than it entails the necessity of assuming other contingent properties (e.g., various heights, weights, colors). So Gregory's axiom only requires that the Son assumed a *full* and *true* human nature, not necessarily a *fallen* one.

Additionally, we should also recognize that the argument only works if you are willing to grant the idea that there is such a thing as a universal human nature that can be assumed and healed in the incarnation. If you think instead that a human nature is a concrete particular that exemplifies the properties necessary for qualifying as a specifically *human* particular, this argument loses much of its validity. As Crisp contends,

The claim here is not that God the Son assumes some sort of universal humanity, so that by becoming human God the Son

---

50. Gregory of Nazianzus, Ep. 101.

51. O'Collins thus distinguishes between "truly essential and merely common or universal properties" (Gerald O'Collins, *Christology* [New York: Oxford University Press, 1995], 269).

somehow changes all human natures from the inside out, so to speak. This is to confuse two things: the property that all human beings share in virtue of being human; and the particular instance of a human nature that is assumed by God the Son. God the Son assumes a human nature, that is, a particular human nature, the nature of Jesus of Nazareth. The human nature of Jesus is *his* human nature; it is made *for him* by the miraculous work of the Holy Spirit in the womb of the Virgin. But it is a particular human nature, not some universal human nature (whatever that might mean).[52]

If a human nature is a concrete particular, then even if the Son assumed and healed a fallen nature, that would not result in the complete transformation of humanity itself. Instead, Crisp rightly notes that his account would require a greater emphasis on being united to the Son through mysterious working of the Holy Spirit rather than a union that takes place simply in virtue of the Son's assumption of a human nature. This does not establish the falsity of the fallenness view, only that there are ways of understanding the metaphysics of the incarnation that render a healing view of the incarnation problematic.

Finally, even if we grant that the Son needed to assume a fallen nature in order to heal humanity, this would not resolve the *fallenness* debate itself. Remember that according to *Unfallen B* the Son assumed a fallen human nature that was immediately sanctified. Consequently, while this argument would help somewhat by excluding *Unfallen A* from consideration, it would not resolve the underlying question.

For all three reasons, then, we should be careful about arguing that Jesus had to assume a fallen human nature in order to redeem humans from their sin. Yet McFarland also points out that "though it is difficult to see how one could insist on soteriological grounds

52. Oliver D. Crisp, "Incarnation without the Fall," *Journal of Reformed Theology* 10, no. 3 (2016): 224–25.

that Christ *had* to assume a fallen human nature, that does not rule out the possibility that he *did* in fact assume one."[53] Hebrews itself offers material that would at least be consistent with such an interpretation. Without implying that Jesus was actually sinful, the author of Hebrews claims that it was still fitting for God to "make the pioneer of their salvation perfect through what he suffered" (2:10). Later we hear that "he learned obedience from what he suffered" and that it was only after he was "made perfect" that he could be "the source of eternal salvation for all who obey him" (5:8–9). Jesus is pictured as living a life in which humanity was somehow perfected through his faithful suffering. We could understand this as a reference to the teleological orientation of human nature which we discussed in the first chapter, claiming that the "perfection" in view here has to do with bringing humanity from its creational state to its eschatological telos. Throughout, though, Hebrews emphasizes Jesus's faithful obedience in the midst of pain and suffering, which suggests more than just living out God's creational purposes for humanity. Although the author of Hebrews does not address the underlying metaphysics—namely, whether he had to assume a fallen nature to accomplish this—he still tells a story in which the eternal Son became fully human to the extent that he experienced the same temptation, suffering, and death that we associate with the fallen condition, and that this was necessary for him to bring humanity to its intended telos.

If we ask whether fallenness is strictly required by the incarnation, then, I think we need to say no. However, if we shift our focus to Hebrews's own description of the incarnation, we may have reasons for beginning to lean in that direction.

Fallenness vs. Sinfulness

The question before us in this section is whether we should reject fallenness for being incommensurate with Christ's sinlessness. Although people on both sides of the debate affirm the sinlessness

53. McFarland, "Fallen or Unfallen?," 406–7.

of Christ, as I mentioned earlier, many worry about whether either of the *fallen* views can do so coherently. If we receive corrupt human natures (fallenness) as a consequence of guilt (sinfulness), then there does not seem to be any way of saying that the incarnate Son had the former without concluding that he also had the latter.[54] So both *fallen* options either need to reject the fallenness view or find some way of breaking the link between fallenness and sinfulness. According to Crisp, "This is the issue upon which the fallenness view stands or falls."[55]

Before we deal with that issue directly, though, it might help to clarify the relationship between a *person* and a *nature* with respect to things like *fallenness* and *sinfulness*. According to McFarland, sinfulness is a moral category that involves agency, responsibility, and guilt, things we must associate with *persons* because only persons can be moral agents. But natures are not the kinds of things that engage actions for which they can be held responsible. Instead, we associate agency and morality to the person, the *who* that is responsible for every intentional action, rather than the nature, the *what* that comprises the basis of the action. Consequently, it would make no sense to describe a nature as "sinful" with all of the corresponding implications of responsibility and blameworthiness. Instead, these properly belong to the person. "Fallen," on the other hand, is a category that describes a situation in which a nature has become damaged or disfigured in some way. Such defects may well come as a consequence of sin, yet they do not become blameworthy in and of themselves. He thus concludes, "Quite simply, fallenness is a property of nature and sin of hypostasis (or person)."[56]

This terminological distinction helps us see that the real issue: whether we can find a coherent way of affirming that Jesus's nature was fallen without the corresponding implication that he must be a

---

54. See esp. Crisp, "Did Christ Have a Fallen Human Nature?"; Crisp, *God Incarnate: Explorations in Christology* (London ; New York: T&T Clark, 2009), 122–36.

55. Crisp, "Did Christ Have a Fallen Human Nature?," 286.

56. McFarland, "Fallen or Unfallen?," 412.

sinful person (the guilt problem). And even if this were a coherent position, would Jesus need to be condemned for his corrupt nature regardless of whether he had any personal guilt (the corruption problem)? Let's take the guilt problem first. On many accounts of original sin, all humans receive a corrupt nature as a punishment for participating in the guilt of Adam's sin. If this is the case, then even if there is a conceptual distinction between fallenness and sinfulness, the former entails the latter. One way of breaking the link would simply be to deny this view of original sin. For example, many theologians maintain instead that humans receive corruption but not guilt from Adam.[57] If this is the case, then corruption should be viewed more as a *consequence* of the fall rather than a *punishment* for personal guilt. Imagine that the story goes something like this. Adam and Eve personally chose to sin, as a result of which, they became guilty before God and their natures became corrupted and inclined toward further sin. Their children were thus born into a state that was already corrupted by sin, and they too were inclined toward further sin, so strongly, in fact, that they would inevitably participate in actual sin. Despite receiving this corrupt nature, however, they do not actually participate in the guilt of their parents any more than my children participate in my guilt even though they routinely experience the consequences of my broken parenting. They only become guilty when they participate culpably in their sinful condition. On this story, Jesus could have a corrupt nature (fallenness) without personal guilt (sinfulness) as long as he never participates culpably in that sinful condition. Although sinfulness inevitably results from fallenness for all other humans, Jesus alone resists his fallen condition and lives a life of perfect faithfulness before God.

Even if you reject the argument above and affirm instead that fallenness should be viewed as a punishment for sin, rather than

---

57. Michael Allen contends that it is even possible to read Calvin as supporting something similar to this (Allen, "Calvin's Christ: A Dogmatic Matrix for Discussion of Christ's Human Nature").

a mere consequence of sin, it may be possible to affirm fallenness without sinfulness. One way of doing this would be to maintain that although fallenness was *originally* a punishment for sinfulness, it is possible for the punishment to continue even when people are no longer guilty of sin.[58] The fact is that I still struggle with a fallen human nature despite the fact that I have become "not guilty" in Christ. So even if I think that my own fallenness originally came as a punishment guilt (inherited from Adam), it is reasonable to maintain the possibility of experiencing fallenness without the corresponding implication of guilt.

The difficulty here is understanding why such a punishment would continue despite the removal of guilt. Consider, for example, a person who gets sent to prison for committing some crime. After a few years, the prisoner receives a pardon from the governor, removing all guilt for the crime. Once this has happened, the prisoner must be released from jail. It simply makes no sense to continue *punishing* someone if they no longer have the corresponding guilt. An alternative would be to consider that punishments can have lingering consequences even after the punishment itself has been removed. Returning to our hypothetical prisoner, suppose he spent twenty years in prison before he was pardoned. Although both guilt and punishment have now been addressed, it would be foolish to think that there will be no lingering consequences. Some of those consequences would be largely circumstantial (e.g., the difficulty of finding work and housing), but others run deep. After so many years in prison, this person's mind and body will have been shaped by the experience, indelible marks that will likely remain with him for the rest of his life. These aftereffects of incarceration are not the punishment itself but the lingering effects of the punishment. Maybe something similar is at work with fallenness. Even after our guilt has been addressed through Christ and our liability to punishment has been removed, we continue to experience the indelible consequences

---

58. Oliver D. Crisp, *Divinity and Humanity: The Incarnation Reconsidered*, Current Issues in Theology (Cambridge: Cambridge University Press, 2007), 96.

of living sin-shaped lives in a broken world. Our bodies continue to disintegrate as we move toward death, no longer as a punishment for our guilt, but now as a consequence of that punishment, one that can only be addressed once our bodies have been completely remade in the resurrection. If we can imagine the "corruption" of humanity in this way, it becomes possible to think of Jesus assuming a human nature that is fallen in the sense of still experiencing the effects of fallenness.

If one of the arguments above works, then we have resources for making a coherent distinction between fallenness and sinfulness, which enables us to envision the possibility of having the former without the latter. Even if this succeeds, though, we still face a question about whether God would still condemn Jesus for possessing such a corrupt human nature regardless of whether he participated in original guilt. Crisp draws this conclusion, arguing, "God could refuse such an individual a place in heaven even should the individual never actually sin, or have original guilt, merely because, in virtue of having a fallen human nature (original corruption), he is loathsome to God and must have the blessings of heaven withheld from him."[59] Yet I wonder if this is truly the case for two reasons. First, whether fallenness should itself be condemned seems to depend on the circumstances that led to the condition. For example, in the third season of *24*, counterterrorism agent Jack Bauer voluntarily becomes a heroin user so he can infiltrate a dangerous Mexican cartel. Along the way, he becomes addicted to the drug and experiences the corresponding symptoms of drug addiction. In normal situations, we would find such addiction to be morally repugnant. In this case, though, the negative condition was freely undertaken for the benefit of others. This does not change the fact that the condition itself is still negative, yet our evaluation of the situation is shaped at least partly by the motivations that led to the condition. Similarly, given the redemptive motives behind the

---

59. Ibid., 106.

Son's decision to assume a fallen nature, I find it difficult to believe that God would condemn the Son for this particular state of affairs.

We also need to remember that the redemption of our fallen natures lies at the heart of the fallenness position. Like with *Unfallen B*, both versions of fallenness emphasize that the Son assumes a fallen human nature so he can redeem and sanctify it. Although they argue that this takes place throughout the Son's life rather than just at the moment of the incarnation, that does not change the transformative focus of the position. Consequently, it would not be accurate to suggest that the fallenness advocate envisions the Son arriving in heaven with a vitiated human nature, as though he showed up at the Father's banquet without his wedding clothes (Matt 22:11–13). They instead stress that the fallen nature is redeemed through some combination of the incarnation, Jesus's faithful obedience, the sanctifying work of the Spirit, and ultimately the resurrection.

All of this suggests that it is at least possible to affirm that Jesus had a fallen nature without the corresponding implication that he was also sinful. Although I argued in the prior section that fallenness is not required by our commitment to the incarnation, neither do I think that *rejecting* fallenness is required by our commitment to the sinlessness of Christ.

Our Sympathetic High Priest

Even if we cannot move directly from claims about the incarnation to conclusions about the fallenness of his human nature, however, we might still be able to strengthen the relevant concern. Although sin is not essential to humanity in itself, perhaps it is such a fundamental aspect of *our* human existence that Jesus needed to assume a fallen human nature in order to truly become one of us. Indeed, that seems to be the logic of Hebrews when it emphasizes not only that Jesus had to be tempted like us in "every way," but that this requires a kind of solidarity in which Jesus can empathize with our weaknesses sufficiently enough for him to be a *merciful* High Priest

(2:17). The emphasis on mercy here suggests that being fully human involves experiencing our broken condition sufficiently for Jesus to sympathize with the struggles of fallen humans. In the following verse, Jesus's temptations become the basis for his ability to minister to those who are tempted (cf. 4:15). Throughout Hebrews, then, the emphasis is not just on the Son's *full* humanity, but also on the fact that he experienced humanity in the same way that we do, which is why he can represent us so faithfully before the Father. For Barth, this is the "concrete form" of humanity that requires us to affirm that the Son assumed a fallen nature in the incarnation.[60]

Yet it remains entirely possible for proponents of either *unfallen* view to affirm that Jesus experienced all of the common infirmities that come from living in a broken world—suffering, temptation, hunger, weariness, and probably even the awkwardness of puberty—they will simply differ in the explanation for *why* he experienced these things. Unlike the rest of us who experience these infirmities as a consequence of our fallenness, the Son could experience them as a consequence of his own free choice. In other words, without actually being fallen the Son could choose to experience what it is like to be fallen. This would be like someone voluntarily choosing to live in prison, experiencing the reality of prison life without the corresponding realities of guilt and punishment. Crisp thus points out that "exemplifying the effects of the fall is not the same as being fallen," contending that this would be like a person who displays "the symptoms of measles without . . . having the virus."[61] Since Jesus was "without sin," he did not have to suffer. Yet in his love, the Son freely chose to immerse himself so fully in our fallen condition that he actually experiences the pain and brokenness of the world in precisely the same way we do.[62]

Some might object that this makes it sound as though Jesus is merely pretending to identify with us. Responding to Crisp's analogy,

---

60. *CD* II/1, 151.

61. Crisp, *Divinity and Humanity*, 116.

62. For a classic account, see Thomas Aquinas *Summa Theologica* III, Q. 14.

McFarland worries that although "such a person might appear to have measles, measles sufferers in the know would have to confess that she was not really one of them."[63] At first glance, the worry seems ungrounded. We have already established that Jesus need only assume a true human nature to be one of us. Yet the concern here has to do with whether his experiences are sufficiently similar to our own that he can serve as our merciful High Priest. For that to be the case, *why* Jesus experiences these infirmities does not seem as relevant as *whether* he experiences them.

We could strengthen the worry further by explaining why the *why* matters. Returning to the idea of someone voluntarily living in prison and having the same experiences as the other prisoners, it seems that the innocence of the volunteer would necessarily shape his experiences differently from those had by the others. At the very least, he would be able to go through those experiences knowing that he had done nothing to deserve them. This might suggest that even if Jesus freely chose to experience the same kinds of things that those with fallen human natures experience, he would necessarily have those experiences in importantly different ways from the rest of us. This would weaken the claim that Jesus can sympathize with us in virtue of our shared experiences.

Yet this question afflicts both accounts. Advocates of fallenness also maintain that the Son assumed a fallen nature freely. But this is not true for other humans, at least according to most traditional views of original sin, since we did not choose to receive a fallen human nature at birth. Consequently, Jesus would experience fallenness for a different reason than the rest of us. We could try to block this response by claiming that maybe in the incarnation the Son was *unaware* that he had freely chosen to enter this condition.[64] Using our prison analogy, maybe he is like someone who freely

63. McFarland, "Fallen or Unfallen?," 408.

64. This would be similar to the "two minds" explanation sometimes offered for how to resolve the omniscience of the eternal Son with the limited knowledge of the incarnate Christ (see esp. Thomas V. Morris, *The Logic of God Incarnate* [Ithaca, NY: Cornell University Press, 1986]).

chose to enter prison *and* freely chose to undergo a procedure that would remove the relevant memories, making him unaware of his own innocence. On this view, the Son could have all the same experiences as the rest of humanity despite the fact that he freely chose to enter their fallen condition. If such a thought experiment succeeds, however, it would apply to the unfallen view as well. We could simply stipulate that in the incarnation the Son was not aware that he had freely chosen to experience all the effects of fallenness without actually being fallen.

The reality is that both positions need to wrestle with the fact that although Jesus is *fully* human, he is not *merely* human. The incarnation itself requires that we affirm some level of discontinuity between Jesus and the rest of us; a similar discontinuity arises here given that Jesus is the only instance of a sinless human. While we should not emphasize this discontinuity to the extent that we lose sight of Jesus's full and true humanity, we should also realize that the discontinuity means Jesus's experiences will always be importantly different from that of other humans. If this alone is adequate to render him unfit to be our merciful High Priest, then every orthodox Christology is at stake. At the same time, we have seen that even most proponents of fallenness shy away from claiming that Jesus's *fallenness* entails his *sinfulness* (i.e., guilt). If that is the case, though, they too must argue that Jesus's human experiences are different from our own, at least in the fact that he does not experience them through the lens of guilt. In the end, while we must maintain that Jesus's experiences were sufficiently similar to our own that he can serve as our merciful High Priest, I see no significant differences in the various ways of explaining *why* he has those experiences.

The Temptation of Christ

Many worry that any kind of *unfallen* view undermines belief that Jesus was "tempted in every way, just as we are" (Heb 4:15). However, if we can say that Jesus experienced the effects of fallenness irrespective of whether he actually had a fallen nature, we should be able to say the same about the experience of temptation.

Before we deal specifically with temptation, we need to address the question of whether Jesus *could* have sinned. Traditionally theologians have maintained Jesus's *impeccability*—that is, it was not possible for him to sin—while others have argued on the basis of Christ's temptations that it must have been possible for him to sin. It would be easy to correlate this discussion with the fallenness debate, associating impeccability with the unfallen view and peccability with fallenness. Rightly understood, though, the discussion of whether Jesus could have sinned is not necessarily about the nature of his humanity at all. Although it is possible to contend that Jesus's human nature was incapable of sinning in itself,[65] theologians commonly affirm instead that Jesus's human nature considered in abstraction from the incarnation is fully capable of being actualized in sinful ways. The impeccability of Jesus results from the peccable human nature being united with the impeccable divine nature, or sometimes from the gracious work of the Spirit.[66] Importantly, then, people on both sides of this particular discussion can agree that Christ's human nature was peccable. Yet if impeccability results from the hypostatic union and not from some quality of the human nature itself, it does not seem to matter whether that human nature is fallen or unfallen. Either way, you would be left with the question of whether the union of that human nature with a divine nature renders the person of Jesus incapable of sinning.

Moving on to the nature of Jesus's temptations, the issue here has to do with whether those temptations are relevantly similar to our own. Most importantly, it seems that our temptations require both external circumstances and internal desires to qualify as real temptations. For example, suppose my family is away for the

---

65. Crisp contends that this is the position of most theologians in the Augustinian tradition (Crisp, "Did Christ Have a Fallen Human Nature?," 272).

66. For a thorough summary of various perspectives on impeccability, see John E. McKinley, *Tempted for Us: Theological Models and the Practical Relevance of Christ's Impeccability and Temptation* (Colorado Springs: Paternoster, 2009).

weekend, and I have a major paper to complete while they are gone. Suppose as well that Netflix just released an entire season of my favorite show. I could sit at my desk and take care of my responsibilities, or I could curl up on the couch for a serious Netflix binge. Here I have both external circumstance and internal desire, which combine to produce a significant temptation. Indeed, if we were to record this situation on my personal temptometer, it would probably register a seven out of ten, possibly higher depending on the show. Suppose as well that my family left a giant jar of pickles in the refrigerator and told me that I was not allowed to eat any while they were away. Technically this qualifies as a temptation since I have been placed in a situation with the possibility of disobedience. However, I think it's absurd to soak a perfectly good vegetable in vinegar before consuming it; consequently, there will be no internal temptation of any kind. My temptometer will hover pretty close to zero on this one. At the same time, I would not experience any temptation to spend the weekend playing video games. Although I probably would desire to play video games in such a circumstance, I don't own any.[67] So there is no external circumstance that would offer the opportunity for an internal desire to express itself as a real temptation.

Our experience of real temptation thus involves a combination of both external circumstances and internal desires.[68] Since the argument of Hebrews rests on the fact that he was tempted "just as we are" and that this is what renders him fit to serve as our merciful High Priest, it would seem necessary to affirm that Jesus also experienced both external and internal temptation. That he encountered

---

67. This is intentional since I discovered years ago that I cannot be trusted with video games.

68. Some might suggest the possibility of temptation without the corresponding external circumstance. For example, we could imagine a drug addict locked away in a rehab facility who desperately wants to use drugs. Yet it is hard to see how this would involve a real *temptation* since no drugs are present. The mere existence of a desire does not seem to constitute a true temptation. Instead, we would at least have to revise the scenario so that the drug addict has been tricked into *thinking* that drugs are present. Yet that introduces precisely the kind of circumstantially relevant fact I have in mind.

external temptations is without dispute (e.g., Matt 4:1–11). Without the corresponding internal temptation, however, Jesus's temptom-eter would always be zero, making his experience of temptation radically unlike our own. Moreover, since the issue is a qualitative one, we cannot address it with a quantitative response. Some have appealed to the fact that since Jesus resisted these temptations, not giving in like we do, his temptations would have lasted far longer. Therefore, Jesus experienced temptation to a (quantitatively) greater degree than other humans.[69] But the question is about the quality of Jesus's temptations rather than their quantity. I could resist the temptation of eating pickles for the rest of my life without feeling like I had accomplished anything of great significance. Only a real temptation, one that included some attraction, would involve the kind of real struggle that makes enduring in the face of the temp-tation noteworthy.

If this is the case, then this issue would affect *Fallen A* as well as both versions of *unfallenness* since none of them think that Jesus experienced these kinds of desires. Consequently, advocates of these positions invest considerable time in defending the conclusion that Jesus could be truly tempted even if he did not have the same kinds of desires that we do.[70] Yet it is not clear to me that such arguments are necessary. Instead of denying that Jesus had the requisite desires, we can draw on the arguments made in the previous section to contend that the Son freely chose to experience the desires through which we are tempted, even the desire for sinful things, without having to assume a nature that is itself fallen.[71] His desires would

---

69. In C. S. Lewis's famous words, "Christ, because He was the only man who never yielded to temptation, is also the only man who knows to the full what temptation means" (C. S. Lewis, *Mere Christianity*, rev. ed. [San Francisco: HarperOne, 2015], 142).

70. Most commonly, they appeal to the ways in which even good desires can come into conflict, creating a situation in which Jesus could be tempted to choose a good thing in the wrong way.

71. I think even those committed to the principle that the Son did not assume concu-piscence or the "fomes of sin" (e.g., Weinandy, *In the Likeness of Sinful Flesh*) might be able to affirm something like this, arguing that although Jesus experiences the desires that typically correspond to the fallen human nature, he does not experience these desires as a consequence of the fallen nature itself.

still be unlike ours in that they do not result from a condition of sinfulness, but I would again argue that the reasons Jesus has the requisite experiences are less significant than the experiences themselves.

The fallenness view might have the harder challenge in this discussion since it needs to maintain that Jesus experienced tempting desires that arise from his own fallen nature without drawing the corresponding conclusion that such desires are evidence of actual sinfulness.[72] However, here as well we can draw on our prior discussion of consequences that linger as the aftereffects of punishment. Consider a drug addict who overcomes the addiction and has now been clean for several years. Nonetheless, it is quite likely that such a person would continue to experience a desire for drugs as a lingering consequence of living in a broken state, one that may not be addressed until their entire neurophysiological system has been healed and reconstituted in the resurrection. Although it seems appropriate to view those continued desires as the lingering consequence of sin, it is not clear to me that we need to view them as "sinful" in ways that would create christological problems if Jesus were to assume a human nature that also experienced those same kinds of desires.

At the end of all this, we can safely conclude that all of the various positions offer compelling arguments. Most importantly, it seems that all four can affirm coherently the two fundamental propositions we noted at the beginning of the discussion: (1) Jesus experienced many of the things we associate with the consequences of the fall, and (2) Jesus was sinless. Nonetheless, although I think the *unfallen* positions can affirm both of these coherently, some of the arguments seem rather *ad hoc*. The prima facie evidence of Christ's historic existence suggests a humanity like ours, including all the things we

---

72. Although the fact that Adam and Eve were tempted in the Garden demonstrates the possibility of temptation without sinful desire, that alone will not satisfy the fallenness advocate. The issue in question is not merely whether Jesus experienced desires that could lead to temptation but whether those desires are sufficiently like our own to render him our sympathetic High Priest.

associate with being human in a fallen world with the exception of Christ's unbroken faithfulness. The most natural interpretation of the evidence would be that Christ has a fallen nature like our own. Because of the prior commitment to the connection between sinfulness and fallenness, however, the unfallen advocate cannot accept this and must create ways of explaining how Christ could have all of the requisite experiences anyway. This comes across as an *ad hoc* solution to a problem that could more easily be addressed by reconsidering the relationship between sinfulness and fallenness.

CONCLUSION

We started this chapter by looking at the paradigmatic humanity of Jesus in Hebrews, focusing particularly on the first two chapters. The author of Hebrews consistently identifies Jesus not just as *fully* human but also as the one who reveals what it means to be *truly* human. He is the true heir of the inheritance God promised to his people (1:2), the perfect expression of the *imago Dei* (1:3), the "first-born" who inaugurates a new stage of human existence (1:6), the true *anthrōpos* who fulfills God's creational purposes for humanity (2:6–9), the "pioneer" who prepares the way for others to follow (2:10), and the faithful one who fully entered our fallen condition and lived a life of perfect obedience (2:13; 3:6; 12:1–3). Without undermining the significance of the Son's eternal relationship with the Father, Hebrews offers a clear picture of Jesus as the one in whom we see what it means to be truly human.

Yet Hebrews also alerted us to a difficult question. In Jesus we see someone who suffers and dies, who struggles with temptation and grows through obedience. Where we might have expected a picture of perfect humanity in all its glory, we see instead humanity in the midst of sin. We thus wrestled with a number of issues that surround the question of whether Jesus himself assumed a fallen human nature. Yet many worry that such a conclusion would mean Jesus was actually sinful, making it impossible for Jesus to be the pure and unblemished sacrifice who could atone for the sins of God's

166 | ReSourcing Theological Anthropology

people. Both sides thus have compelling concerns and interesting arguments. Although I find the argument for fallenness slightly stronger, the fact remains that certain versions of the unfallen position can account for most, if not all, of that which motivates the fallenness position. If we maintain that the Son assumed a fallen nature at the incarnation, one that was immediately redeemed through the work of the Spirit, and if we maintain that the Son also freely chose to experience everything that normally comes as a consequence of having a fallen nature, *Unfallen A* seems to have all the resources necessary to maintain that the Son immersed himself in our fallen condition in all the ways that matter.

In the next chapter, we will consider the implications of all this for christological anthropology. On the one hand, we have clearly established that Hebrews presents good grounds for affirming that in Jesus we have the revelation of what it means to be truly human in the midst of a broken world, and he offers a glimpse of the eschatological telos toward which God is directing his people. Yet this discussion also highlights the discontinuity that stands between Jesus and the rest of us. He alone is the incarnate God-man who lived a life of sinless obedience. Any christological anthropology needs to account for these two points of discontinuity as it moves from Christology to anthropology. At the same time, the discussion raises the question of how the fallenness debate affects christological anthropology. What difference does it make if we conclude that Jesus had a fallen or an unfallen nature? That will be one of the key questions in the next chapter.

CHAPTER 5

Eleven Theses for Christological Anthropology

WITH THIS CHAPTER, we begin to move in a different direction. The preceding four chapters all carry with them the temptation of the abstract. It would be all too easy to focus entirely on the interesting biblical discussions and challenging theological issues involved in developing a christological vision of humanity without addressing how this all relates to the difficult anthropological questions we face every day. How does understanding the relationship between Christology and anthropology help me understand the painful reality of death, the racial tensions in the world, or the questions my prepubescent daughter asks after her most recent health class?

Questions like these take us into the second half of this book as we seek to apply the decisions made in the first four chapters to at least some of the issues involved in understanding humanity today. Before dealing with specific issues, however, we need to say something about the *how* of christological anthropology. The first four chapters focused on the biblical basis for christological anthropology and some of the key theological issues those discussions generated. However, we have not yet said anything about how we should use Christology to inform anthropology. Consequently, we need to pause for a moment and pull together the various insights generated by the preceding discussions, and use them to develop methodological principles that can guide the practice of christological anthropology. We will see in the end that christological anthropology does not comprise a particular "method" for approaching the study of humanity. Nonetheless, these principles offer clear guidance for how to view humanity through the lens of Jesus Christ.

As I mentioned in the introduction, the issues we covered in the earlier chapters are complex, and many will disagree with the conclusions I have drawn along the way. I do not presume to suggest that the approach taken here offers the only way of thinking christologically about the human person. I will not even claim that this approach offers a more robust christological anthropology. Consequently, I readily admit, even invite, the possibility of alternate ways of developing a christological anthropology down one of the paths I have not taken. Nonetheless, the following eleven theses identify some of the core claims generated by our earlier discussions. Those who reach different conclusions will need to modify these theses accordingly. I will list the eleven theses first, before unpacking them in a bit more detail.

1. Jesus is the unique revelation of what it means to be truly human.
2. The epistemological centrality of Jesus derives from the fact that his humanity is ontologically fundamental for the existence of all other humans.
3. The fact that Jesus is epistemologically and ontologically fundamental to humanity means that christological anthropology is inherently teleological.
4. The fact that Jesus's humanity is ontologically fundamental for the existence of all other humans does not result in either soteriological universalism or anthropological exclusivism.
5. The epistemological and ontological centrality of Jesus for anthropology entails that ultimate truths about the human person must be grounded in Christology.
6. Christologically grounded truths about humanity provide an interpretive framework for understanding other anthropological truths.

7. Christological anthropology must pay close attention to the concrete particularities of Jesus's existence.
8. The particularities of Jesus's existence mean that we must affirm both the continuity and the discontinuity between Jesus and other humans.
9. There can be no direct move from Christology to anthropology.
10. Christological anthropology must be robustly pneumatological and Trinitarian.
11. Jesus's humanity primarily reveals what it means to be truly human in the midst of a fallen world.

Although each of these flows in some way from the discussions of the prior chapters, it will help to address each of them in a bit more detail to see how they relate to that material and how they shape the way we approach and understand theological anthropology.

1. JESUS IS THE UNIQUE REVELATION OF WHAT IT MEANS TO BE TRULY HUMAN.

This first thesis should come as no great surprise since it is the basic claim of what we have been calling a christological anthropology throughout. One of the primary concerns of the first four chapters was to establish the claim that the New Testament authors consistently portray Jesus as the only one in whom we see what it truly means to be human. We saw that he is the true *anthrōpos* (John 19–20), the second Adam (1 Cor 15), the *imago Dei* (Col 1:15), and the paradigmatic human (Heb 1–2), each establishing the truth of this thesis.

If we had more time and space, we could expand the biblical grounds for this claim even further. From the synoptic Gospels, we might examine the ways Jesus is presented as the new Israel and how this correlates to an Old Testament motif in which Israel comes as the new Adam.[1] God called Israel to be his faithful people, offering

---

1. See, for example, N. T. Wright, *The Climax of the Covenant: Christ and the Law in Pauline Theology* (Minneapolis: Fortress, 1992); Peter J. Leithart, *A Son to Me: An Exposition of 1 & 2 Samuel*

the promises of the new covenant as a way of declaring his own faithfulness to his own creational purposes despite humanity's fall into sin. Yet it is only with Jesus that we have the true Israel in whom those promises find their fulfillment. Here as well, then, we have the theme of true humanity revealed in Christ. If we needed more evidence from Paul, we might well have considered Philippians 2:5–11. Although some have argued that this passage also has echoes of an Adam Christology, others remain unconvinced.[2] Regardless, the idea that Jesus manifests what it means to be truly human seems difficult to refute. Not only does he *become* truly human, but he exemplifies humanity in such a way that Paul calls his readers to contemplate and emulate what they see. This leads to yet another unexplored motif: the *imitatio Christi*. As I mentioned in the introduction, I chose not to address this theme directly because, unlike other areas in christological anthropology, this is one that has already received considerable attention. Nonetheless, if our aim was comprehensiveness, we would need to consider the numerous ways the New Testament authors present Jesus as the one who is so perfectly human that we should all seek to model our own ways of being human around his (e.g., John 13:12–15; 1 Cor 11:1; Phil 2:3–8; 1 Pet 2:21).

Notably, each of these presents Jesus as the *unique* revelation of true humanity. Although others might play an exemplary role as models of faithful human living (e.g., Heb 11), Jesus is the only one identified by the biblical authors as truly revealing what it means to be human. The New Testament authors do not even place Adam and Eve in that role despite the sinlessness of their initial existence. Paul does occasionally draw insight from the state of humanity in the garden (e.g., 1 Cor 11:7; 1 Tim 2:13–15), but as we will see in

---

(Moscow, ID: Canon, 2003); Scott Hahn, *The Kingdom of God as Liturgical Empire: A Theological Commentary on 1–2 Chronicles* (Grand Rapids: Baker Academic, 2012); Seth D. Postell, *Adam as Israel: Genesis 1–3 as the Introduction to the Torah and Tanakh* (Cambridge: James Clarke, 2012).

2. See Charles A. Wanamaker, "Philippians 2:6–11: Son of God or Adamic Christology?," *New Testament Studies* 33, no. 2 (1987): 179–93; James D. G. Dunn, "Christ, Adam, and Preexistence," in *Where Christology Began: Essays on Philippians 2* (Louisville: Westminster John Knox, 1998), 74–83; Morna D. Hooker, "Adam Redivivus: Philippians 2 Once More," in *Old Testament in the New Testament: Essays in Honour of J. L. North* (Sheffield, England: Sheffield Academic, 2000), 220–34.

the following theses, the anthropological centrality of Jesus does not entail that we must derive *everything* we know about humanity directly from the humanity of Christ. Yet the fact remains that the New Testament emphasizes the uniqueness of Jesus's revelatory significance for our vision of humanity.

2. THE EPISTEMOLOGICAL CENTRALITY OF JESUS DERIVES FROM THE FACT THAT HIS HUMANITY IS ONTOLOGICALLY FUNDAMENTAL FOR THE EXISTENCE OF ALL OTHER HUMANS.

Without an ontological foundation, the epistemological claim of the first thesis would hang in midair like a treehouse with no tree. Although we must begin with the epistemological claim that Jesus reveals true humanity, such a claim needs explanation. The New Testament does not grant this paradigmatic status to any other human, so why draw that conclusion here? What makes it the case that Jesus plays this revelatory role?

We might be inclined to think that the incarnation itself can establish this claim. Yet, as I noted in the introduction, that will not suffice. Simply affirming Christ's *full* humanity would not explain the uniqueness of his anthropological centrality since presumably all humans are fully human. We would at least need to strengthen this and claim that he is also *perfectly* human. Let's say we strengthened it in the strongest way possible, affirming with *Unfallen A* that Jesus assumed a human nature untouched by sin. Although that would establish the purity of his humanity, it still would not be enough to ground the epistemological claim of the first thesis. After all, Adam and Eve also had an unfallen nature, and as we have just discussed, the New Testament authors do *not* present them as having the same paradigmatic significance for anthropology. We might also question whether "humanity" is the kind of thing that can even have a perfect instantiation or an ideal form. Given the variety and flexibility of human existence, perhaps there are numerous ways of being flawlessly human. Maybe there is no single "perfect" or "ideal" human. If so, even affirming *Unfallen A* only entails that Jesus's humanity is *an* instance of flawless humanity, which would be *useful* rather than *necessary* for understanding humanity in general.

Many ground the ontological significance of the incarnation in the idea that the Son assumed some kind of universal human nature, transforming and healing humanity in itself, which would have obvious implications for all of us who participate in that same nature. But not only does this argument depend on the idea of a universal human nature, which many contemporary theologians would not affirm, but it also fails to address the matter at hand. Indeed, it falls prey to the same argument as the previous paragraph since before the fall Adam and Eve would also have participated flawlessly in this same universal human nature.

A more likely approach would retain the emphasis on the incarnation but focus instead on the divine identity of the eternal Son as the ground for Jesus's anthropological significance. We might do this by contending that the eternal Son just *is* the paradigm of humanity. Consequently, the incarnation entails the revelation of true humanity since it involves the paradigm himself becoming flesh. Although this would provide an explanation for the unique revelatory significance of Jesus, we have seen that such an approach struggles to account for the embodied nature of the *imago Dei* (ch. 3). Images are material things. If this is the case, it becomes difficult to understand how the preexistent Son, the *logos asarkos*, could himself be the paradigm of true humanity. We might adjust this somewhat and affirm instead that the paradigm of humanity somehow resides in the eternal Son, maybe as a divine idea. Yet we must notice that the biblical authors never talk about some abstract, eternal idea of humanity as the paradigm of what it means to be human. Instead, it is always Jesus himself.

Consequently, I argued in chapter 3 that we should view the humanity of Jesus itself as the eternal paradigm. Jesus just is God's eternal determination of what it means to be human. His humanity has ontological significance for that of all other humans simply because Jesus is the one in whom God establishes what it means to be human.

3. THE FACT THAT JESUS IS EPISTEMOLOGICALLY AND ONTOLOGICALLY FUNDAMENTAL TO HUMANITY MEANS THAT CHRISTOLOGICAL ANTHROPOLOGY IS INHERENTLY TELEOLOGICAL.

At several points in our study, we encountered the importance of eschatological consummation for understanding what it means to be human. In essence, eschatological consummation involves the idea that God always intended some kind of movement from creation to new creation in which the latter state was not simply a return to the former. Although the state of Adam and Eve in the garden was good (i.e., not "fallen"), that does not preclude the possibility of further growth. We did not go into the details of this eschatological consummation because all that is necessary for our purposes is that there is some kind of upward movement between creation and new creation (e.g., from the creational state of being able to sin to the eschatological state where sin is no longer a possibility).

It is entirely possible to generate a theological anthropology that affirms eschatological consummation as the telos of the human person apart from Jesus, one that speculates on the possibility God could have brought about this finality through some means other than the incarnation. So an emphasis on eschatological consummation is not *unique* to christological anthropology. Nonetheless, eschatological consummation seems *inherent* to christological anthropology. All four of the previous chapters pointed to Jesus as the fulfillment of God's creational purposes in a way that seems to require this kind of teleological perspective. We saw this most clearly in John's story of the *anthrōpos*, in which Jesus completes the plans God had for creation "in the beginning," by bringing about new creation through the outpouring of the Spirit. As its fulfillment, new creation stands in continuity with original creation, yet not as a mere restoration. The same framework was at work in our discussion of the Adam/Christ relationship in 1 Corinthians 15. By comparing the "spiritual" body of Christ in the resurrection to the "natural" body of Adam in creation, we have another way of talking about the teleological movement toward eschatological consummation. Although we have continuity between the two states here as well—like the continuity between a seed and the plant it produces—Paul argues that the very bodies that comprise human existence will in some way be transformed in the new creation reality. It may seem at first glance that the *imago Dei* moves in the opposite direction since God declares humans to be his images at the beginning of the story. Nonetheless, we also saw that the full reality of the image comes only with the incarnation. For other humans, the image of God is an ongoing story of being transformed into the likeness of the Son through the power of the Spirit so that we become ever more conformed to the Son who is the true *imago Dei*, a process that will certainly not be complete this side of the eschaton. Finally, the eschatological orientation of christological anthropology came up again with Hebrews's emphasis on the ascension as the state in which true humanity will be most fully revealed. At every step along the way, then, we find that eschatological consummation is inherently part of a christological perspective on the human person.

As we saw in the first chapter, such an approach raises difficult questions about the nature/grace relationship and whether we should affirm that humans have a natural telos in addition to the eschatological finality we have in Christ. If we take seriously the claims of the first two theses, however, it becomes difficult to think that there is any value in speculating about a hypothetical form of humanity in which we are not ontologically and epistemologically grounded in Jesus. Instead, to be *human* simply is to be related to Jesus in these ways.

4. THE FACT THAT JESUS'S HUMANITY IS ONTOLOGICALLY FUNDAMENTAL FOR THE EXISTENCE OF ALL OTHER HUMANS DOES NOT RESULT IN EITHER SOTERIOLOGICAL UNIVERSALISM OR ANTHROPOLOGICAL EXCLUSIVISM.

Construed in certain ways, christological anthropology could easily suggest either that everyone will eventually be saved (soteriological universalism) or that only Christians qualify as human beings (anthropological exclusivism). Each of these results from combining the following claims: (1) all humans are united with Jesus in such a way that his humanity can serve as the epistemological and ontological ground of their humanity and (2) only the saved are united with Christ. If we lead with the first claim, emphasizing that *all humans* are somehow united with Christ, we end up with soteriological universalism when we add the second claim. Contrarily, if we lead with the second claim and emphasize that *only the saved* are united with Christ, we end up with anthropological exclusivism when we add the first claim.

For example, Gregory of Nyssa and Karl Barth both offered christological anthropologies that either explicitly endorsed soteriological universalism or at least struggled with its implication.[3] Gregory of Nyssa grounded his christological anthropology in the actuality of the incarnation in which the eternal Son united himself with universal humanity and began transforming humanity so that it could be united to the greatest extent possible with the divine being. The Son uniting himself with universal humanity is what grounds the anthropological significance of the Son's humanity, yet it is also what generates the worries about universalism. If the Son transforms universal humanity and unites it to the greatest extent possible with the divine being, why wouldn't that result in the salvation of all human persons, a conclusion Gregory explicitly endorsed?[4] Although Karl Barth consistently rejected the idea that his christological anthropology necessarily entails soteriological universalism, many remain unconvinced.[5] Barth grounded the anthropological significance of Jesus in the divine decree of election: God eternally chooses to be God-for-us-in-Christ, where "us" refers

---

3. See Marc Cortez, *Christological Anthropology in Historical Perspective: Ancient and Contemporary Approaches to Theological Anthropology* (Grand Rapids: Zondervan, 2016), chs. 1, 5. Friedrich Schleiermacher and Julian of Norwich similarly espoused christological anthropologies that generate universalist concerns.

4. E.g., Gregory of Nyssa, *On the Soul and the Resurrection* (Crestwood, NY: St. Vladimir's Seminary Press, 1993), 86.

5. As Barth famously declared, "I am not a universalist [*Ich bin keine universalist*]" (quoted in Lewis Smedes, *My God and I: A Spiritual Memoir* [Grand Rapids: Eerdmans, 2003], 99).

to all of humanity. Indeed, to be "human" on this account just is to be one of the creatures included in this divine decree of election. Yet if God eternally says "yes" to all humans in Christ, it becomes difficult to conceive how any could fall outside the scope of salvation. Irrespective of how Barth addressed the issue, both Gregory and Barth demonstrate how soteriological universalism might arise from the two claims above.

On the other side of the equation, Martin Luther and John Zizioulas illustrate the exclusivist concern.[6] Luther grounded his anthropology in the doctrine of justification by faith alone, defining humanity in terms of a particular kind of relationship to God. This strongly suggests that only the justified qualify as truly human. Zizioulas raises similar concerns with his argument that human personhood is something that only occurs in the church. Like Barth, Zizioulas rejects this as a necessary entailment of his position, though the fact remains that his position presses strongly in this direction.[7]

Although some might not be troubled by the universalist implication, I will assume without argument that we should avoid articulating christological anthropology in such a way that it leads to soteriological universalism. Similarly, it seems best to avoid any theological system in which we state, or even imply, that some *homo sapiens* are not truly human. The history of the *imago Dei* contains many instances in which people called into question the full humanity of certain groups, with consistently devastating effects (e.g., women, those with disabilities, racial minorities).[8] Consequently, we need to understand the relationship between Christology and anthropology in such a way that it avoids both concerns.

Fortunately, the argument presented in thesis 2 requires neither conclusion, as seen in thesis 4. Although thesis 2 affirms that all

---

6. Ibid., chs. 3, 6.

7. See esp. Jonathan Martin Ciraulo, "Sacraments and Personhood: John Zizioulas' Impasse and a Way Forward," *Heythrop Journal* 53, no. 6 (2012): 993–1004.

8. See esp. John Kilner, *Dignity and Destiny: Humanity in the Image of God* (Grand Rapids: Eerdmans, 2014), 17–37.

humans are only human insofar as they stand in some relationship with Jesus, the paradigm of true humanity, it does not follow from this that all humans will be saved. It does mean that all humans have been designed for eschatological consummation as the outworking of God's creational plans, but it says nothing about how many humans will actually arrive at this telos. Similarly, this framework does not limit the scope of humanity only to those who are already united with Christ soteriologically. Instead, it maintains that all humans are human insofar as they have been patterned after the humanity of Christ and that all humans have been called to the eschatological telos we see revealed in Christ, even though it remains the case that not all humans will ultimately experience that eschatological blessing.

5. THE EPISTEMOLOGICAL AND ONTOLOGICAL CENTRALITY OF JESUS FOR ANTHROPOLOGY ENTAILS THAT ULTIMATE TRUTHS ABOUT THE HUMAN PERSON MUST BE GROUNDED IN CHRISTOLOGY.

This thesis follows directly from theses 1 and 2. If Jesus is the only one who is both epistemologically and ontologically fundamental for humanity, then our truth claims about what it means to be human must somehow be grounded in Christology.[9] Yet we need to consider the kinds of claims we have in mind here. It would be absurd to think that we could reduce anthropology to Christology such that all truths about the human person could be derived directly from a consideration of Christ's humanity. Take for example any number of claims generated today by the neurosciences. None of these claims depend on Christology in any way, yet they involve some of the more important developments in contemporary anthropology. If these claims are true of human persons in general, then they will

---

9. I will not make any attempt here to argue for a particular view of what qualifies a claim as being properly "grounded" in Christology, which would require a rather lengthy and distracting epistemological excursus. It should suffice for this thesis to maintain simply that the truth of ultimate claims about what it means to be human must be established on the basis of claims about the humanity we see in Jesus. He is the epistemological norm for ultimate truth claims about humanity.

in fact be true of Jesus in virtue of his true humanity. But that does not mean we must derive them from Christology.

Instead, this thesis focuses only on "ultimate" truths about the human person. To understand what I have in mind by "ultimate truths," consider the truth claims we might make about *me* as a human person. Some of those, like the number of hairs currently on my head, will be rather peripheral. Others, like the fact that I am a father and a husband, are far more central. We cannot change those truths without radically altering my identity, which would in turn affect how we understand more peripheral truths. Although changing my status as "husband of Mary" would not necessarily affect the number of hairs on my head, it would change the one to whom they belong. The more central a truth is for the nature of the individual in question, the greater the ramifications are for other truths about that person. Ultimate truths, then, would be whatever truths we take to be most fundamental for the nature and identity of the human person. If we are going to maintain the epistemological centrality of Jesus Christ, we must at least affirm that he is the one who reveals that which is ultimately true about the human person.

It would be a mistake at this juncture to try and offer a list of truths that qualifies as ultimate in this sense. Any such list needs to be the outworking of a christological anthropology, not its starting point. Although some truths stand out as likely candidates (e.g., the importance of sexuality), we need to be careful about assuming that we already know those things that are ultimately true about humanity before we have done the work of exploring the christological basis of those truth claims. On the basis of the first four chapters, however, we tentatively claim that things like the *imago Dei*, the indwelling of the Holy Spirit, and faith/obedience all qualify as anthropologically ultimate.

We also should not conclude that if a truth is non-ultimate it is therefore inconsequential. Nonultimate truths may still be quite important. Consider again the truth that I am "husband of Mary." Although I believe that to be one of the more important truths about who I am as a person, it does not qualify as an ultimate truth in the same way as "made in the image of God." Changing the former would result in a radical adjustment to the shape of my human existence, while changing the latter would affect my status as *human*. Yet the nonultimacy of my marital status does not in any way detract from its marcological significance.[10]

Finally, it is important to note that such claims need to be "grounded in" rather than "derived from" Christology. I suspect that many of the truth claims delivered by a christological anthropology are the same kinds of claims that could be generated by anthropologies that would not qualify as christological in the same way. Consider, for example, the *imago Dei* itself. Given the way we defined the image of God in chapter 3, it seems reasonable to conclude that the *imago Dei* qualifies as an ultimate truth about humanity. Yet one could argue quite reasonably that this truth derives from the creation narratives rather than Christology. After all, we first learn about the image from Genesis 1. However, although we may not have *derived* that claim from Christology, we saw in the New Testament texts that this claim is *grounded* in Christology. Rather than a generic anthropological truth we know in abstraction from Jesus, the image of God is something we only know properly in light of what we see in his person and work. We might say something similar about the fundamental significance of human embodiment. While many anthropologies would affirm this basic truth, only Christology can ground the claim in the eternal paradigm for humanity itself.

6. CHRISTOLOGICALLY GROUNDED TRUTHS ABOUT HUMANITY PROVIDE AN INTERPRETIVE FRAMEWORK FOR UNDERSTANDING OTHER ANTHROPOLOGICAL TRUTHS.

We have already noted that we can derive anthropological truths from sources other than Christology. Indeed, the biblical authors themselves do not derive statements like "humans excrete" or "humans

---

10. Marcology is a rapidly growing discipline in which people spend most of their time talking about me.

normally have thirty-two teeth" from a christological starting point. Instead, it seems likely that they received most of their information about humanity from other sources. This is true for us as well. Christological anthropology does not try to constrict the range of sources available to us for understanding humanity—such as experience, the sciences, philosophy, the arts, history, and tradition. This includes the robust anthropology we have in the Old Testament scriptures. All of these comprise important and legitimate sources of anthropological information.

Christological anthropology focuses far less on our sources for anthropological claims than on the interpretive framework within which we understand them. The epistemological centrality of Jesus Christ for theological anthropology means that in light of him we must interpret and understand all other anthropological claims. Regardless of the source, if a particular claim is not adequate to the ultimate truths about humanity revealed in Christ, we must reconsider the claim. We should also be open to the possibility that we have misunderstood what is required by our christological starting point, though we will need to guard here against the temptation to adjust Christology simply to meet the needs of our changing anthropologies.

This should help address the concern in the first chapter about the intelligibility of human nature. As we saw, some contend that we need a clear distinction between the *natural* and the *supernatural*, identifying each as a distinct order of existence with its own capacities and finalities; otherwise, we make it impossible to affirm that humanity is the kind of thing that can be studied and understood from nontheological perspectives. On the approach taken here, however, it is entirely possible to argue both (1) that what it means to be *human* cannot be known independently of the true telos that God offers through grace and (2) that the human person can be studied—partially but legitimately—from the perspective of nontheological disciplines. The situation seems similar to what thinkers in other disciplines encounter in the difference between lower order and higher order systems. For example, physicists study the entire material world using a certain set of methods and principles. Their understanding of the material universe is impressive, to say the least. Other than a few hardcore reductive materialists, however, few think it possible or even desirable to reduce everything we know about the universe to those things physics can analyze. Instead, we recognize that higher order realities like living systems and human societies need to be analyzed with a different set of principles and methods (e.g., biology and sociology). These higher order principles have the potential to make us reinterpret what we think we know about lower order systems. That is because we think these higher order systems involve realities that cannot be predicted or comprehensively understood in terms of lower order disciplines alone. This does not denigrate the value of studying the underlying systems, but it does suggest that the disciplines studying those systems have built-in limitations.

Consequently, despite concerns to the contrary, christological anthropology does not undermine or marginalize nontheological perspectives on the human person. Instead, such an anthropology often depends on these other sources of anthropological insight to provide the material upon which it can reflect christologically.[11]

7. CHRISTOLOGICAL ANTHROPOLOGY MUST PAY CLOSE ATTENTION TO THE CONCRETE PARTICULARITIES OF JESUS'S EXISTENCE.

In the four previous chapters, we spent relatively little time examining the particular details of Jesus's historic existence, focusing instead on a number of theological claims about Jesus that were necessary for establishing the christological orientation of theological anthropology. Yet it would be a mistake to conclude that christological anthropology can function without careful attention to Jesus's life. Christological anthropology does not have at its center

---

11. For more on the importance of interdisciplinary dialogue for christological anthropology, see Marc Cortez, *Embodied Souls, Ensouled Bodies: An Exercise in Christological Anthropology and Its Significance for the Mind/Body Debate* (London: T&T Clark, 2008), 40–74.

an abstract idea about humanity—and not even an abstract idea about Jesus. Instead, as I have argued throughout this project, the paradigm of true humanity is the humanity of the incarnate Christ himself. Consequently, his historic existence must serve as a basic starting point for christological anthropology.

This will certainly mean spending considerable time in the gospels as a primary source of information about Jesus's life.[12] Yet emphasizing Jesus's historic life does not mean that we need to neglect other sources as well. The prior studies have already demonstrated that you can maintain the centrality of Jesus's historic life while also affirming that the sweep of Christology covers everything from God's eternal determinations to eschatological consummation. Christological anthropology would be tragically limited if we restricted ourselves to those details of what took place between Christmas and the crucifixion or maybe the ascension. Consequently, while christological anthropology must focus on the life of Jesus revealed in the gospels, we should not bifurcate between the Jesus of the Gospels and the material we find in the rest of the New Testament. Additionally, just as the Old Testament is necessary for understanding the person and work of Jesus Christ, so must our vision of humanity be informed by the robust anthropology of the Old Testament.

We must reject a similar mistake that often arises with respect to later theological developments. Scholars often make a sharp distinction between the Jesus we see in the biblical narratives and the complex Christologies developed in the third and fourth centuries. It would be easy to conclude from this thesis that only the former provides the proper source for christological anthropology. However, if we understand those later developments as the church's best attempts at understanding Jesus, and if christological anthropology takes this same person as the starting point for understanding

---

12. Although this does not commit us to any particular position regarding the various quests for the historical Jesus, I take it that the gospels themselves provide the best resources for understanding Jesus's life, while affirming at the same time that historical background studies will often facilitate their proper interpretation.

humanity, then it would be foolish to ignore these later reflections. Instead, we can maintain a commitment to the historic existence of Jesus as the primary focus of christological anthropology without denigrating these later attempts to understand the identity of the one revealed in those accounts.

8. THE PARTICULARITIES OF JESUS'S EXISTENCE MEAN THAT WE MUST AFFIRM BOTH THE CONTINUITY AND THE DISCONTINUITY BETWEEN JESUS AND OTHER HUMANS.

If we pay close attention to the particularities of Jesus's existence, we will notice the many ways that Jesus's humanity is continuous with our own. He ate, drank, slept, cried, felt pain, and died. It would not seem too much of a stretch to assume that he also experienced other facets of human existence not explicitly mentioned in the text. He probably laughed, belched, daydreamed, and yelled when he stubbed his toe in the middle of the night.[13] Once again we need to be careful about merely projecting our own understanding of humanity onto Jesus. Nonetheless, the clear biblical testimony that Jesus was fully human, as well as the contention that his human experience was sufficiently like our own for him to qualify as our merciful High Priest, means that the burden of proof rests on anyone who denies that Jesus experienced something that seems likely to be a normal aspect of human existence.

At the same time, careful attention to Jesus requires that we also recognize several important discontinuities. First, the particularities of his concrete existence create discontinuities of their own. Jesus not only had universal human experiences like eating and sleeping, but he was also a particular human person whose identity was shaped by things like ethnicity, gender, culture, geography, and more. Taken together, these particularizing features of Jesus's existence are the things that make him a distinct individual; consequently, they are also the things that make his existence discontinuous with all other human persons. He alone is the particular human *Jesus of Nazareth*.

---

13. I won't speculate about *what* he might have yelled in such a situation.

The more obvious discontinuity arises from the incarnation. He alone is the hypostatic union of deity and humanity, the eternal Son of God in human form. We cannot allow this fundamental truth to override the continuities mentioned earlier, lapsing into a form of docetism in which Jesus has only the outward form of humanity but not the corresponding subjective experience of being human. Nonetheless, the uniqueness of the incarnation requires us to maintain discontinuity as well, which makes it difficult to say much about the actual nature of Jesus's subjectivity. While we must affirm that Jesus experienced whatever was necessary for him to be our merciful High Priest, this discontinuity means that providing specific content for the meaning of that *whatever* will always prove elusive.

Finally, close attention to Jesus's life also requires that we recognize the discontinuity created by his sinlessness. Regardless of how we handle the question of whether the Son assumed a fallen human nature at the incarnation, we must affirm with the biblical authors that Jesus was not "sinful," at least not in the sense of being personally guilty (culpable) for any sin. That is what enables him to be our *faithful* High Priest and perfect sacrifice. Yet his sinlessness means that, even though sin is not essential to humanity, his human existence will be importantly different from our own. At the very least, he will not process life through the lenses of guilt, judgment, and alienation from God.

9. THERE CAN BE NO DIRECT MOVE FROM CHRISTOLOGY TO ANTHROPOLOGY.

This thesis gets us into the "scandal of particularity" in Christology. In other words, no matter how unique or significant we claim Jesus to be, he remains a single instance of humanity, one limited by the particularities of race, gender, culture, and time, among many other things. How do we generate truth claims about humanity in general in the midst of all this particularity? And how do we avoid the risk of universalizing these particularities so that, for example, we end up suggesting that the *male* is the norm for what it means to be fully *human*? Satisfactory answers to these questions will have to wait for the case studies that follow, particularly chapters six (sexuality) and seven (race). Yet we can identify here three mistakes that we must avoid.

First, we should not respond to this challenge by downplaying the details of Jesus's historic existence clearly limited by particularity (e.g., his Jewishness); instead, we should emphasize aspects of his existence that offer better material for making universal claims about humanity (e.g., embodiment). Any attempt to do this immediately runs into the problem of selectivity. How do I *know* which aspects of Jesus's existence are universally normative? On what basis can I conclude that embodiment is more fundamental than ethnicity (or vice versa)? Rather than allowing Christology to shape our understanding of humanity, such a move places our intuitions about humanity at the center of an ostensibly christological anthropology.

A second mistake would be thinking that we can move directly from the particularities of Jesus's life to anthropological claims about humanity in general. This is obviously the case with particular historical claims like "lived in Galilee." I am fairly confident we want to avoid universalizing such a particularity into the conclusion that true humanity can only be expressed in Galilee. Instead, it is far more likely that we would handle a particular detail like this by viewing it as part of an overall picture of Jesus's humanity from which we might derive implications for other humans. Yet if a particular historical detail like this cannot be the basis of a direct anthropological claim, then we should be careful about making such claims on the basis of *any* particular detail alone. As we will see in chapter 6, theologians have sometimes drawn anthropological conclusions from the particular detail of Christ's maleness in precisely this way.

The last mistake to avoid with respect to this thesis is in thinking that we can resolve the dilemma through some form of principalization. In other words, we might argue that the way to handle the problem is by moving from the particular (maleness) to the more general (sexuality) and making our anthropological claims only on the basis of the latter. Although there will probably be an element of this in any christological anthropology, this again runs into the problem that it seems driven by our existing anthropological intuitions. Otherwise, on what basis do we determine when we are operating with a concept that is generally applicable to all humans?

10. CHRISTOLOGICAL ANTHROPOLOGY MUST BE ROBUSTLY PNEUMATOLOGICAL AND TRINITARIAN.

One worry commonly expressed about christological anthropology, indeed about "christocentric" theologies in general, is that such an approach necessarily downplays the importance of the Holy Spirit and/or the Trinity for understanding humanity. By focusing our attention solely on Jesus Christ, we marginalize the Father and the Spirit, reducing them to secondary considerations at best.

Yet that is clearly not a necessary consequence of a christological approach to anthropology. Instead, taking Jesus as our anthropological starting point leads directly to emphasizing the importance of pneumatological and Trinitarian perspectives for understanding humanity for the simple reason that *you cannot understand Jesus* apart from these same considerations. If our method requires paying close attention to Jesus's particular identity, we cannot avoid recognizing that his identity is indissolubly related to the Father who sent him, the Spirit who empowers him, and ultimately the Trinitarian relationships that comprise the divine being itself. Properly done, a christocentric approach to theology should result in *emphasizing* rather than *marginalizing* both pneumatology and the Trinity.[14]

Even though our study of the *imago Dei* had a clearly christological

---

14. For more on this, see Marc Cortez, "What Does It Mean to Call Karl Barth a 'Christocentric' Theologian?," *Scottish Journal of Theology* 60, no. 2 (2007): 127–43. Some might contend that, while downplaying pneumatology and the Trinity might not be a *necessary* consequence of a christological anthropology, the approach has led to such consequences often enough to generate concerns nonetheless. That being said, such a claim would need to be carefully defended rather than simply assumed.

structure, that discussion led us to the centrality of the Father as the one whose presence is being manifested through his image bearers and the Spirit as the one who manifests that divine presence. We could make a similar argument from our study of the *anthrōpos* in John, which likewise emphasized the importance of both the Son and the Spirit in carrying out the creational purposes of the Father. From such discussions alone we would have to draw the conclusion that we cannot understand humanity properly apart from viewing the human person in relation to all three persons of the Trinity.

If this is the case, though, some might wonder about the wisdom of referring to this as a *christological* anthropology. Maybe we should call it a *Trinitarian* anthropology instead. Or maybe we could even explore the possibility of developing *pneumatological* anthropologies that take the Spirit as the anthropological starting point rather than Christ. Yet the label *christological* is intended to capture the Bible's own emphasis on Jesus as the one in whom true humanity is both inaugurated and revealed. While such a christological starting point necessarily and immediately leads us to view other theological truths as absolutely fundamental to understanding the human person, that does not change the fact that *Jesus* is the one in whom these anthropological truths find their firm and certain basis.

11. JESUS'S HUMANITY PRIMARILY REVEALS WHAT IT MEANS TO BE TRULY HUMAN IN THE MIDST OF A FALLEN WORLD.

This thesis also flows from the importance of paying close attention to the concrete particulars of Jesus's existence. If this is the case, then we must deal with the fact that the majority of what Jesus reveals about humanity comes in the context of fallenness. Jesus does not enter the world in an isolation bubble that protects him from the messy reality of life in a broken world. Instead, he lives out his humanity in a world shaped by sin. Even if we affirm that Jesus assumed an unfallen human nature like that of Adam and Eve in the garden, Jesus's life still would not show us a picture of Edenic humanity because of the radical differences introduced by the fall.

Neither does the life of Jesus reveal much about the eschatological condition of humanity, although we catch glimpses of it in the resurrection, ascension, and occasional descriptions of his return and future kingdom. Yet even those glimpses rarely provide the kind of detail necessary to formulate confident claims about the nature of eschatological humanity. If we simply look at the *context* in which Jesus reveals humanity, then we must affirm that the vast majority focuses on what it means to live humanly in a fallen world.

The same holds true for the *kind* of humanity we see in Jesus regardless of our position on the fallenness issue. As we discussed in chapter 4, even those who maintain that Jesus assumed an unfallen human nature contend that Jesus freely chose to adopt many of the infirmities associated with fallenness (e.g., pain) in order to better empathize with those he came to save. Therefore, the humanity we actually see in the life of Christ is a humanity shaped by the fall irrespective of whether his human nature was in fact fallen. Once again, we must recognize that the primary emphasis of christological anthropology will be on understanding what "true humanity" means in this present world rather than speculating about the lost condition of Edenic humanity or the nature of humanity's eschatological state.

Consequently, the kinds of anthropological proposals generated by a christological anthropology should likewise focus on understanding what it means to live humanly in the midst of a world shaped by the reality of sin. That does not mean we completely ignore the nature of prelapsarian or postresurrection humanity, and it may well be the case that those topics provide an opportunity for the kind of "productive speculation" we discussed in chapter 2.[15] Indeed, we will see an example of this when we address the nature of death in chapter 8. Nonetheless, if theological anthropology is truly to be guided by its christological starting point, it too needs to be shaped by the reality of life in a broken world.

With the biblical/theological framework of the first four chapters

---

15. See p. 84–85.

as well as the eleven theses articulated here, we can now move forward to deal with a few case studies in christological anthropology. In the space remaining, of course, we cannot deal with everything. Given the complexity of being human in this broken and fragmented world, I can't imagine how many books it would take to deal with everything necessary to think christologically about the entirety of what it means to be human today. Yet we can do enough to illustrate some of the ways in which a christologically shaped vision of the human person can address specific issues in theological anthropology.

CHAPTER 6

The Male Messiah

Sexuality, Embodiment, and the Image of God

───────●────────●───────

IN THE FIRST FOUR CHAPTERS, we explored a variety of ways in which the biblical authors present Jesus as the one who inaugurates and reveals what it means to be truly human in the midst of this fallen world. However, this raises a fundamental question that we have not yet addressed: How should we understand the claim that Jesus is normative for *all* humans in light of the fact that he is *male*? Many worry that when we connect Jesus's normativity with his maleness, we necessarily imply that true humanity somehow correlates more directly with maleness than with femaleness. We may *say* that women are equally human, but such a christological account *implies* a hierarchy of being in which men stand higher than women.

The question of Christ's maleness has received significant atten-tion in recent years, so much so that some might wonder if the topic really warrants further discussion.[1] However, the question raised here has such tremendous significance for understanding christolog-ical anthropology and its implications for women in particular that

───────────────

1. For good discussions of the topic, see Elizabeth A. Johnson, "The Maleness of Christ," in *Special Nature of Women* (London: SCM, 1991), 108–16; Nonna Verna Harrison, "The Maleness of Christ," *St. Vladimir's Theological Quarterly* 42, no. 2 (1998): 111–51; Elizabeth E. Green, "More Musings on Maleness: The Maleness of Jesus Revisited," *Feminist Theology* 20 (1999): 9–27; Julia Baudzej, "Re-Telling the Story of Jesus: The Concept of Embodiment and Recent Feminist Reflections on the Maleness of Christ," *Feminist Theology* 17, no. 1 (2008): 72–91; Elisabeth Schüssler Fiorenza, *Jesus: Miriam's Child, Sophia's Prophet: Critical Issues in Feminist Christology*, 2nd ed. (New York: Bloomsbury, 2015).

it cannot be ignored. Elizabeth Schüssler Fiorenza has identified this as "one of the most central issues in christology,"[2] and Julia Baudzej recently reaffirmed that conclusion, noting its perennial significance in feminist literature.[3] To discuss the issue thoroughly would require an extensive study on the nature of gender in dialogue with other disciplines like biology, psychology, and sociology, among others. Yet we will focus our attention on three key christological issues that people often use as loci for discussing the anthropological significance of Christ's maleness: the *imago Dei*, the resurrection, and biblical portrayals of Jesus that stretch or challenge gender conceptions.[4] All three discussions will demonstrate that we should not address this issue by attempting to minimize the historic reality of Christ's male body. But Eleanor McLaughlin rightly warns against the temptation to "leave the male Jesus of childhood piety for the Christ of mature theological reflection."[5] These discussions will thus illustrate a variety of ways in which people have sought to affirm the importance of Jesus's gendered body while addressing the maleness problem.

THE *IMAGO DEI* AND THE BODY OF CHRIST

The maleness of Christ raises the most direct questions with respect to the *imago Dei*. If Jesus is the true *imago Dei* (chapter 3), and if this presents Jesus as the true human, then how do we handle the fact that Jesus is male? As Patricia Wilson-Kastner explains, "In light of the two figures of Adam and Jesus, the imago dei in humanity unmistakably had a male face. Even if that was not made explicit in strict theological terms, it was driven home in sermons, devotional literature, poetry, and art. In this life the Christian could be

---

2. Schüssler Fiorenza, *Jesus*, 36.

3. Baudzej, "Re-Telling the Story of Jesus," 72.

4. Johnson also emphasizes the importance of this issue for debates about women's ordination and understanding the nature of God (Johnson, "The Maleness of Christ," 108–9); however, we will have to reserve those discussions for another time.

5. Eleanor McLaughlin, "Feminist Christologies: Re-Dressing the Tradition," in *Reconstructing the Christ Symbol: Essays in Feminist Christology* (New York: Paulist, 1993), 127.

sure that woman was an inferior human, and her nature and her behavior, actual and hoped for, was lesser than a male's."[6] Elizabeth Johnson argues that this logic has consistently led to the conclusion that men are more closely related to Christ than women, along with the implication that men somehow exemplify true humanity more adequately: "The belief that the Word became flesh and dwelt among us as a male indicates that thanks to their natural bodily resemblance, men enjoy a closer identification with Christ than do women. Men are not only theomorphic but, by virtue of their sex, also christomorphic in a way that goes beyond what is possible for women."[7] In light of all this, Delfo Canceran concludes, "Thus, Jesus's maleness has become a problem, if not the problem, in feminist theology. The maleness of Jesus seems to justify patriarchy and thereby defeats feminist struggles."[8]

Paul himself appears to exacerbate these concerns with the way he relates the *imago Dei* to human sexuality in 1 Corinthians 11:7. In the midst of a famously difficult passage involving head coverings, authority, and gender relations in the church, Paul declares: "A man ought not to cover his head, since he is the image and glory of God; but woman is the glory of man" (1 Cor 11:7). Here Paul apparently limits the image to men, suggesting that he thinks women participate in the image *indirectly*: men image Christ, while women only image men. When Paul elsewhere identifies the Son as the true image, then, maybe he is merely reinforcing a gendered view of the image.

---

6. Patricia Wilson-Kastner, "Contemporary Feminism and Christian Doctrine of the Human," *Word & World* 2, no. 3 (1982): 238.

7. Johnson, "The Maleness of Christ," 109. See also Elizabeth A. Johnson, "Jesus, the Wisdom of God: A Biblical Basis for Non-Androcentric Christology," *Ephemerides Theologicae Lovanienses* 61, no. 4 (1985): 262. Although the majority of theologians have historically affirmed that both men and women are full and equal participants in the *imago Dei*, a few have either disagreed explicitly or have argued in such a way as to raise questions about whether they truly affirmed this theological truth. For a good summary of the historical discussion, see Maryanne Cline Horowitz, "The Image of God in Man: Is Woman Included?," *Harvard Theological Review* 72, no. 3–4 (1979): 175–206.

8. Delfo Canceran, "Image of God: A Theological Reconstruction of the Beginning," *The Asia Journal of Theology* 25, no. 1 (2011): 14.

Yet this cannot be the case. Just a few chapters later Paul refers to the image in a way that clearly includes all believers without differentiation (1 Cor 15:49). Every other instance of the *imago Dei* in Paul's writings clearly associate the image with all believers regardless of gender. The logic of the *imago* appears to follow that of union with Christ in general: "There is neither Jew nor Gentile, neither slave nor free, nor is there male and female" (Gal 3:28). Indeed, to see Paul as limiting the image only to men in 1 Corinthians 11:7, we would have to contend that he is doing so in direct contrast to every other image passage in the Bible.[9]

Before drawing such a drastic conclusion, then, we would do well to look more closely at what Paul actually says. Most importantly, we should note that although Paul does not *attribute* the image to women in this passage, neither does he *deny* that women are made in the image of God. Instead, immediately after referencing the image, he turns his attention to "glory."[10] Given that glory fits naturally in the overall language of honor and shame that dominates the passage (1 Cor 11:4–6, 15), and the relationship between image and glory that we noted in chapter 3, it is entirely possible that Paul introduces the image here as a way of connecting the head covering issue (11:4–6) with the creational argument he develops (11:8–9). In other words, rather than trying to limit the *imago Dei* to men alone, Paul makes a quick reference to the image as a way of introducing the related concept of glory to his broader discussion of practices that bring dishonor and shame to the people of God.[11]

---

9. Even those who disagree fundamentally about the implications of Paul's argument for male/female relations in the church agree that Paul is not denying here that women are made in the image (e.g., Gordon D. Fee, *The First Epistle to the Corinthians*, The New International Commentary on the New Testament (Grand Rapids: Eerdmans, 1987), 516; Bruce A. Ware, "Male and Female Complementarity and the Image of God," *Journal for Biblical Manhood and Womanhood* 7 [2002]: 20). Nonetheless, some remain unconvinced (e.g., Lone Fatum, "Image of God and Glory of Man: Women in the Pauline Congregations," in *Image of God and Gender Models in Judaeo-Christian Tradition*, ed. Kari Elisabeth Børresen [Minneapolis: Fortress, 1995], 71; Urs von Arx, "The Gender Aspects of Creation from a Theological, Christological, and Soteriological Perspective: An Exegetical Contribution," *Anglican Theological Review* 84, no. 3 [2002]: 530).

10. John Kilner, *Dignity and Destiny: Humanity in the Image of God* (Grand Rapids: Eerdmans, 2014), 241–52.

11. C. K. Barrett, *A Commentary on the Second Epistle to the Corinthians* (New York: Harper

However, if Paul does not restrict the image to maleness, what do we do with his claim that the true *imago Dei* is a man (Col 1:15)?[12] We could deal with this question by eliminating the body itself from our definition of the image, associating it exclusively with the human soul or spirit.[13] Theologians have long viewed the image as primarily a spiritual reality, particularly in the Eastern tradition. Since such theologians also tended to maintain that souls do not have gender by restricting sexuality to the realm of the body alone,[14] this approach would allow us to affirm that Jesus is the true image without involving his embodied sexuality in any way. This approach clearly will not work with the view presented in chapter 3, which entails that the image is essentially embodied, but some might be inclined to think that the maleness problem is serious enough to warrant reconsidering our definition of the image itself. Even if you reject the argument of chapter 3, however, you must still contend with the fact that most scholars now view the *imago Dei* as something that refers to the whole person and not just the "spiritual" aspects of the person,[15] especially since Genesis 1:26–28 does not indicate that only certain aspects of human persons are made in the image

---

& Row, 1973), 252; Judith M. Gundry-Volf, "Gender and Creation in 1 Corinthians 11:2–16: A Study in Paul's Theological Method," in *Evangelium, Schriftauslegung, Kirche: Festschrift für Peter Stuhlmacher zum 65. Geburtstag* (Göttingen: Vandenhoeck & Ruprecht, 1997), 151–71; David E. Garland, *1 Corinthians*, Baker Exegetical Commentary on the New Testament (Grand Rapids: Baker Academic, 2003), 522–23; Roy E. Ciampa and Brian S. Rosner, *The First Letter to the Corinthians*, The Pillar New Testament Commentary (Grand Rapids: Eerdmans, 2010), 523.

12. The easiest option would be to argue that the *imago Dei* should not be central to theological anthropology. Thus, even if it is true that Jesus's maleness is somehow directly related to his identity as the paradigmatic *imago Dei*, it would not necessarily cause problems for *all* humans. Yet we already addressed this argument in chapter 3, noting several reasons for maintaining the centrality of the *imago Dei* for understanding humanity.

13. For a good historical overview of interpretations, see Stanley J. Grenz, *The Social God and the Relational Self: A Trinitarian Theology of the Imago Dei* (Philadelphia: Westminster, 2001), 141–82.

14. Harrison, "The Maleness of Christ," 138.

15. E.g., Edward Mason Curtis, "Man as the Image of God in Genesis in the Light of Ancient Near Eastern Parallels" (PhD diss., University of Pennsylvania, 1984), 390; Anthony A. Hoekema, *Created in God's Image* (Grand Rapids: Eerdmans, 1986), 64–65; Wolfhart Pannenberg, *Systematic Theology*, trans. Geoffrey W. Bromiley (Grand Rapids: Eerdmans, 1991), 206–7; Andreas Schüle, "Made in the 'image of God': The Concepts of Divine Images in Gen 1–3," *Zeitschrift Für Die Alttestamentliche Wissenschaft* 117, no. 1 (2005): 7.

of God. Additionally, and in my mind most decisively, any attempt to downplay the significance of embodiment necessarily fails on the basis of Jesus himself. I have argued elsewhere that embodiment is one of the central affirmations of a christologically determined anthropology.[16] After all, the incarnation and resurrection both declare the importance of the body for being human. Indeed, at no point in the story of Jesus do the biblical authors make any attempt to discuss Jesus's significance in abstraction from his embodiment. Regardless of how we understand the nature of his existence between his death and resurrection (i.e., Holy Saturday), it remains significant that the Bible is almost entirely silent on the subject. Thus the picture of humanity we receive in Jesus is entirely that of an embodied being carrying out God's purposes in a material world.[17]

Consequently, we need a way of affirming the centrality of Jesus's embodied existence without implying that maleness in itself is normative for humanity in general. Verna Harrison suggests that the way to do this is by making a distinction between the *universal* and the *particular* with respect to Christ's humanity. The universal dimension of his humanity is "the common 'substance' of which the concrete totality of all human persons throughout time and throughout the world are made and which unites them all with each other."[18] Having this common substance is what makes a person human, yet each instantiation of this universal human nature will also involve the particularities that differentiate humans from one another. Thus, "He could not have become incarnate as 'humanity-in-general' because human nature exists only in particular persons. Yet in order to save he has to share the humanity that is common to all people."[19] On this account, Jesus's maleness is a function of the fact that sexuality is one of the particularities he had to assume in

---

16. Marc Cortez, *Embodied Souls, Ensouled Bodies: An Exercise in Christological Anthropology and Its Significance for the Mind/Body Debate* (London: T&T Clark, 2008).

17. Although some might take this as an argument in favor of a materialist anthropology, it is entirely possible to affirm substance dualism and still maintain this emphasis on the body.

18. Harrison, "The Maleness of Christ," 115.

19. Ibid.

order to become human, but as a particularity it is not normative for other humans. In other words, it is entirely possible to say that viewing Jesus as paradigmatic for the image requires us to affirm the importance of *embodiment* (universal) but not necessarily the individual aspects of a given *body* (particular). Of course, you cannot be embodied without a particular body, yet it does not follow from this that both have the same significance for understanding the *imago Dei*.

The challenge of this approach for many is that it requires the existence of a universal human nature in which we all somehow participate. Yet this is not the only way of making this kind of universal/particular distinction. For example, drawing on Gregory of Nyssa's theology, David Bentley Hart explains the universality of humanity this way: "If the 'essence' of the human is none other than the plenitude of all men and women, every essentialism is rendered empty: all persons express and unfold the human not as shadows of an undifferentiated idea, but in their concrete multiplicity and hence in all the intervals and transitions belonging to their differentiation; and so human 'essence' can only be an 'effect' of the whole."[20] In other words, the universality of humanity derives from the very particularity and multiplicity of all those individuals who comprise totality of the *humanum*, which is itself grounded in Jesus. Rather than leading with the undifferentiated essence and then dealing with particularity as a problem, this approach emphasizes particularity as essential to being human.

Either way, we end up with a universal/particular distinction that seems necessary for understanding how Christ's humanity relates to the rest of us. To illustrate this further, let's return to the idea of the *imago Dei* as an idol discussed in chapter 3. Suppose that I decide to make an idol for Marduk. (It's not clear to me why I would do this since it violates pretty much everything I believe in. But just go with me on this.) For it to be a true idol, it will need

---

20. David Bentley Hart, "The 'Whole Humanity': Gregory of Nyssa's Critique of Slavery in Light of His Eschatology," *Scottish Journal of Theology* 54, no. 1 (2001): 64.

to be a material object, the physical means by which Marduk will manifest his presence in my living room. But the particular details of the idol can vary. I could make it taller or shorter, with legs or without. I could even create an idol that is more abstract rather than explicitly anthropomorphic.[21] Yet none of these variants impact its status as an idol. We should not go so far as to say that the particular details are irrelevant, yet it remains the case that the materiality of the object (universal) is more central to meaning/function of the idol than the details (particular).

It seems entirely possible to affirm something similar about Jesus and the *imago Dei*. To be an image bearer, Jesus must be an embodied being. (Or, more appropriately, we see from Jesus that to be a true image bearer is to be an embodied being.) Jesus thus had a body, which entails having the individuating characteristics that go along with having a physical body (height, weight, shape, etc.). Thus, the fact that Jesus was embodied makes embodiment central to the image. And the fact that Jesus had a particular body with individual characteristics may even entail that having a particular body with individual characteristics is central to the image. But none of this entails that any particular characteristic would also need to be viewed as similarly paradigmatic.

One danger with this argument is that it could easily lead to a christological anthropology that ignores the details of Jesus's historic existence. After all, each of those details would itself be a particularity of Jesus's humanity and, consequently, not something universally true of all humans. Yet how could we pretend to have a christologically informed vision of humanity if we neglect the specific details that comprise Jesus's particular life? The key here will be to recognize that we only have access to the universal *through* the particularities of Jesus's humanity. Proclamations about that which is universally true of all humans must come as a result of considering the particular details of Jesus's life. Consequently, even

---

21. David J. A. Clines, "The Image of God in Man," *Tyndale Bulletin* 19 (1968): 92; Grenz, *The Social God and the Relational Self*, 199; Kilner, *Dignity and Destiny*, 57.

if we make the necessary affirmation that Jesus's maleness is part of the particularity of his individual humanity rather than a universal norm for humanity in general, it still provides an opportunity for reflecting on the reality of what it means to be human. At the very least, the fact that the Son became incarnate as a gendered individual would seem to require us to affirm that sexuality is an essential feature of human existence. Yet we will see in the next section that some would challenge even this conclusion.

TRANSCENDING GENDER THROUGH THE RESURRECTION

The resurrection is often viewed as providing another option for people seeking to deal with the relationship between Christ's maleness and his anthropological normativity. One way of doing this has been by arguing that humans will no longer be gendered in the resurrection but will instead have resurrection bodies that have been transformed into some kind of nongendered state.[22] This might then provide space for thinking about Jesus's own body without the difficulties generated by his maleness. Rather than taking his male body as somehow paradigmatic for the rest of humanity, it would be his resurrected and nongendered body that would play this role.

For example, Gregory of Nyssa argued that in Jesus we see the transformative power of the incarnation, which begins the process of remaking human nature so that it becomes capable of participating in the divine life to the greatest extent possible.[23] This begins with his christological argument that sexuality cannot be part of the meaning of humanity as seen in the *imago Dei*. "I presume that every one knows that this is a departure from the Prototype: for 'in Christ Jesus,' as the apostle says, 'there is neither male nor female.'"[24]

---

22. Verna Harrison lists Clement of Alexandria, Basil the Great, Gregory the Theologian, Gregory of Nyssa, John Chrysostom, and Maximus the Confessor as all affirming this position (Harrison, "The Maleness of Christ," 122–23).

23. See esp. Marc Cortez, *Christological Anthropology in Historical Perspective: Ancient and Contemporary Approaches to Theological Anthropology* (Grand Rapids: Zondervan, 2016), 31–55.

24. Gregory of Nyssa, "On the Making of Man," in *A Select Library of the Nicene and Post-Nicene Fathers*, ed. Philip Schaff, vol. 5, series 2 (Grand Rapids: Eerdmans, 1978), 16.7.

Although sexuality is necessary for procreation in this life,[25] being created male and female means that humans are "divided according to this distinction."[26] Our union with Christ, on the other hand, demonstrates a fundamental unity in the nature of humanity that transcends this division and reveals the truth that sexuality is a secondary feature of human existence rather than something that defines humanity at its core. In addition, Gregory also espoused a form of gender essentialism in which only some characteristics (virtues) are primarily associated with each nature. Consequently, while our gendered bodies facilitate the development of certain virtues, they hinder us from experiencing others. In Jesus, though, we see the ultimate promise of a form of humanity in which the virtues are no longer distributed among and divided between the sexes. On such an account, it stands to reason that the resurrection body would not possess the characteristics of sexuality that divide us from one another and hinder our acquisition of the full range of the virtues, especially when we no longer need these characteristics for procreation.[27]

However, if we take seriously Jesus's entire history (thesis 7), then we also need to account for the fact that Jesus retains his identity as *Jesus* in the resurrection, an identity that is unavoidably linked to the fact that he is male. Although the resurrection narratives present Jesus's body as transformed in some way, nothing about those narratives suggests a transformation of identity such that he is no longer the same male individual the disciples knew him to be. Indeed, Harrison notes that even theologians like Gregory did not draw the expected conclusion regarding Jesus's gendered identity: "We do not find the fathers stating that Christ is no longer male after his resurrection. Instead the Church's experience is that he continues to be known to the faithful in the form known to the

---

25. Ibid., 17.2.

26. Ibid., 16.7.

27. Verna E. F. Harrison, "Gender, Generation, and Virginity in Cappadocian Theology," *Journal of Theological Studies* 47 (1996): 56.

apostles."[28] I have argued elsewhere that Gregory might be able to account for this by drawing on a distinction between biological sexuality and gendered identity, maintaining that although the former no longer characterizes the resurrection body, the latter remains.[29] Kevin Corrigan thus argues, "Just because physical sexuality and genitalia are accidental [i.e., nonessential], this does not mean that everything resulting from them is accidental."[30] It may be that while Jesus no longer has a male *body*, he retains a male *identity* because his identity is at least partially shaped by the reality of his earthly existence. Consequently, eschatological humanity is "de-genitalized" but not de-gendered.[31]

While this might succeed at defending the coherence of Gregory's argument, this approach still has two key weaknesses. First, as Harrison points out, Gregory follows a pattern common to many early theologians in assuming that individuality is a problem.[32] Since salvation requires all humans to be united intimately with Jesus, the resurrection must involve overcoming as many features of particularity as possible without losing personal identity entirely. It is difficult to see, though, why we would draw such a conclusion from our christological starting point. We certainly must emphasize union with Christ as a central theological truth, but nothing in Jesus's own existence suggests that particularity constitutes a problem for this union. Instead, the incarnation seems to affirm the importance of particularity for being human, suggesting that it is precisely in our particular humanity that we are united with Jesus through the power of the Spirit. Ruether thus rightly critiques a pervasive

---

28. Harrison, "The Maleness of Christ," 123.

29. Cortez, *Christological Anthropology in Historical Perspective*, 52–54.

30. Kevin Corrigan, *Evagrius and Gregory: Mind, Soul, and Body in the Fourth Century*, Ashgate Studies in Philosophy and Theology in Late Antiquity (Burlington, VT: Ashgate, 2009), 139. See also Morwenna Ludlow, *Gregory of Nyssa, Ancient and (Post)modern* (Oxford: Oxford University Press, 2007), 178.

31. Sarah Coakley proposes this as an apt way of describing Gregory's vision of protological humanity, but the language serves here as well. See Coakley, *Powers and Submissions: Spirituality, Philosophy, and Gender* (Oxford: Blackwell, 2002), 163.

32. Harrison, "The Maleness of Christ," 118.

tendency to "dissolve most aspects of Jesus's particularity . . . in order to make him the symbol of universal humanity," arguing instead that "an insistence that the historical particularity of his maleness is essential to his ongoing representation."[33]

A second problem relates more directly to the focus of this chapter. Even if the above distinction between sexuality and gender works for explaining Gregory's argument, it would still leave us with the question about the normativity of Jesus's maleness. If Jesus remains *Jesus* in the resurrection, and if this entails that he remains male in some sense, then this argument does not succeed in avoiding the maleness problem. It has simply shifted the issue from biological sexuality to gendered identity.

A second way that people might use the resurrection when dealing with Christ's maleness draws on a different aspect of Gregory's understanding of eschatological consummation. According to Gregory, the christological transformation of humanity that we see in the incarnation and resurrection means that eschatological humanity is incomprehensible on the basis of current anthropological knowledge and experience.[34] As Gregory concluded at the end of *On the Soul and the Resurrection*, "Every reasoning which conjectures about the future restoration will be proved worthless when what we expect comes to us in experience."[35] Elizabeth Johnson argues that this kind of apophatic anthropology is precisely what we need in order to maintain that Jesus retains the particular features of his humanity that constitute him as a distinct person, including his maleness, while still maintaining that this does not make maleness *as we know it* normative for all humans. Contending that the resurrection involves "a transformation of his humanity so profound

---

33. Rosemary Radford Ruether, "The Liberation of Christology from Patriarchy," *Religion and Intellectual Life* 2, no. 3 (1985): 127.

34. This is what Brian Daley referred to as Gregory's "Christology of transformation" (Brian E. Daley, "'The Human Form Divine': Christ's Risen Body and Ours according to Gregory of Nyssa," in *Studia Patristica Vol 41* [Leuven: Peeters, 2006], 316).

35. Gregory of Nyssa, *On the Soul and the Resurrection* (Crestwood, NY: St. Vladimir's Seminary Press, 1993), 113.

that it escapes our imagination," she thus concludes that theological humility requires us to affirm an apophatic view of his resurrected humanity, which "acknowledges that language about the maleness of Christ at this point proceeds under the negating sign of analogy, more dissimilar than similar to any maleness known in history."[36] Consequently, his maleness is no longer problematic for anthropology today precisely because, although we affirm that he is male in the resurrection, we no longer know what that means.[37]

It is true that we need to exercise considerable theological humility when talking about eschatological humanity. As it stands, though, this argument would render a christological anthropology entirely vacuous. Almost any claim we might make about the human person would immediately need to be bracketed in the same way. While Jesus would still *be* the true human, we could no longer claim that he *reveals* true humanity in any meaningful way. This entire argument also runs into the problem that the biblical authors do not defer entirely to Jesus's resurrection humanity when portraying him as paradigmatically significant for other humans. Instead, as we have seen, it is precisely as an embodied human living an earthly existence that Jesus is the true *imago Dei*. This is why christological anthropology should focus its attention on the ways in which Jesus reveals what it means to be human *now* and not just what it will mean to be human in the eschaton (thesis 11).

This does not mean that we entirely have to reject the possibility of using the resurrection for understanding humanity. Indeed, the resurrection plays a vital role in reminding us that our current experiences of humanity do not reveal everything that God intends for his creatures. Yet I remain skeptical that resurrection-based arguments provide the best framework for dealing with the maleness of Jesus.

---

36. Johnson, "The Maleness of Christ," 113.

37. E.g., Ian A. McFarland, *The Divine Image: Envisioning the Invisible God* (Minneapolis: Fortress, 2005), 41–50; Linda Woodhead, "Apophatic Anthropology," in *God and Human Dignity*, ed. R. Kendall Soulen and Linda Woodhead (Grand Rapids: Eerdmans, 2006), 233–46; Kathryn Tanner, *Christ the Key*, Current Issues in Theology (New York: Cambridge University Press, 2010), 54.

MASCULINITY, FEMININITY,
AND THE SUBVERSION OF GENDER

A final set of questions about Christ's maleness arises when we consider its significance for understanding things like *masculinity* and *femininity*, where we take those as referring to aspects of gender that go beyond mere biological differences. In other words, while most affirm that *male* and *female* correspond to certain biological generalities (e.g., genitalia, chromosomes, hormone production), some contend that they also correspond to certain qualities (e.g., aggressiveness, nurturing) and behaviors (e.g., roughhousing, playing with dolls), and that this correspondence holds because these qualities and behaviors are in some way essential to their respective genders.[38] Thus, *masculinity* and *femininity* describe gendered qualities and behaviors that correspond essentially with the biological realities of *male* and *female*. Others reject this kind of *gender essentialism*, contending that most (maybe all) of the qualities and behaviors we associate with the genders derive from cultural norms and expectations rather than underlying biological realities. The question for us is whether Christ's own maleness has anything to say on the matter.

The starting point for any such discussion is to appreciate the many ways that the biblical authors portray Jesus as one who challenges cultural notions of masculinity.[39] He washes feet, touches sick people, shows compassion to sinful women, loves children, and more. Although we have become accustomed to such images through our familiarity with the stories, these were countercultural actions that should cause people to rethink what it means to be "male." Elizabeth Green thus points to a number of ways in which the gospel writers portray Jesus transgressing social boundaries: "I am thinking of those numerous episodes in the gospels which

---

38. As I mentioned earlier, whether the genders also correspond to particular roles, especially roles in the church, is not an issue we will be getting into here.

39. See esp. McLaughlin, "Feminist Christologies"; Rosemary Radford Ruether, *To Change the World: Christology and Cultural Criticism* (New York: Crossroad, 1981); Baudzej, "Re-Telling the Story of Jesus."

portray Jesus as transgressing the boundaries which separated men from women, Jew from Gentile, prophets from prostitutes, healthy from sick, sane from insane, law abiders from outlaws as well as of the God-human divide set up and bridged by Chalcedon."[40] In many ways, Jesus broke down socially erected barriers, challenging people to appreciate unity where they saw only division.

However, it is entirely possible to agree that Jesus's maleness challenges cultural expectations and still disagree about what this entails for understanding gender essentialism. Some might retain gender essentialism and contend that what we see in Jesus challenges only certain *illegitimate* ways of understanding the characteristics essential to each gender. We could try and make this argument in three ways. First, we could maintain gender essentialism and contend that Jesus's own maleness was also limited by these essential differences. Although Jesus helps us see that true maleness includes more than we might have realized (e.g., qualities like compassion and patience), this does not require us to jettison entirely the notion that there are fundamental differences between men and women. It may be the case that there are just fewer differences than we thought, or maybe we see in Jesus that there are distinctively male ways of expressing shared qualities like these.

However, a response like this makes the maleness problem almost insoluble. If Jesus exemplifies a distinctively male way of being human that is essentially different from a female way of being human, *and* if Jesus is the paradigmatic human, then two conclusions seem inevitable: (1) the male way of being human is more paradigmatic; and (2) Jesus cannot be the normative model for women. Indeed, the latter conclusion seems to lie behind at least some of the arguments for emphasizing the Eve/Mary typology as a model for women rather than Adam/Christ.[41] While there are excellent reasons for exploring Eve and Mary as resources for theological anthropology, we can-

---

40. Green, "More Musings on Maleness," 21.

41. Benjamin H. Dunning, *Christ without Adam: Subjectivity and Sexual Difference in the Philosophers' Paul* (New York: Columbia University Press, 2014).

not do so because we have defined Jesus's humanity in a way that excludes women.[42] We also encounter the significant difficulty that the biblical authors expect the Spirit to reproduce in all Christians the same kinds of virtues and behaviors we see in Jesus (e.g., Gal 5:22–23). The Bible never claims that some Christian qualities are limited either to men or women, nor does it imply that there are distinctively male and female ways of exemplifying those qualities. The Bible simply calls on all believers to be Christlike.

A second approach would retain gender essentialism as it relates to men and women generally, but view Jesus as one who combined both sets of qualities in a single person. Although Jesus remains biologically male, he is not limited just to a subset of human qualities and virtues. According to Ruether, such Christologies take as their starting point "the basic Christian affirmation that Christ redeems the whole of human nature, male and female."[43] Yet this must also mean that in some way Jesus transcends the differences between male and female, including in himself the fullness of what it means to be human.

Although this approach resolves the normativity problem above since Jesus's humanity includes both maleness and femaleness, it runs into problems of its own. By affirming that Jesus can incorporate both sets of properties in a single person, it undermines the gender essentialist framework. Generally speaking, gender essentialists hold that there is a direct link between the underlying biology and the corresponding qualities. However, if Jesus can be biologically male *and* possess the qualities typically associated with being female, then it follows that such qualities are not in fact *essentially* female. Additionally, this approach extends the concerns about Christlikeness raised above so that they now apply to men

---

42. Maja Weyermann, "The Typologies of Adam-Christ and Eve-Mary and Their Relationship to One Another," *Anglican Theological Review* 84, no. 3 (2002): 609–26; John VanMaaren, "The Adam-Christ Typology in Paul and Its Development in the Early Church Fathers," *Tyndale Bulletin* 64, no. 2 (2013): 275–97.

43. Rosemary Radford Ruether, *Sexism and God-Talk: Toward a Feminist Theology* (London: SCM, 1983), 127.

as well as women. Since Jesus combines both sets of properties in himself, neither group can exemplify Christlikeness as a whole, but only a subset of those properties.

A third option would be to retain gender essentialism but severely restrict its scope for understanding the human person. For example, we could stipulate that maleness tends to correspond to higher levels of testosterone, which in turn correlates with things like larger muscles and higher activity levels.[44] But we would then deny that any of this has significance for the fact that men are also called to exemplify virtues like patience, gentleness, and kindness. This would be the case for all of the most important qualities of the human person, creating significant commonality between men and women. We would still affirm the existence of some essential differences, but deny their significance for understanding what it truly means to be human.

Probably the most significant question for this last option is whether such a weakened and revised understanding of gender essentialism is worth retaining. Consequently, many push for an alternate interpretation of Christ's maleness, one that views it as challenging the masculinity/femininity paradigm itself. Feminist theologians question the value of viewing Jesus as one who combines in himself the properties of both maleness and femaleness, contending that such "androgynous" Christologies still portray these as fundamentally distinct realities.[45] They are merely juxtaposed within the person of Christ in a way that Mary Daly once described as something like "John Travolta and Farrah Fawcett-Majors scotch-taped together."[46] Instead, they contend that Jesus is one who subverts gender itself.[47]

---

44. Note that I am not defending this claim, just using it as an example of how such an argument might proceed.

45. Green, "More Musings on Maleness," 19.

46. Mary Daly, *Gyn/Ecology: The Metaethics of Radical Feminism* (Boston, MA: Beacon, 1979), xi.

47. Schüssler Fiorenza, *Jesus*, 45. Eleanor McLaughlin thus contends that Jesus functioned like a "transvestite" in society, one who makes ambiguous that which society holds to be

This is most commonly done by appealing to the wisdom/logos/sophia tradition.[48] As we saw in chapter 3, many scholars maintain that Paul associates Jesus with the wisdom tradition by describing him as the *eikōn* (image) and *prōtotokos* (firstborn) through whom God creates and sustains the universe (Col 1:15–16). Many argue for a similar wisdom background behind John's prologue and the exordium of Hebrews.[49] Although I argued earlier that we should still understand these texts as referring to the *imago Dei* (chapter 3), this does not mean we should just ignore the wisdom material. The significance of this material for our discussion comes from the fact that although "the Logos-Sophia of God is neither male nor female," she "was imaged in the major Jewish tradition that lies behind Christian Trinitarian thought in female personification."[50] By using this conceptual framework to describe Jesus, then, the New Testament authors present him "in terms of the powerful female figure of Sophia who is creator, redeemer and divine renewer of the people of Israel, and indeed of the whole earth (Wisdom 7.10)."[51] These thinkers contend that by identifying Jesus with a female figure like this, the biblical authors provide resources for understanding his humanity in ways that transcend the limitations we typically associate with masculinity. Canceran thus concludes, "This Sophia tradition can provide hope for feminists in neutralizing the heavily andocentric interpretation of the maleness of Jesus."[52]

Julian of Norwich offers a similar example from the tradition of the church. Reflecting on her visions of Christ's self-giving love and

clear and certain (Eleanor McLaughlin, "Feminist Christologies: Re-Dressing the Tradition," in *Reconstructing the Christ Symbol: Essays in Feminist Christology* [New York: Paulist, 1993], 138).

48. See esp. Johnson, "Jesus, the Wisdom of God"; Schüssler Fiorenza, *Jesus*.

49. E.g., Henry R. Moeller, "Wisdom Motifs and John's Gospel," *Bulletin of the Evangelical Theological Society* 6, no. 3 (1963): 92–99; Kenneth Schenck, "Keeping His Appointment: Creation and Enthronement in Hebrews," *Journal for the Study of the New Testament* 66 (1997): 91–117; Andrew T. Glicksman, "Beyond Sophia: The Sapiential Portrayal of Jesus in the Fourth Gospel and Its Ethical Implications for the Johannine Community," in *Rethinking the Ethics of John: "Implicit Ethics" in the Johannine Writings* (Tübingen: Mohr Siebeck, 2012), 83–101.

50. Ruether, "The Liberation of Christology from Patriarchy," 120.

51. Johnson, "The Maleness of Christ," 113.

52. Canceran, "Image of God," 16.

sacrificial service, Julian routinely drew on feminine imagery as the most apt for explaining what she had seen.[53] In what is a startling move for many modern readers, Julian thus provides extensive reflections on the idea that Jesus is "our true Mother, in whom we are endlessly born and out of whom we shall never come,"[54] routinely describing the persons of the Trinity in terms of fatherhood, motherhood, and love.[55] For Julian, the mother/child relationship was the most apt description of the sacrificial love Jesus willingly endured that his people might see new life.

According to this approach, then, if we take seriously the fact that Jesus is soteriologically united to all humans, men and women alike, as well as biblical portrayals that present Jesus as one who transcends masculinity/femininity stereotypes, especially in the wisdom/sophia/logos tradition, we should reject gender essentialism and not restrict behaviors and qualities to particular genders. Some might worry that such an approach would eliminate recognizing *any* distinctions between men and women, but that would be an overextension of this argument. It is entirely possible to reject gender essentialism while still affirming the importance of biological differences related to sexuality. Neither does this approach entail the rejection of all cultural norms for masculinity and femininity. It simply challenges the assumptions that these are *essential* expressions of maleness and femaleness. Others may worry about the implications that such might have for things like sexual ethics and roles in the church. If masculinity and femininity are merely the products of our societies rather than the essential entailments of underlying biological realities, then

---

53. For additional information on this aspect of Julian's theology, see Brant Pelphrey, *Christ Our Mother: Julian of Norwich*, Way of the Christian Mystics (Wilmington, DE: Glazier, 1989); Margaret Ann Palliser, *Christ, Our Mother of Mercy: Divine Mercy and Compassion in the Theology of the "Shewings" of Julian of Norwich* (New York: de Gruyter, 1992); Marilyn McCord Adams, "Julian of Norwich on the Tender Loving Care of Mother Jesus," in *Our Knowledge of God* (Dordrecht, Netherlands: Kluwer, 1992), 197–213; Kerry Dearborn, "The Crucified Christ as the Motherly God: The Theology of Julian of Norwich," *Scottish Journal of Theology* 55, no. 3 (2002): 283–302.

54. Julian of Norwich, *Showings*, trans. Edmund Colledge and James Walsh, The Classics of Western Spirituality (New York: Paulist, 1978), 292.

55. See esp. Julian of Norwich, *Showings*, chs. 57–60.

why continue to limit *any* behavior, including sexual relationships or church leadership, according to biological realities? Although I mentioned in the introduction that we would not be getting into issues related to sexual ethics in this book, at least a brief comment is needed here. Most importantly, I would argue that gender essentialism is *not* required for maintaining either a traditional sexual ethic or a complementarian view of church governance. In both cases, it is entirely possible to argue that God can stipulate norms for human life irrespective of underlying biological realities. Indeed, he frequently does so. Consider, for example, that God chose the Levites as the ones who would serve as priests in the temple. He does not seem to have done so because of any qualities they had that made them essentially different from the other tribes. Similarly, when God forbade Israel from intermarrying with the Canaanites, he instituted a sexual norm that had nothing to do with biology. Consequently, if you are convinced that God has instituted certain norms for sexuality and church governance, nothing about the gender essentialist discussion prevents you from continuing to affirm those norms.

The more significant challenge for this position will likely come from those who are simply unconvinced that the biblical portrayals of Jesus are sufficiently strong as to warrant the corresponding conclusion. Even if we grant that the New Testament uses the wisdom tradition as a way of explaining the significance of Jesus and that Wisdom was commonly portrayed as a female in the Old Testament, it would not follow that these authors were trying to attribute femininity to Jesus by association any more than associating Jesus with the *Logos* means attributing to him all the properties of the Stoic *logos*, the principle of reason that animates the universe. When the New Testament authors *adopt* language from various spheres of discourse, they also *adapt* that language to serve new christological purposes. The same principle is almost certainly at work with the sophia/wisdom material.

If we take seriously the Jesus we see revealed in the New Testament, we must recognize the ways in which his male existence challenged conceptions about what it means to be *masculine* and *feminine* in his cultural context, preparing us to hear a similar challenge to our own assumptions today. At the same time, the importance of being brought into union with Christ through the power of the Spirit so that we come to take on the very characteristics of Christ should lead us to question the extent to which we should emphasize maleness and femaleness as distinct realities that differ essentially as a consequence of underlying biological processes. Instead, despite our variations the unity of the body of Christ presses us to emphasize "one human nature celebrated in an interdependence of multiple differences."[56] Or, at least, those who think they have good reasons to maintain gender essentialism should consider ways to do that without undermining these important christological convictions.

CONCLUSION

If we are going to claim that Jesus somehow reveals what it means to be truly human without allowing that to collapse into some kind of abstract generalization with little connection to his actual identity, we need to deal with the particularities of his historic existence. One of those details that has generated the most discussion and concern is that of his gendered body, his maleness. In what ways can we view Jesus's particular humanity as having normative significance for *all* humans in light of his maleness? That is a challenging question that we could pursue in a variety of ways, only a few of which have we explored here. If we had more time, we could also investigate the implications of Christ's teachings, the oft-debated question of whether the eternal Son could have been incarnated as a woman, or the perennial debates regarding the significance of his maleness for understanding gender roles in the church. Each of these would potentially generate further insight into the anthropological significance of Christ's gendered body.

For our purposes, though, we focused on only three issues. In the first, we reflected on the relationship between Jesus's body

---

56. Johnson, "The Maleness of Christ," 110.

and the *imago Dei*, arguing that although Jesus's body is central to the image of God, it does not follow that all the particular details of his body are universally normative. We then considered the significance of the resurrection and the state of Jesus's humanity in the eschaton. The key issue here was the extent to which we should allow an apophatic understanding of eschatological humanity to shape anthropological claims today. Finally, we looked at several ways to engage the issue of gender essentialism from a christological perspective. The conclusions drawn here were less decisive since it would take a much broader range of dialogue partners to address the issue comprehensively. Nonetheless, we still saw how viewing human sexuality through the lens of Christology can challenge existing conceptions of masculinity and femininity and the extent to which men and women differ essentially from one another.

CHAPTER 7

The Jewish Jesus and the Racialized Self

———•———

W. E. B. Du Bois begins his classic *The Souls of Black Folk* by declaring that "the problem of the Twentieth Century is the problem of the color-line."[1] Though published in 1903, those words accurately reflect the continuing challenges of the twenty-first century as well. Indeed, although people have always found ways of differentiating themselves from the "other" (gender, class, language, religion, etc.), typically using those differences as occasions for suspicion and hostility, Kumar Rajagopalan rightly points out that in many ways race is "the defining divide."[2] Even more than other anthropological categories, race plays a central role in how we divide humanity into its various subgroups. Consequently, few would contest the fact that race is a vital topic for theology today. Brian Bantum goes so far as to state, "Our world is indelibly marked by race, by violent differentiations of ethnicity, culture, and gender. I have no use for a Christianity that does not account for the ways our bodies are named and shaped."[3] In our second study of the ways that people have used Christology as a source of insight into specific issues in theological anthropology, we will thus focus on theological accounts of race. A truly adequate discussion of race would also delve into the

---

1. W. E. B. Du Bois, *The Souls of Black Folk* (New York: Penguin, 1994), 1.

2. Kumar Rajagopalan, "What Is the Defining Divide? False Post-Racial Dogmas and the Biblical Affirmation of 'Race,'" *Black Theology* 13, no. 2 (2015): 166–88.

3. Brian Bantum, *The Death of Race: Building a New Christianity in a Racial World* (Minneapolis: Fortress, 2016), 8.

almost impossibly challenging question of racism and corresponding discussions surrounding racial reconciliation today. Given our limited space, though, we will have to reserve those for another time, focusing specifically here on ways that several key theologians have used Christology to understand the nature of race itself.

To do this, we first need to understand what terms like *race* and *ethnicity* mean in modern discourse. People commonly use those terms to capture aspects of human existence that are more biological (race) or cultural (ethnicity). As we will see, though, such distinctions are impossible to maintain once we begin to appreciate the complex history of racial discourse and the numerous ways in which embodied realities are always already shaped by cultural dynamics. Most importantly, in this section we will also see why several significant thinkers have argued that race is a fundamentally *theological* problem, one that is intrinsically linked to Christology. As we will see, these thinkers contend that the rejection of Jesus's *Jewish* identity was central to the rise of the modern view of race. With this background in hand, the second section will focus on the insight that might be generated by further emphasizing Jesus's Jewish identity. We will do this by looking specifically at the approaches taken by James Cone and Virgilio Elizondo. In the third and final section, we will consider some challenges raised by these two approaches and what adjustments might be necessary to think christologically about this important topic.

THE STORY OF RACE

When discussing biblical/theological perspectives on race, we need to be careful not to confuse our categories. People often point quickly to Old Testament texts on caring for the foreigners in our midst (e.g., Lev 19:34; Deut 10:19) or New Testament texts that focus on breaking down the divisions between Jew and Gentile (esp. Eph 2:11–22), concluding that such texts relate directly to modern discussions of race and racism. The difficulty with this move which often goes unnoticed is that such categories differ substantially from the modern idea of *race*.

Xenophobia is not a new phenomenon, and people in the ancient world had many ways of identifying differences between people groups and using those differences as the basis for hatred and exclusion. However, they generally did not develop prejudices based on skin color or the other phenotypical characteristics we traditionally associate with race today. "The classical period attaches no stigma to color and there is no evidence in antiquity of a well-developed theory of race. There may have been stereotypes employed about dark-skinned Africans, but the stereotypes were in no way *racial*. Ethiopians were another ethnic group, but were not fundamentally different from those with lighter skin, and whatever differences were recognized had nothing to do with skin color."[4] Instead, ancient people focused on characteristics like religion, kinship, geography, and language as the primary categories of differentiation. While such categories could still be the basis for considerable hostility and violence, they were relatively malleable.[5] Religious conversions were certainly less common in the ancient world, but they were not impossible: a "barbarian" could learn to speak Greek and be integrated into Greek society, and even kinship relationships could shift through intermarriage. While the ancient world had certain ways of clearly identifying difference, their categories were not based on permanent, biological/phenotypical characteristics like skin color and facial features.

Accounts differ on when the modern view of race began to develop.[6] Many have argued that it was a product of the Enlightenment,[7]

---

4. Shawn Kelley, *Racializing Jesus: Race, Ideology, and the Formation of Modern Biblical Scholarship* (New York: Routledge, 2002), 26, emphasis original. See also Frank M. Snowden, *Before Color Prejudice: The Ancient View of Blacks* (Cambridge, MA: Harvard University Press, 1983). This does not mean that ancient people ignored skin color entirely, only that they did not interpret skin color as an indicator of essential/biological differences.

5. For more on classical views of race, consult the various readings in Rebecca F. Kennedy, C. Sydnor Roy, and Max L. Goldman, eds., *Race and Ethnicity in the Classical World: An Anthology of Primary Sources in Translation* (Indianapolis: Hackett, 2013).

6. The first anthropological use of the word does not occur until the sixteenth century (Michael Banton, "The Idiom of Race: A Critique of Presentism," in *Theories of Race and Racism: A Reader*, ed. Les Back and John Solomos, 2nd ed. [London: Routledge, 2009], 53) and even then it did not convey the same ideas as our use of the term today (Ivan Hannaford, *Race: The History of an Idea in the West* [Washington, DC: Johns Hopkins University Press, 1996], 4–6).

7. See esp. Carol Chapnick Mukhopadhyay, Rosemary C. Henze, and Yolanda T. Moses,

while others begin the story in the Middle Ages,[8] and some find at least the seeds of race in the ancient world as well.[9] Yet most agree that the Enlightenment played a key role. During the Age of Exploration and the corresponding growth of the African slave trade, Europeans increasingly began to focus on skin color and other phenotypical characteristics as the fundamental way of differentiating *us* from *them*.[10] At the same time, the rise of nationalism in early modern Europe also contributed to modern racial theories as thinkers sought new ways of defining what constitutes a "people."[11] Throughout the period, then, we have a combination of economic, political, and social factors that together led European intellectuals to use skin color as a fundamental way of demarcating humanity into distinct groups.[12] Additionally, since humans have always struggled to notice differences without establishing qualitative hierarchies between those differences, these distinctions led to the development of racial hierarchies in which lighter skinned peoples were viewed as culturally, morally, religiously, and intellectually superior to darker skinned people.

At the same time, the rise of the modern sciences, especially biology, provided an apparently rational way of explaining these

---

How Real Is Race? A Sourcebook on Race, Culture, and Biology, 2nd ed. (Lanham, MD: AltaMira, 2014); Robert W. Sussman, *The Myth of Race: The Troubling Persistence of an Unscientific Idea* (Cambridge, MA: Harvard University Press, 2014); Tanya Maria Golash-Boza, *Race & Racisms: A Critical Approach* (New York: Oxford University Press, 2016).

8. See esp. the collection of essays in Miriam Eliav-Feldon, Benjamin Isaac, and Joseph Ziegler, eds., *The Origins of Racism in the West* (New York: Cambridge University Press, 2013).

9. E.g., Robert E. Hood, *Begrimed and Black: Christian Traditions on Blacks and Blackness* (Minneapolis: Fortress, 1994); Dwight N. Hopkins, *Being Human: Race, Culture, and Religion* (Minneapolis: Fortress, 2005); Denise Kimber Buell, *Why This New Race: Ethnic Reasoning in Early Christianity* (New York: Columbia University Press, 2008).

10. Hopkins, *Being Human: Race, Culture, and Religion*, 136–38.

11. Anthony Appiah, *In My Father's House: Africa in the Philosophy of Culture* (New York: Oxford University Press, 1992), 48. Justin Smith offers a nice overview of how various prominent philosophers contributed to the development of racial views in early modern Europe (*Nature, Human Nature, and Human Difference: Race in Early Modern Philosophy* [Princeton: Princeton University Press, 2015]).

12. Michael Omi and Howard Winant, *Racial Formation in the United States: From the 1960s to the 1990s*, 2nd ed. (New York: Routledge, 1994); Philip Yale Nicholson, *Who Do We Think We Are? Race and Nation in the Modern World* (Armonk, NY: M. E. Sharpe, 1999).

phenotypical and behavioral differences. Early biologists were already busily categorizing living things into their various species and subspecies, so it was relatively easy to use the same biological reasoning to categorize humanity as well, identifying anywhere from four to thirty different subspecies (races) of humanity.[13] Each race was understood to be biologically unique in such a way that their biological differences led directly to the corresponding phenotypical and behavioral differences. With the development of evolutionary views of the human person and the advent of modern genetics in the nineteenth century, we seemed to have even more certain biological mechanisms for developing and transmitting these racial differences.[14]

By the time we reach the modern period, then, race has surpassed and even replaced the more ancient categories of religion, geography, kinship, and language as the way of identifying what fundamentally divides people into distinct groups. Unlike those other categories, though, the biological account of race presents this fundamental distinction as something far less malleable, almost permanent. As a biological reality, one cannot simply shift from one race to another. Although the races themselves are not permanent since they can be altered over time through reproduction, explaining the racialized rhetoric against "interbreeding," racial identity is now viewed as a permanent, biological feature of a self-identity.[15] This means that the corresponding intellectual, moral, and behavioral qualities of each race are also relatively stable and permanent features of a person's identity. In many ways, the identity of the human person has been reduced almost entirely to the shape and color of his or her body. Jennings explains it this way: "Racial agency and especially whiteness rendered unintelligible and unpersuasive any narratives of the collective self that bound

---

13. Stephen Molnar, *Human Variation: Races, Types, and Ethnic Groups*, 6th ed. (Upper Saddle River, N.J: Pearson Prentice Hall, 2006).

14. See esp. Sussman, *The Myth of Race*.

15. Kelley, *Racializing Jesus*, 16–17.

identity to geography, to earth, to water, trees, and animals. People would henceforth (and forever) carry their identities on their bodies without remainder."[16]

In light of this history, then, race involves far more than perceived differences between various kinds of human bodies. Instead, it is the story of how one group comes to define its identity and personhood over against and at the expense of some other group. "Slowly, out of these actions, whiteness emerges, not simply as a marker of the European but as the rarely spoken but always understood organizing conceptual frame. And blackness appears as the fundamental tool of that organizing conceptuality. Black bodies are the ever-visible counterweight of a usually *invisible* white identity."[17] Consequently, although race is intrinsically linked to human bodies, it transcends these bodies as "a social system that establishes the personhood of one people through the dehumanization of others."[18]

By the mid-twentieth century, the biological aspects of the modern conception of race had been widely debunked with most scholars arguing that biological differences between the races are not substantial enough to justify differentiating humans into distinct subspecies.[19] Even if we could identify genotypical variations between distinct human subgroups,[20] we would not be able to ground the behavioral distinctions that typically accompany racialized ways of thinking given the widespread rejection of the kind of genetic determinism such a view requires.[21] At the same

---

16. Willie James Jennings, *The Christian Imagination: Theology and the Origins of Race* (New Haven, CT: Yale University Press, 2010), 59.

17. Ibid., 25.

18. Bantum, *The Death of Race*, 57.

19. The work of anthropologist Frank Boas was particularly important in this regard, but the key moment came with Ashley Montagu's book, *Man's Most Dangerous Myth: The Fallacy of Race* (New York: Columbia University Press, 1942).

20. While rejecting the hierarchical conclusions of earlier approaches, some have recently argued that we can still identify genotypical variations between people groups sufficient to continue talking about distinguishable races (see, for example, Nicholas Wade, *A Troublesome Inheritance: Genes, Race and Human History* [Penguin, 2014]). For a nice series of essays on the topic, see Sheldon Krimsky and Kathleen Sloan, eds., *Race and the Genetic Revolution: Science, Myth, and Culture* (New York: Columbia University Press, 2011).

21. Sussman, *The Myth of Race*, 3.

time, though, few think we can jettison the concept of race entirely and embrace the "color-blind" society. Instead, they point out that even if biological race is a myth, race continues to structure society and shape our views of ourselves and the world around us.[22] "We cannot be post-racial because race is not about the differences that we see. It is about how those differences have come to form who we think we can be for one another."[23]

Given criticisms of the biological basis of race, people often shift to an emphasis on *ethnicity* as a better category for understanding human persons. Rising to popularity in the middle of the twentieth century, this term seeks to emphasize a diverse range of factors that differentiate people groups (especially culture and language).[24] Although there is a sense in which this is a helpful move, affirming that human identity should not be reduced to biological realities alone, others have argued that the lines between these two categories are not as clear as they first appear. The cultural distinctiveness of each group is often presented as relatively stable, which is what allows it to serve as a marker of identity.[25] However, this means that ethnicity often has the same quasi-essentialist character as race, with "culture" simply serving as the essentializing feature rather than biology. Malcolm Chapman thus claims, "In many ways, 'ethnicity' is 'race' after an attempt to take the biology out."[26] Additionally, since we often reserve the language of ethnicity for minority or immigrant groups, this framework even retains the racial framework of categorizing people against the universal norm provided by the dominant cultural group.[27] Jennings thus contends

---

22. See esp. Eduardo Bonilla-Silva, *Racism without Racists: Color-Blind Racism and the Persistence of Racial Inequality in America*, 4th ed. (Lanham, MD: Rowman & Littlefield, 2014).

23. Bantum, *The Death of Race*, 17.

24. Kenan Malik, *The Meaning of Race: Race, History, and Culture in Western Society* (Washington Square, NY: New York University Press, 1996), 175. See also Stephen Steinberg, *The Ethnic Myth: Race, Ethnicity, and Class in America*, 3rd ed. (Boston: Beacon, 2001).

25. Malik, *The Meaning of Race*, 177.

26. Malcolm Chapman, ed., *Social and Biological Aspects of Ethnicity* (New York: Oxford University Press, 1993), 21.

27. Malik, *The Meaning of Race*, 177.

that ethnicity "takes its modern cues from the racial imagination."[28] Although the two forms of discourse are not identical, they overlap sufficiently that the rest of this chapter will not make a strong distinction between them.

Several scholars have recently argued that in addition to this largely sociopolitical narrative, we also need to understand the role of theology in the rise of the racialized self. According to Jennings, Christians operate today with a "diseased social imagination"[29] that stems largely from a failure in theology. Without dismissing the historical narrative above, Jennings roots modern racial thinking in theological moves that sought to "universalize" the gospel for new cultural contexts by stripping away its Jewish identity. In reality, though, this simply provided the occasion for Europeans to establish a new universal norm for humanity: whiteness. Thus, for Jennings, "supersessionist thinking is the womb in which whiteness will mature."[30] J. Kameron Carter agrees, contending that "modernity's racial imagination has its genesis in the theological problem of Christianity's quest to sever itself from its Jewish roots."[31] This unfolded in two steps. "First, Jews were cast as a race group in contrast to Western Christians, who . . . were also subtly and simultaneously cast as a race group. . . . Second, having racialized Jews as a people of the Orient and thus Judaism as a 'religion' of the East, Jews were then deemed inferior to Christians of the Occident or the West."[32] Importantly, both thinkers present Christology itself as fundamental to this process. To establish whiteness as the new universal, Christians needed to strip Jesus of his own Jewish identity, treating him instead as a symbol of white humanity.[33]

---

28. Jennings, *The Christian Imagination*, 343n18.

29. Ibid., 6.

30. Ibid., 36.

31. J. Kameron Carter, *Race: A Theological Account* (New York: Oxford University Press, 2008), 4.

32. Ibid.

33. Lest we think that this is only a problem for theologians, Shawn Kelly offers an excellent account of how racial thinking affected a broad range of key biblical scholars as well (Kelley, *Racializing Jesus*).

Jennings thus laments the "sad and grotesquely ironic reality that the supersessionist movement in Christian theology was enabled through Christian reflection on Jesus Christ."[34] Carter similarly critiques "the way in which Christology . . . was problematically deployed to found the modern racial imagination. For at the genealogical taproot of modern racial reasoning is the process by which Christ was abstracted from Jesus, and thus from his Jewish body."[35] According to these thinkers, then, Christology is both part of the problem of race and essential to its solution. We cannot understand ourselves rightly until we have come to grips with the reality of Jesus's Jewish identity.

JESUS'S JEWISH IDENTITY: TWO CASE STUDIES

We now turn our attention to two scholars who sought to address the problem of race by focusing specifically on Jesus's Jewishness, though from considerably different perspectives: James Cone and Virgilio Elizondo.

The Black Christ (James Cone)

According to James Cone, the only way we can understand Jesus and the implications he has for understanding humanity today is by focusing on the historical Jesus. This alone provides the "indispensable foundation of christology."[36] Without a proper historical ground, we have no protection against the unceasing temptation to wield Christology as an ideological sword. However, such a starting point requires us to affirm the fundamental significance of Jesus's social and ethnic identity: "The basic mistake of our white opponents is their failure to see that God did not become a universal human being but an oppressed Jew, thereby disclosing to us that both human nature and divine nature are inseparable from oppression

---

34. Jennings, *The Christian Imagination*, 259.

35. Carter, *Race*, 6.

36. James H. Cone, *A Black Theology of Liberation*, 40th anniv. ed. (Maryknoll, NY: Orbis, 2012), 126.

and liberation. To know who the human person *is* is to focus on the Oppressed One and what he does for an oppressed community as it liberates itself from slavery."[37] Consequently, "The particularity of Jesus's person as disclosed in his Jewishness is indispensable for christological analysis."[38]

Cone offers several reasons for emphasizing the centrality of Jesus's Jewishness. First, and most basically, his Jewishness is fundamental for understanding Jesus's concrete particularity. "He was not a 'universal' man but a particular Jew who came to fulfill God's will to liberate the oppressed. His Jewishness establishes the concreteness of his existence in history, without which Christology inevitably moves in the direction of docetism."[39] In his Jewishness, Jesus confronts us as a discrete individual who demands that we see the theological task as one that must engage real people.

In a related move, Cone also emphasizes that Jesus's Jewishness is central to seeing Jesus as one who engages us as a *Thou* and not an *It*.[40] According to Cone, one of the fundamental dynamics of modern racism is that they have been shaped by *I-It* relationships rather than *I-Thou*.[41] Forgetting that they are mere creatures, humans first usurp God's rightful place as the true *I* who establishes the identity of all beings. They then turn this stolen authority against other humans by treating them as mere objects rather than true persons. Yet they can only do so because they have failed to appreciate the significance of the fact that God chose to encounter them in the form of Jesus in all his concrete, and consequently Jewish, particularity.

Finally, Jesus's Jewishness is that which connects him to God's covenant relationship with Israel, which includes a hope for Gentiles

---

37. Ibid., 91.

38. James H. Cone, *God of the Oppressed* (Maryknoll, NY: Orbis, 2014), 109.

39. Ibid.

40. Here Cone manifests the early influence of Karl Barth's theology, which in turn mediates Martin Buber's personalist philosophy (see esp. *CD* III/2, 274–285).

41. Cone developed this most extensively in his first book *Black Theology and Black Power* (New York: Seabury, 1969). For a good summary of this point, see J. Kameron Carter, "Christology, or Redeeming Whiteness: A Response to James Perkinson's Appropriation of Black Theology," *Theology Today* 60, no. 4 (2004): 525–39.

as well. In other words, Jesus's Jewishness demonstrates that personal identity does not need to be oppositional, establishing his Jewishness over against the identity of the Gentiles. Instead, Cone's position involves the conviction that "covenantally understood, Jewish flesh is flesh that receives those by 'nature' not in its family to be in its family, to carry forward its bloodline. It is in this way that Israel is a nation and people unlike any other, a nation without analogy."[42] Cone also highlights the fact that Jesus's Jewishness means that he stands in direct relationship to the Exodus-Sinai event, which was the paradigmatic witness in the Old Testament of God's identity as one who aligns himself with the oppressed and against the oppressors. The incarnation of the Son in Jewish flesh thus stands as an enduring witness to the fact that God is the Great Liberator. Cone then traces the themes of oppression and liberation throughout Jesus's life.[43] He was born to a family with low social status, in a land oppressed by occupying forces, yet he consistently refused "to identify himself with any of the available modes of oppressive or self-glorifying power."[44] In his public ministry, he aligned himself with the physically and economically poor, the outcasts of society, demanding that those who follow him similarly dedicate themselves to the marginalized. Consequently, all of Jesus's actions, which culminate in his life-giving sacrifice on the cross, "represent God's will not to let his creation be destroyed by non-creative powers."[45] Throughout Jesus's life, then, we see the outworking of the truth etched in his Jewish flesh: "God in Christ becomes poor and weak in order that the oppressed might become liberated from poverty and powerlessness."[46]

This connection between Jesus's Jewishness and God's preference

---

42. Carter, *Race*, 170.

43. For a useful summary, see Michael Joseph Brown, "Black Theology and the Bible," in *The Cambridge Companion to Black Theology*, ed. Edward P. Antonio and Dwight N. Hopkins (New York: Cambridge University Press, 2012), 170–71.

44. Cone, *A Black Theology of Liberation*, 122.

45. Ibid., 74.

46. Ibid., 73.

for the powerless then becomes the link with Cone's argument that Jesus is *black*. "It is on the basis of the soteriological meaning of the particularity of his Jewishness that theology must affirm the christological significance of Jesus's present blackness. He *is* black because he *was* a Jew."[47] Who Jesus *was* becomes the best indicator of who he *is*. Consequently, we should expect to find Jesus identified today with those people who are similarly associated with poverty, powerlessness, and the cry for freedom. For Cone, that means seeing Jesus as essentially black. He is "the black Christ."[48] Cone does not go so far as to claim that Jesus himself was literally black,[49] yet he maintains "the *literal* color of Jesus is irrelevant, as are the different shades of blackness in America."[50] This is because Cone thinks Jesus reveals that human persons are defined not by some underlying, metaphysical *essence*, but by the concrete *history* of their actions in the world. The same holds true for the idea of racial identity. According to Cone, terms like "blackness" and "whiteness" denote *modes* of human living, ways of orienting ourselves for or against the oppressive realities of the world.[51] True human *being* arises from right human *living*.

The *Mestizo* Christ (Virgilio Elizondo)

Virgilio Elizondo also argues that theology today must take more seriously the fact of Jesus's Jewishness. "The overwhelming originality of Christianity is the basic belief of our faith that not only did the Son of God become a human being, but he became *Jesus of Nazareth*. Like every other man and woman, he was culturally situated and conditioned by the time and space in which he lived."[52]

---

47. Cone, *God of the Oppressed*, 123.

48. Cone, *A Black Theology of Liberation*, 127.

49. Cone thus differs from Albert Cleage who called for a literally black Messiah (Albert B. Cleage, *The Black Messiah* [New York: Sheed and Ward, 1968]).

50. Cone, *A Black Theology of Liberation*, 130.

51. See ibid., 125–36; Cone, *God of the Oppressed*, 127–49.

52. Virgilio P. Elizondo, *Galilean Journey: The Mexican-American Promise* (Maryknoll, NY: Orbis, 2000), 49.

Unlike Cone, though, Elizondo contends that this means we need to understand Jesus not simply as a *Jew* but specifically as a *Galilean* Jew. "We cannot really know Jesus of Nazareth unless we know him in the context of the historical and cultural situation of his people. Jesus was not simply a Jew, he was a Galilean Jew; throughout his life he and his disciples were identified as Galileans."[53]

Elizondo thus focuses on the importance of Galilee for establishing the nature of Jesus's sociocultural identity.[54] Indeed, one question has shaped much of Elizondo's work: "Why does the New Testament put such great emphasis on Galilee when Galilee played no important role in the Old Testament?"[55] Despite the relative unimportance of Galilee both regionally and biblically, Elizondo notes that it "must have been of special salvific signification to the first Christians, since it plays an important role in the post-Easter memory of the followers of Jesus and becomes part of the earliest kerygma (Acts 10:37–41)."[56] Consequently, he wonders, "Why is Jesus's ethnic identity as a Jewish Galilean from Nazareth an important dimension of the incarnation, and what does it disclose about the beauty and originality of Jesus's liberating life and message?"[57] For Elizondo, the answer lies in the idea of *mestizaje*. Elizondo describes Galilee as a border territory, on the periphery of Israel, between the more traditionally Jewish territory that surrounded Jerusalem and the Greco-Roman culture of the broader society. A crossroads of sorts, it was constantly invaded by neighboring rulers and frequently visited by caravans traveling the trade routes that passed through its territory. Consequently, it was culturally and ethnically diverse, a people constantly having to negotiate their identity in the tension between

53. Ibid.

54. See esp. Elizondo, *Galilean Journey* and Virgilio P. Elizondo, *The Future Is Mestizo: Life Where Cultures Meet* (Boulder: University Press of Colorado, 2000).

55. Virgilio P. Elizondo, "What Good Can Come out of Galilee?," *Church & Society* 93, no. 4 (2003): 58–59.

56. Virgilio P. Elizondo, "Jesus the Galilean Jew in Mestizo Theology," *Theological Studies* 70, no. 2 (2009): 270.

57. Ibid.

the dominant Greco-Roman and Jerusalem-Jewish cultures. Yet this is precisely the context in which new possibilities emerge. This is what Elizondo refers to as *mestizaje*, "the origination of a new people from two ethnically disparate parent peoples (from *mestizo*, 'mixed', 'hybrid')."[58] In Galilee, a "natural, ongoing biological and cultural *mestizaje* was taking place."[59]

Reflecting on the sociological realities of *mestizaje*, however, Elizondo emphasizes how difficult this process can be for everyone involved. From the perspective of the dominant culture, *mestizaje* comes across as "a threat to the barriers of separation that consolidate self-identity and security."[60] Rather than producing new ethnic and cultural realities, the dominant culture would prefer "acculturation" or "accommodation" to existing ways of being human.[61] They thus oppress and marginalize *mestizos*, rejecting them because of the impurity that results from mixing with another people group. "The tendency of *group inclusion/exclusion* seems to be a fundamental law of human nature."[62] Consequently, the *mestizo* experiences the pain of being "doubly marginated and rejected," despised by *both* parent cultures.[63]

Elizondo could have stopped here, merely arguing for the historical picture of Galilee as a diverse land that produced new cultural possibilities through the often-painful reality of *mestizaje*. But he contends further that this has theological significance given that *this* is the place the Son became incarnate. Born into this land, Jesus's self-identity would have been that of the *mestizo*. In addition to the broad cultural realities of Galilee, Elizondo suggests that Jesus would also have faced the same challenges as anyone perceived as having mixed parentage. Without rejecting the Virgin Birth,

---

58. Elizondo, *Galilean Journey*, 5.

59. Ibid., 51. For a more recent articulation of this point, see Virgilio P. Elizondo, *A God of Incredible Surprises: Jesus of Galilee*, Celebrating Faith (Lanham, MD: Rowman & Littlefield, 2003).

60. Elizondo, *Galilean Journey*, 18.

61. Ibid., 17.

62. Ibid.

63. Elizondo, "Jesus the Galilean Jew in Mestizo Theology," 20.

Elizondo nonetheless concludes that many would have suspected him in that cultural context of being the illegitimate child of a Roman soldier. Consequently, his self-identity would still have been shaped by the perceptions of those around him as someone who had a mixed background.[64] If the Son was incarnated as a *mestizo*, though, Elizondo suggests that this should have some theological significance: "Since grace builds upon nature, I wondered if Jesus's Galilean experience could have been a cultural preparation for the new humanity inaugurated by him and promoted by the New Testament, one that would not be limited by blood or ethnicity."[65] He draws support for this from Matthew's reference to the land as "Galilee of the Gentiles" (Matt 4:15), quoting the prophecy in Isaiah 9:1. Elizondo concludes, "The influence of Isaiah's perspective in the New Testament seemed to suggest a unique and unsuspected role for Galilee in God's salvific plan for the restoration of unity among the human family."[66]

He derives from all of this "the theological meaning of Galilee."[67] First, Galilee is the "Symbol of Multiple Rejection."[68] As a *mestizaje* reality, Galilee was a land rejected by both dominant cultures. Nonetheless, this is the land God chose for his redemptive purposes. "That God had chosen to become a Galilean underscores the great paradox of the incarnation, in which God becomes the despised and lowly of the world."[69] Galilee thus serves as a symbol of both rejection and election at the same time: "What the world rejects, God chooses as his very own."[70] That leads directly to the second theological meaning of Galilee: it is the "Symbol of Universal Acceptance, Welcome, and Love."[71] By choosing Galilee to be the land of the

---

64. Elizondo, *The Future Is Mestizo*, 79.

65. Elizondo, "Jesus the Galilean Jew in Mestizo Theology," 274.

66. Ibid., 271.

67. Elizondo, *Galilean Journey*, 50.

68. Ibid.

69. Ibid., 53.

70. Ibid.

71. Ibid.

Messiah, God declares that everyone is welcome in the kingdom, regardless of social status or ethnic identity. The kingdom itself has a *mestizaje* identity, which means that the kingdom transcends existing expectations and presses toward new realities. Thirdly, then, Galilee is a "Symbol of the Rupture that Inaugurates Liberation."[72] By choosing this land with its *mestizo* people, God initiates a break with existing structures, initiating the birth of a new people in whom God will bring about liberation.

The contemporary significance of this interpretation of Jesus's identity is that it offers a way of finding theological significance in the *mestizaje* experience of others. Elizondo thus uses this as a framework for interpreting his own identity as a Mexican American who grew up in South Texas. "These insights into the life of Jesus in Galilee enabled me to see our situation of border-crossings and *mestizaje* in South Texas not as deficient but as pregnant with multiple possibilities for a broader, more generous future for humanity."[73] Viewed through the theological meaning of Galilee, "We started to see our rejection and marginalization as an element of our election by God to start something new."[74] Like Cone, then, Elizondo uses his analysis of Jesus's identity as a way of interpreting race and ethnicity today. Although he similarly devotes considerable time to understanding the dynamics of poverty and oppression, which often accompany *mestizaje* given the reality of double rejection, Elizondo focuses more of his attention on the redemptive possibilities generated by *mestizaje* itself, redemptive possibilities that are themselves grounded in the fact that the eternal Son chose to identify himself with God's people as a *mestizo*.

HISTORICIZING JESUS WITHOUT ONTOLOGIZING RACE

Cone and Elizondo both offer excellent examples of thinking christologically about race by focusing specifically on Jesus's Jewishness.

72. Ibid., 65.

73. Elizondo, "Jesus the Galilean Jew in Mestizo Theology," 278.

74. Ibid.

We can and should appreciate their emphasis on Jesus's historical particularity (thesis 7) and the importance of both his Jewishness and his sociocultural context for shaping his self-identity. In some theological circles, a strong emphasis on the Son's eternal identity prevents robust reflection on what it would have meant for him to have also been a specific human person living in and being shaped by a concrete social context. Cone and Elizondo provide resources for reflecting on these dynamics and the ways in which they are similar to cultural processes at work in the world today.

However, we need to be mindful of at least two important concerns that arise in these approaches as well. The first has to do with what it means to focus on the *historic* Jesus. Each of these thinkers argues that we need to focus on the concrete particularity of Jesus's Jewishness. Indeed, they both offer interesting ways of responding to the obfuscation of Jesus's Jewishness that, as we discussed earlier, some think led directly to the rise of modern racism. They avoid this specifically by *not* viewing Jesus's Jewishness as a problem to be solved. Instead, they contend that it is only by focusing on the particularity of Jesus's Jewishness that we see the truth of who God is and what it means for us to live humanly in this broken world. Thus, as we have seen, they both emphasize the importance of focusing on the *historical* Jesus, which includes his Jewish identity.

Nonetheless, some problems arise here. As Siker points out, Cone's approach can be critiqued for what he calls its "minimalist approach to the historical Jesus."[75] In other words, although Cone argues that our view of Jesus must be based on the particular details of his historic existence, he spends relatively little time exploring those details. Instead, Cone seems satisfied with just those details that are necessary to establish the conditions of oppression in Jesus's life. Yet why focus on only those details? Surely Jesus's Jewish identity involved more than the mere fact that he was a member of an oppressed group. If Jesus's Jewishness is really as important

---

75. Jeffrey S. Siker, "Historicizing a Racialized Jesus: Case Studies in the 'Black Christ,' the 'Mestizo Christ,' and White Critique," *Biblical Interpretation* 15, no. 1 (2007): 33.

as Cone claims, should we not expect a more robust analysis of the broad range of features that characterize that identity? Cone does spend some time on the history of Israel as the necessary background for understanding Jewishness, but most of that focuses on the Exodus as the definitive expression of God's identity as the Liberator. Throughout, Cone's analysis gives the appearance of only engaging the details of Jesus's historic existence selectively, which leads to corresponding questions about what presuppositions are guiding the selection process and what aspects of Christ's human experience are being neglected along the way.

Elizondo, on the other hand, offers much more extensive reflections on particular details of Jesus's historical context in Galilee, making detailed claims about the social context and how it would have informed Jesus's identity. Unlike Cone, then, Elizondo escapes the concern about a "minimalist" approach to history. Yet Elizondo illustrates a different challenge that can arise here. By making specific, historical claims about Jesus's life, Elizondo opens himself up to questions about the accuracy of those claims. Siker thus rejects Elizondo's portrayal of the region as predominantly Gentile, contending that Elizondo has anachronistically applied his own *mestizo* culture to the biblical material.[76] "Such a reading of Galilee is highly problematic given Elizondo's own strong emphasis on the importance of the historical particularity of Jesus, and presumably the most probable and reliable historical portrait of Jesus that scholars can re-construct."[77] To such worries, Elizondo points out that Matthew is the one who refers to the region as "Galilee of the Gentiles,"[78] suggesting that the way Galilee is portrayed theologically in the gospels is more significant for his purposes than extrabiblical material about Galilee's cultural composition.

---

76. Ibid., 40. For good discussions of the historical material, see Seán Freyne, *Galilee and Gospel: Collected Essays* (Boston: Brill Academic, 2002); Mark A. Chancey, *The Myth of a Gentile Galilee* (New York: Cambridge University Press, 2002); Chancey, *Greco-Roman Culture and the Galilee of Jesus* (New York: Cambridge University Press, 2005).

77. Siker, "Historicizing a Racialized Jesus," 42.

78. Elizondo, "Jesus the Galilean Jew in Mestizo Theology," 271.

Although I sympathize with that argument, it runs into the difficulty that Elizondo regularly appeals to background information
when it suits his argument. If a christological anthropology com-
mits itself to reconstructing the life of Jesus from extrabiblical
material, it must be willing to follow that material wherever it
leads. If, on the other hand, Elizondo chooses to focus exclusively
on the gospels to determine the theological significance of Galilee,
it is no longer clear that he has sufficient grounds for establishing
Galilee's *mestizo* identity.

Additionally, Elizondo also displays the same lack of attention
to the Old Testament as a necessary background for understanding
Jesus's Jewish identity. Indeed, there seems to be a missed opportunity in both studies. As we noted earlier, it is entirely possible
to appreciate the robust anthropology of the Old Testament and
still have a thoroughly christological understanding of the human
person. Focusing on Jesus's Jewishness may provide an avenue
for making the stronger claim that a christological anthropology
must take Old Testament anthropology seriously because that is a
necessary aspect of understanding Jesus's own self-identity.

As we noted above, these thinkers understand the importance
of addressing who Jesus actually was as a defense against ideological and self-serving reconstructions. As Jennings rightly warns,
"Ideological uses of Jesus begin with the fundamental decoupling of
Jesus from Israel's life. The story of Jesus becomes, through ideological deployment, a social cipher for any and every redemptive vision
of a people."[79] Despite their awareness of the problem, however,
we can raise at least some questions about whether their approach
has adequately addressed all of the concerns. Apart from close and
careful reflection on the details of Christ's historic existence, we
will be tempted to use Christology as a tool for implementing our
own vision of what it means to be human, often unintentionally.

A second concern stems from the way that both of these figures
conceptualize Israel as a distinct racial or ethnic group, with the

---

79. Jennings, *The Christian Imagination*, 259.

consequence that they run the risk of exclusivism (thesis 4). Cone and Elizondo both offer christological analyses of race that affirm the particularity of Jesus's Jewish identity while also maintaining that the incarnation provides reasons for privileging that identity in some way. The fact that the eternal Son chose to become "the black Christ" or "the *mestizo* Christ" means that blackness and *mestizaje* uniquely reveal who God is and what it means to be human in relation to him. While this does not necessarily lead to the conclusion that other identities are subhuman, it does seem to suggest that they are less apt ways of being human. Cone makes this explicit by rejecting "whiteness" as in any way adequate to understand the Jesus we see in the gospels. If the incarnation involves the Son electing a particular racial group such that certain aspects of that racial identity should be viewed as normative for all humans (e.g., liberation and marginality), and if only some racial identities correspond adequately to that christological norm (e.g., blackness and *mestizaje*), it seems to follow necessarily that other racial identities are either excluded entirely or are at least placed lower on a new anthropological hierarchy.

Cone and Elizondo could respond to this by appealing to the idea that race is an existential category, a mode of living in the world. Consequently, while certain modes of living would be deemed christologically inadequate (whiteness), it would not follow that the *people* in that category are similarly excluded since there remains the possibility that they could "convert" to a new racial identity by adopting a new way of living. This is what Cone has in mind when he calls on white people to "become black."[80] However, both Cone and Elizondo describe the experience of having a racial identity in ways that seem almost ontological. Describing "black experience," Cone contends, "Whites do not understand it; they can only catch glimpses of it in sociological reports and historical studies. The black experience is possible only for black persons. . . . Black soul is not learned; it comes from the totality of black experience, the

---

80. Cone, *A Black Theology of Liberation*, 130.

experience of carving out an existence in a society that says you do not belong."[81] This account of race sounds far more exclusivist than Cone's conversion rhetoric might suggest. Similarly, although Elizondo does not deal with this question as directly, the fact that *mestizaje* involves the production of a new racial identity through both biological and cultural mixing would strongly suggest that one cannot become a *mestizo* simply by adopting a new way of living. Consequently, it is not clear to me that this way of responding to the exclusion problem will work as it stands.

The alternative is to reconsider how these thinkers understand the nature of Jewishness itself. Cone and Elizondo both respond to the modern problem of race by arguing that the incarnation identifies Israel as the optimal race and then aligning their understanding of humanity with what they see revealed in that racial identity. But Jennings rightly questions what he calls "a novel reading of Israel," namely the attempt to view Israel "not as God's people but as an ethnic group."[82] According to Jennings, this fails to appreciate that Israel's identity derives not primarily from cultural, biological, spatial, or familial relations, but fundamentally through God electing them as his covenant people. Referring specifically to the importance of land in Israel's story and in the construction of identity for most people in the ancient world, Jennings writes, "This God enfolds the holy people in the truth that YHWH, not the land, is the giver of life; YHWH, not the land, defines their identity; YHWH imparts into their collective life the divine *dabarim*, the divine word and demands they live by that word."[83] Jennings thus portrays the story of Israel as a story that disrupts and destabilizes human identity so it can be reestablished in and through the covenant. This is what allows Israel to have a discernible identity that freely accommodates those not included in Israel. God's election of Israel constitutes "an irrepressible distinction between the elect and those outside Israel," yet it is "not

---

81. Ibid., 26.
82. Jennings, *The Christian Imagination*, 254.
83. Ibid., 256.

first a boundary of difference but a marking of entrance."[84] Rather than being defined as a people in opposition to some racial other, Israel's identity is established by being the people into whose story God invites the other to participate.

Israel itself failed to appreciate this theological truth, often viewing itself in primarily ethnic/tribal ways. Yet Jennings contends that what we see in Jesus is the reaffirmation of the fundamental truth of Israel's identity. "Jesus will challenge the very foundations of social life by challenging the power of the kinship network, which organized the central social, economic, and geographic realities of life in Israel. Jesus entered fully into the kinship structure not to destroy it but to reorder it—around himself."[85] If this is the case, then it would be a mistake to understand Jesus's Jewish identity as an ethnic identity, along with the dynamics of exclusion and opposition that typically inform such identities. He does not come to destroy Israel's identity but to reestablish it as an identity firmly grounded in God's covenant with them, and through them with the other peoples of the world.

Cone and Elizondo, on the other hand, seem to reify the very racial realities they seek to critique by presenting Israel as a racial/ethnic group. If Israel is primarily a racial entity, then God's election of Israel would be a direct declaration that God affirms racialized ways of thinking about humanity. However, if Jennings is correct and Israel's identity is fundamentally covenantal and inclusive, then we can see the story of Israel, as well as the story of Jesus's own Jewishness, as disrupting *any* racialized understanding of humanity.

Although approaching the discussion from a slightly different perspective, Bryan Bantum agrees that a properly christological approach to this discussion ultimately subverts the very category of race.[86] Instead, he draws on Christology to emphasize the

---

84. Ibid., 257.

85. Ibid., 263.

86. See esp. Brian Bantum, *Redeeming Mulatto: A Theology of Race and Christian Hybridity* (Waco, TX: Baylor University Press, 2010).

fundamental importance of *embodied difference* for being human. The story of race is about how we present the differences in other people's bodies as a problem to be solved through power. "Race is a way of resisting difference by violently determining which differences matter. Race is about power, sovereignty, and how words can become enfleshed, part of our daily, bodily lives, shaping who we are."[87] Reductionistic and destructive, "The story of race reduces me to my body and to a narrow, shallow story of what my body means."[88] The solution is to tell an alternative story, one that celebrates the centrality of embodied difference. For Bantum, that story is thoroughly christological.

By uniting the divine and the human in a single person, the incarnation presents a different interpretation of the body, celebrating embodied difference as essential to human flourishing. Jesus thus offers "a new logic of difference" in which we view our embodied differences as a gift.[89] "The power of our bodies lies in their limitations. Our senses help us to know and understand so much. But our bodies can only see and hold and know so much. Because of this, difference is always an opportunity to understand God, the world, others, and ourselves more deeply. Our bodies and their differences are not impediments to loving God. They are what make love, faith, and hope possible."[90] Although starting from the incarnation more than Jesus's Jewish identity, Bantum thus arrives at a similar conclusion: *a christological perspective on the human person subverts the logic of the racialized self.*

CONCLUSION

As we have seen throughout this chapter, a number of key thinkers have argued that the problem of race in the world today is at least partly a theological problem. More specifically, it is a *christological*

---

87. Bantum, *The Death of Race*, 14.

88. Ibid., 35.

89. Ibid., 108.

90. Ibid., 40.

problem. While Christology was not the only factor contributing to modern conceptions of race and racism, Jennings, Carter, and others have offered compelling arguments that Christology was an important part of the process as theologians sought to "universalize" the gospel by whitewashing Jesus and erasing his Jewish identity. If that is the case, then an important part of any properly theological response to race will be a renewed appreciation for Jesus's Jewish identity and what it reveals about humanity today.

However, we have also seen that there are different ways of reappropriating Jesus's Jewishness. While Cone and Elizondo offer powerful examples of examining race from a christological perspective, their approaches raise challenging questions about what it means to focus on the concrete (historical) humanity of Christ and how we should understand the nature of his Jewishness. This should not be taken as a critique of their contributions as a whole. Many of their reflections on power, oppression, liberation, and marginality remain salient and worth consideration. Nonetheless, Jennings rightly challenges what looks like a subtle reification of race in these ways of understanding Israel's identity, contending instead that a properly christological view of race will understand Jesus's Jewishness as locating him within a story that is about a people whose identity is established in and through the covenant, making it both particular and inclusive at the same time. Bantum adds to this by emphasizing the ways in which Christology requires us to resist the logic of the racial story in which embodied differences are used to fragment humanity into distinguishable "others" who can then be categorized and controlled. Instead, Christology leads to a new story of humanity, one in which the human body in all its quirky and often confusing diversity is received as a gift and the source of new life.

CHAPTER 8

Even Jesus Died

Christology and the Normativity of Death

———◆———

With a loud cry, Jesus breathed his last.

MARK 15:37

FEW TRUTHS HAVE AS MUCH SIGNIFICANCE for Christianity as the death of Christ. All four gospel writers devote considerable space to the events surrounding his death, and each pays particular attention to Jesus's final moments (cf. Matt 27:45–56; Luke 23:44–49; John 19:28–37). We have also seen that the author of Hebrews considers Jesus's death as one of the primary truths for establishing that he became one of us by entering our fallen condition and suffering as we do (Heb 2:5–18).

Yet we may not notice that a fundamental ambiguity arises when we consider that even Jesus experienced the reality of death. On the one hand, we clearly need to affirm that Jesus's death was thoroughly shaped by the reality of sin. He was "delivered over to the hands of sinners" (Luke 24:7) and crushed by the violence of a broken world, yet he did this so he could redeem God's people from their own sins (1 Cor 15:3; 1 Pet 3:18). When Paul reflects on the relationship between Christ and Adam, he affirms this same connection between sin and death: "Just as sin entered the world through one man, and death through sin, and in this way death came to all people, because all sinned" (Rom 5:12). Rather than presenting death as a creational reality, Paul declares that "death came through a man [Adam]" so that "in Adam all die" (1 Cor 15:21–22). The entire New Testament seems to validate this approach by presenting death as a part of the punishment for sin that Jesus assumed on the cross. Indeed, the very reason that he needed to die was to redeem us from the "enemy" to which we had been enslaved as a consequence of sin (1 Cor 15:26; Heb 2:14–15).

On the other hand, though, a number of modern theologians have argued that death is somehow intrinsic to the creaturely condition of humanity.[1] Although they recognize that all of these biblical passages emphasize that humans universally *experience* death in ways shaped by sin, which is the focus of the biblical passages above, they deny that this entails that *death itself* is a consequence of sin. Instead, they suggest that we view death as a creational reality that, like everything else in creation, has become twisted by the corrupting influence of sin.

Thus, our final case study will wrestle with the reality of death by addressing the question of whether death is intrinsic to human persons as created beings or whether it is a consequence of the fall, a fundamental aspect of God's judgment on sin. Fortunately, though, we do not have to imagine what it might look like to approach this issue from a christological perspective since we have an excellent example in the theology of Karl Barth. As we will see, Barth begins with the fact that even Jesus died. This fact serves as his basis for maintaining that death is intrinsic to human nature and, consequently, part of God's creational design for humans. Although we could engage the issue by diving directly into Barth's christological argument, we will first consider some of the biblical material, particularly in the Old Testament, that drives the conviction that we

---

1. For other modern theologians who affirm a similar position, see Karl Rahner, *On the Theology of Death*, trans. Charles H. Henkey (New York: Herder and Herder, 1961); Eberhard Jüngel, *Death, the Riddle and the Mystery* (Philadelphia: Westminster, 1975); Ray S. Anderson, *Theology, Death and Dying* (Oxford: Basil Blackwell, 1986); Wolfhart Pannenberg, *Systematic Theology*, trans. Geoffrey W. Bromiley (Grand Rapids: Eerdmans, 1991); Henry Novello, *Death as Transformation* (Burlington, VT: Ashgate, 2011).

should view death as the "enemy" of humanity. This biblical material provides an important anthropological perspective that needs to be accounted for in a christological anthropology (thesis 6). The second section will take us into Barth's christological argument, offering an opportunity to reflect on how an important theologian uses Christology to engage a difficult issue in theological anthropology. In the final section, however, I will argue that Barth's approach runs into problems with respect to several of our christological theses. Consequently, we will need to revise his conclusions before developing a christological view of human death.[2]

FRIEND OR ENEMY: BIBLICAL PERSPECTIVES ON DEATH

We do not have to look far to find biblical perspectives on death as the enemy. Although we will soon engage with those who argue that the Old Testament views death as a natural aspect of human existence, we need to acknowledge that many of the Old Testament authors talk about death in distinctly negative ways. Death is the realm where people are cut off from God and unable to praise his name or perform any meaningful actions (Num 16:33; Ps 6:5; Isa 38:18). Consequently, death is something to be approached with fear and trembling (Pss 55:4; 116:3). Even Job, who often longs for death as an escape from his painful existence (Job 3:11; 6:8–9; 7:8–10; 10:1; 14:13; 17:13–16), laments the fact that his life is fleeting and will terminate only in the forgetfulness of death (7:6–10). Similarly, although Ecclesiastes views death as an escape from the futility of life in this world (4:2–3), he also maintains that "a live dog is better off than a dead lion!" (Eccl 9:4). Throughout the Old Testament, then, the biblical authors routinely portray death as an enemy, something that tragically cuts us off from the only things that provide meaning, purpose, and hope. They even go so far as to personify death as a power that has invaded the realm of the living (Ps 116:3; Hos 13:4). God himself declares his judgment on death:

---

2. Throughout this chapter, I will use "death" to refer to the cessation of biological life unless I indicate otherwise.

"For I take no pleasure in the death of anyone. . . . Repent and live!" (Ezek 18:32). He promises that someday "he will swallow up death forever" (Isa 25:8).

Moving into the New Testament, of course, those statements become even clearer. Along with sin and the demonic powers, death is one of the three great enemies Jesus came to defeat. Rather than portraying death as simply part of the natural order, Paul routinely associates death with sin and Adam's disobedience (Rom 5:12–21; 6:15–23; 7:13; 8:2; 1 Cor 15:54–56). Consequently, the New Testament authors portray death as an enemy that needs to be destroyed (1 Cor 15:26) through the death of Jesus (Heb 2:14–15), which is finally realized when death itself is thrown into the lake of fire (Rev 20:14).

Throughout the bible, then, we seem to have a consistent picture of death as the enemy. Death is not something God established as part of the created order. Death is an intruder, something to be feared and resisted despite its inevitability. God declares his opposition to death and eventually delivers on his promise to defeat death by sending his own Son to suffer it on our behalf.

However, an ambiguity lurks beneath the apparently clear surface of this account. All this material pertains to the nature of death *after the fall*. But sin shapes every aspect of postlapsarian existence, including those things that we generally consider to be part of God's design plan for humanity. We eat, often enjoying the food God gives us as a creational blessing, yet we also wrestle with eating disorders, alcoholism, and other food-related manifestations of sin. Our rest shifts to restlessness, dreams turn to nightmares, and marriages become stifling and oppressive. The gifts remain, preventing existence from becoming a true hell, but sin distorts each so that they become in many ways a parody of their creational goodness. Might we say the same about death? Could it be that death itself is part of God's creational design, something so twisted and tainted by sin that we can only view it now as the "enemy"?

Indeed, many have argued that the Old Testament itself contains at least some hints of a more positive view of death, albeit one that is still affected by the reality of sin. In the Old Testament, the human person is often portrayed as a finite being who lives for a startlingly brief period of time before returning to the dust from which he came (Job 10:9; 34:15; Ps 103:15; Eccl 3:20; 12:7; Isa 40:7). Since these passages do not associate the finite and fleeting nature of the human person with the consequences of sin, some conclude that this suggests a view in which the human person is inherently mortal.[3] Consequently, "death is the destiny of everyone" (Eccl 7:2). In his classic study, Lloyd Bailey argued that despite the material discussed above, many Old Testament texts portray death in far more positive terms.[4] Some focus on the idea of a "good death," one that comes at the end of a life well-lived, surrounded by family and friends (Gen 25:7–11; Job 42:16–17; Jer 34:4–5),[5] while others view death as an escape from suffering (e.g., Job 3:11, 21–22; 7:15), a state of relative peace in comparison to the painful chaos of this world (Job 14:13; Eccl 4:1–2). Such texts suggest to many that "death as the enemy" is not the only interpretive framework necessary for understanding the reality of death in the Old Testament.

Some might be inclined to argue from a scientific perspective that death *must* be a part of the created order. Everything we know about the created universe, from evolution to entropy, requires at least some form of death. Theologians have often argued that all of this death is a consequence of sin, yet it is increasingly difficult to conceive of how this universe could have any continuity with a universe in which there was no death or decay of any kind. Instead of a mere "fall," we would need to talk about "the transformation

---

3. For example, Routledge contends that "death in the Old Testament is viewed as inevitable and natural" (Robin L. Routledge, "Death and Afterlife in the Old Testament," *Journal of European Baptist Studies* 9, no. 1 [2008]: 22).

4. Lloyd R. Bailey, *Biblical Perspectives on Death* (Philadelphia: Fortress, 1979).

5. Ibid., 48–52. Frerichs similarly concludes, "What attitudes did Old Testament people have toward death? For the most part, they seemed to be resigned to it as inevitable and normal, provided the person facing it was old, with family grown and an inheritance to pass on to heirs, was held in honor by the community, and had a grave at hand for burial" (Wendell W. Frerichs, "Death and Resurrection in the Old Testament," *Word & World* 11, no. 1 [1991]: 18).

of all of nature in what amounted to a hostile second creation."[6] Fortunately, though, such a move should not be necessary. When the biblical authors reflect on the theological significance of death, they do so exclusively from the perspective of the human person. If we maintain the traditional view that death entered the world as a consequence of sin, this need only have ramifications for how we understand the death of human persons rather than the broader category of death and decay in the universe at large. Understanding the origin and theological significance of the latter form of death would be an interesting study in its own right, but it lies beyond the scope of this chapter.

From the biblical material, then, although we have a fairly consistent picture in which death is presented as a fundamental problem, one that is closely associated with sin, we still have to account for two things: (1) the possibility that this results from the fact that all of this material deals with death after the fall and (2) the Old Testament texts that offer a more positive account of death and may at least hint at a lingering view in which death is intrinsic to the human person as a finite creature.

"YOU WILL CERTAINLY DIE"

Some will likely view this as an unnecessarily complex way of articulating a problem that has a fairly simple solution. After all, Genesis 2–3 clearly presents death as a consequence of sin. God himself warned Adam before the fall that death would be the result of disobedience: "You are free to eat from any tree in the garden; but you must not eat from the tree of the knowledge of good and evil, for when you eat from it you will certainly die" (Gen 2:16–17). After the fall, God reaffirmed the consequential nature of death, declaring, "By the sweat of your brow you will eat your food until you return to the ground, since from it you were taken; for dust you are and to dust you will return" (Gen 3:19). With such clear texts at

---

6. Ronald E. Osborn, *Death Before the Fall: Biblical Literalism and the Problem of Animal Suffering* (Downers Grove, IL: IVP Academic, 2014), 16.

our disposal, we can easily conclude that death is not a creational reality but that it only intrudes after the fall. This explains the consistency with which other biblical texts view sin as an enemy that needs to be defeated by the Messiah. We can even interpret the more positive portrayals of death as an attempt to make the best out of an unavoidable reality.

However, we run into a problem here as well. When God states that Adam would surely "die" on the day that he eats from the tree, he seems to be saying that biological death would be the inevitable and immediate result of disobedience. Yet Adam and Eve do *not* "die" when they eat from the tree. Indeed, Adam does not die until a few chapters later at the age of 930! Could it be that God was wrong and only the serpent truly understood the situation? Surely not. So we seem to have three options: (1) conclude that "death" refers to the cessation of biological life and find some way of understanding what it means to say that Adam and Eve died that day; (2) conclude that "death" refers to the cessation of biological life and find some way of explaining why Adam and Eve did *not* die that day; or (3) conclude that "death" must refer to something other than the cessation of biological life.[7]

For the first option, we could focus on the fact that Adam dies eventually, thus interpreting "on the day when you eat" as referring to the *certainty* of God's judgment rather than its *timing*.[8] Yet it is counterintuitive to think that God's dire warning to Adam referred to an event that would not occur for almost a millennium.[9] Alternatively, we could claim instead that Adam "dies" immediately in the sense of becoming subject to death. Some suggest that this is the moment when Adam loses his immortality and becomes mortal,

7. For a nice summary of proposals, see Umberto Cassuto, *A Commentary on the Book of Genesis*, trans. Israel Abrahams (Jerusalem: Magnes, 1961), 124–26.

8. Victor P. Hamilton, *The Book of Genesis: Chapters 1–17* (Grand Rapids: Eerdmans, 1990), 172. Others also contend that this phrase "tends to emphasize promptness of action" (Gordon J. Wenham, *Genesis 1–15* [Waco: Word, 1987], 68; cf. R. W. L. Moberly, "Did the Serpent Get It Right?," *The Journal of Theological Studies* 39, no. 1 [1988]: 4).

9. Abraham van de Beek, "Evolution, Original Sin, and Death," *Journal of Reformed Theology* 5, no. 2 (2011): 214.

the consequence of which is realized later when Adam actually dies.[10] However, the phrase used here never refers elsewhere to the idea of becoming mortal, and the argument also makes the problematic assumption that Adam was somehow immortal before the fall. Yet the presence of the Tree of Life suggests that Adam's continued existence came not from some intrinsic property of his own (immortality) but only as a gift that he had to receive from God.

The second option agrees that the warning focused on biological death, but finds some way of explaining why the forewarned consequence did *not* in fact take place. For example, maybe God graciously chose to rescind the death sentence,[11] "repenting" from the punishment as he does in other instances (Exod 32:12–14; Jer 18:8; Jonah 3:9–10). Yet Moberly rightly points out that God repents in those stories in response to the repentance of the people.[12] It would be unusual for God to withdraw a threatened punishment for no apparent reason. We might also appeal to some underlying rhetorical purpose for the warning: maybe he merely wanted to emphasize the importance of the command, offer strong motivation for obedience, or any number of other reasons God may have had for offering a warning about something he knew would not take place.[13] The problem with all such interpretations, though, is that they require us to view the *serpent* as the one who got the story straight when he said that Eve would not die (Gen 3:4).

As it stands, the narrative offers a considerable puzzle. The prima facie meaning of God's warning is that biological death would immediately result from disobedience, yet that clearly does not happen. Many thus opt for the third option and conclude that the narrative itself wants us to pursue a different possibility: "There remains,

---

10. David Jobling, "A Structural Analysis of Genesis 2:4b–3:24," *SBL Seminar Papers* 1 (1978): 64.

11. Claus Westermann, *Creation* (Philadelphia: Fortress, 1974), 306; David J. A. Clines, "Themes in Genesis 1–11," *The Catholic Biblical Quarterly* 38, no. 4 (1976): 490.

12. Moberly, "Did the Serpent Get It Right?," 10–12.

13. Barr explores a number of such options and argues that none of them result in the conclusion that God was a "liar" (James Barr, "Is God a Liar? [Genesis 2–3]–and Related Matters," *The Journal of Theological Studies* 57, no. 1 [2006]: 1–22).

however, one way in which the problem might be resolved, and that is to interpret death itself in a non-literal, metaphorical way to signify something other than the termination of physical existence."[14] Although the specific phrase used here, "you will certainly die," always refers to biological death in the Old Testament, biblical authors frequently refer to death as "a metaphor for those things which detract from life as Yahweh intends it, among them illness, persecution, despair, and nonparticipation in the life of the covenant community."[15] Consequently, many understand the "death" in 2:17 as referring to the fact that Adam and Eve were exiled from the garden, cut off from the presence of God and the bountiful life he had provided for them.[16]

What can we conclude from all of this? Both of the first two options have fatal flaws, suggesting that the third offers the best way of reading the text. Immediately after Adam and Eve's disobedience, they "die" in the sense of being excluded from the blessings that come from living as God's people in God's presence. Though God does not retract the blessings themselves—such as children, marriage, work, food—we experience those blessings through the taint of sin. But none of this tells us whether biological death is a consequence of sin or part of the natural order. It would be easy to argue on this basis that biological death was a part of the human condition before the fall and that the "death" of Genesis 2:17 only refers to other aspects of human existence. After the fall, we do find God talking about biological death in the context of the subsequent curses: "By the sweat of your brow you will eat your food until you return to the ground, since from it you were taken; for dust you are and to dust you will return" (3:19). According to this interpretation, however, the curse refers only to the frustration of Adam's labors, with the reference to death serving to indicate that this frustration will characterize Adam's entire life. In other words, mortality was

---

14. Moberly, "Did the Serpent Get It Right?," 16.

15. Bailey, *Biblical Perspectives on Death*, 39.

16. E.g., Wenham, *Genesis 1–15*, 74; Beek, "Evolution, Original Sin, and Death," 215.

part of Adam's condition before the fall and it remained so after the fall. What changed was the quality of the life Adam will experience before he dies. At the same time, though, it is entirely possible to affirm the metaphorical nature of death in the warning *and* contend that the ongoing sustaining of human life was a creational blessing now lost in the fall.[17] While Adam and Eve were "mortal" in the sense that they had to receive life as a gift rather than possessing "immortality" as an intrinsic feature of their being, death itself was not part of God's creational design for humanity. Instead, death does not become a part of human experience until after the fall as the eventual result of the immediate loss of the creational blessings.

If the first section demonstrated how difficult it is to develop a theology of death on the basis of biblical texts that talk about death *after* the fall, this section has argued that a similar problem occurs even in a text offering a perspective from *before* the fall. That does not mean we should neglect this material, but it does suggest the importance of viewing the issue from a different angle.

A CHRISTOLOGICAL VISION OF DEATH IN THE THEOLOGY OF KARL BARTH

Barth consistently maintained that a proper understanding of the human person must always begin with the humanity we see revealed in Jesus Christ.[18] We should not be surprised to discover, then, that Barth similarly orients his discussion of death around a christological analysis. "His death, resurrection and coming again are the basis of absolutely everything that is to be said about man and his future, end and goal in God."[19] Consequently, Barth's theology offers an excellent opportunity to observe a christological anthropology at work. At the same time, however, Barth's approach

---

17. Cassuto, *A Commentary on the Book of Genesis*, 125.

18. For more on this, see Marc Cortez, "The Madness in Our Method: Christology as the Necessary Starting Point for Theological Anthropology," in *The Ashgate Research Companion to Theological Anthropology*, ed. Joshua Farris and Charles Taliaferro (Aldershot: Ashgate, 2015), 15–26.

19. *CD* III/2, 624.

also demonstrates some important weaknesses, several of which highlight concerns that we need to be aware of when dealing with any anthropological issue from the perspective of Christology.

On the Mortal Messiah

Barth agrees with those who think the Bible consistently portrays death negatively. Indeed, he goes so far as to reject the idea discussed above that the Old Testament occasionally views death in a more positive light. Instead, he contends that any idea of death being "a friendly or at least a conceivably neutral fate" is alien to the biblical material.[20] However, Barth also argues that this entire picture is based on death "as it actually encounters us,"[21] which means death experienced in the context of sin and guilt. Consequently, we need to make at least a conceptual distinction between *death* and *judgment*. While *death* refers to the event in which biological life ceases, *judgment* denotes the fact that we experience this event in ways that are shaped by our sinfulness and guilt. Yet this means we cannot determine on this basis alone whether death is inherently linked to judgment or only contingently so. Only in Christ does the nature of death become clear.

If we take Jesus as our starting point, though, we must immediately acknowledge, "Like all men, the man Jesus has His lifetime: the time bounded at one end by His birth and at the other by His death; a fixed span with a particular duration within the duration of created time as a whole."[22] The basic truth we need to account for is the fact that even Jesus died.[23] The natural response would be to argue that Jesus only died because he took our sins on himself, which means that even his death was a consequence of sin. The fact that Jesus feared his own death (Matt 26:36–46) makes it difficult to

---

20. *CD* III/2, 601. See also IV/1, 307; II/2, 588–93; IV/1, 253; IV/4, 16.

21. *CD* III/2, 596.

22. *CD* III/2, 440.

23. Thus, "there is no human greatness and grandeur which is not exceeded, overshadowed and fundamentally called in question by death: not even that of the promised and manifested Messiah and Son of Man" (*CD* III/2, 601).

think that Jesus saw death as a good and natural aspect of human existence. The cry of dereliction similarly demonstrates the agony of divine judgment that accompanies death (Matt 27:46). Barth agrees with all of this, even arguing that Jesus is the one who most truly experienced death as judgment.[24] This is the cup he chose to drink on our behalf.[25] Nonetheless, he rejects the conclusion that this requires us to affirm an intrinsic link between death and judgment. Instead, Barth maintains that even though Jesus was personally sinless, he voluntarily chose to *experience* death as judgment on our behalf.[26] However, to do this, Jesus "had to be able to die."[27] In other words, although the manner of Jesus's death was clearly shaped by sin, the mere fact that the sinless Messiah was capable of dying means that we need to understand mortality as part of God's creational vision for human persons. Thus, "if it seems to be for Him an anthropological necessity, the determination of His true and natural being as man, how can we maintain that all this has nothing to do with the nature of man as created good by God?"[28]

Somewhat counterintuitively, Barth grounds the distinction between death and judgment in the cross, the one place where the link seems unavoidably clear. Yet he does so by arguing that if even the sinless Savior is capable of dying, mortality and death must be intrinsic features of humanity. Our experience of death as judgment has to do with the nature of death as the door through which we pass on our way to the Father. Even if we believe that the Father is good and loving, we still fear what lies beyond the door because of our sin and guilt. Like a naughty child standing outside her parent's room, we come to fear the door itself because we know we deserve the judgment that lies beyond. But that does not change the fact that the door itself is just a way of moving from one sphere to another.

---

24. See esp. *CD* IV/1, 306–7.

25. *CD* II/1, 420.

26. *CD* III/2, 628.

27. *CD* III/2, 630.

28. *CD* III/2, 630.

If we could approach death without the sin and guilt that makes us fear what lies beyond, would we not experience it differently?

Since Barth views "death" as the language we use to describe the event in which we transition into the state of eschatological consummation, he associates it even with the passing of people like Enoch and Elijah.[29] They provide a clear illustration of the fact that the transition does not have to be experienced as judgment. He similarly contends that the transformation of living believers at the *parousia* constitutes another example of people going through the transition without experiencing death as judgment.[30] Consequently, "Death, as it actually encounters us men, is the sign of God's judgment on us. We cannot say less than this, but of course we must not try to say more either."[31]

The Goodness of Death

Barth's christological argument for distinguishing between death as judgment and death as transition by itself offers plenty of material for consideration. If we stopped here, though, we would be missing out on a key aspect of Barth's argument. Since Barth contends that his christological starting point requires us to view death itself as a creational good, it is worth asking about what constitutes the goodness of death. As difficult as it may be to think about death in abstraction from the sin, guilt, and judgment that necessarily color all of our experiences of death, in what ways could we consider death itself to be a creational blessing?

To a considerable degree, all of Barth's arguments on this point deal with the benefit of being finite, limited creatures. According to Barth, we often go awry in our understanding of the human person because we try to establish our significance and identity by making ourselves infinite in some way, most commonly by viewing the human person as an immortal soul. Yet Barth contends that we

---

29. *CD* III/2, 635–37.

30. *CD* IV/3.2, 924–25.

31. *CD* III/2, 596.

only understand ourselves rightly when we recognize that we are temporally limited beings.

One of Barth's most fundamental reasons for arguing that limitation is good for human persons is that he thinks it is only by having a finite history that we have a meaningful identity. Barth contends that humans constitute themselves as persons in and through their actions in time.[32] Humans are not metaphysical "substances" in which their identity is grounded in some stable, underlying essence. Instead, Barth contends that I establish my identity in and through the history of my personal actions and relations. "And in so far as I am caught up in this movement from my beginning to my end, my life becomes my history—we might almost say my drama—in which I am neither the author nor the producer, but the principal actor. . . . I myself am in this movement."[33] Indeed, "We might almost say that he is himself his time in the sequence of his life-acts."[34] However, such an account requires that my history eventually comes to an end.[35] Without an ending of some kind, *who* I am would continue to unfold through a never-ending sequence of actions in time. No matter how much time transpired, I would never have a determinable identity. "In an infinite and unending time he would obviously be an indefinite being dissolving both behind and before. He would have no centre, and therefore would not be himself. To be himself he must be constituted by his existence in time, by the appointed limits of birth and death."[36] For our histories to be complete, the temporal succession of past, present, and future must someday come to an end. Consequently, death is the blessing that makes it possible for us to have determinate identities.

---

32. This is Barth's famous actualism at work (see esp. George Hunsinger, *How to Read Karl Barth: The Shape of His Theology* [Oxford: Oxford University Press, 1991]).

33. *CD* III/3, 232.

34. *CD* III/2, 521.

35. *CD* III/3, 233.

36. *CD* III/4, 572–73. Indeed, Barth argues that unlimited time would cause problems even for the identity of God himself, arguing that we should think of God himself as having a kind of eternal temporality (see esp. *CD* II/1, 608–77).

Another argument Barth offers for the goodness of death is that without finitude there could be no real salvation. In a state of unending life in which our personal histories had no conclusion, there would be no way to secure our salvation. "What would become of us if in an endless life we had the constant opportunity to achieve a provisional ordering of our relationship with God and our fellows?"[37] For Barth, this could only mean the eternal possibility of breaking fellowship and again falling back toward the nothingness that currently plagues us. "Long life and an ample measure of time can only mean more opportunities. And an infinite measure of human life can only mean an infinite number of opportunities."[38] Instead of unending bliss, this would leave us in the position of being "compelled to aspire continually" and "condemned to perpetual wanting and asking and therefore dissatisfaction."[39] For Barth, this is a better picture of hell than of heaven.

Barth takes the argument a step further and suggests that the atonement itself can only be effective if we are in fact finite beings. "We have to be finite, to be able to die," if Christ's atonement is to have its once-for-all effect on us.[40] He does not unpack this argument in any detail, but the concern again relates to the difficulties of envisioning the human life as an unbounded set. Barth uses the same once-for-all language to describe the idea of being a temporally bounded person. Birth and death are the "two events which give to human life its character of once-for-allness."[41] Barth seems to think, then, that there is a connection between the once-for-allness of the atonement and the once-for-all nature of temporal beings. For the atonement to be a real event that impacts real beings, both Jesus Christ and other human beings must have the kind of identities that come from their historical, and therefore temporally limited, determination.

---

37. *CD* III/2, 631.

38. *CD* III/2, 561.

39. *CD* III/2, 562.

40. *CD* III/2, 631.

41. *CD* III/3, 231.

A fourth benefit is that without the finitude of death, we would have no way to view any particular time, even an extended period of time, with any real urgency.[42] After all, if our years are unlimited, how can we possibly think that a decision I make in *this* moment, or even a series of decisions I make over the course of a few decades, has any real significance? Would not such years and their corresponding actions be a mere drop in the infinite ocean of my unending life? The fact that my history is limited to just *these* years, the ones bounded by my birth and death, means that *these* years are my unique and unrepeatable contribution to what God is doing in creation. These years and these alone are my distinct work as God's covenant copartner. This places particular urgency on how we use the time we have. Since every moment is a unique and precious part of my unrepeatable history, everything I do should be "tested by the question whether it is a seizing or neglecting of the unique opportunity presented to [me] in [my] time."[43]

A Christological Critique of a Christological Argument

Barth thus offers us a compelling example of a christological approach to a specific anthropological issue. He clearly takes Jesus as his starting point, though he does not neglect material that comes from other sources, particularly the Old Testament, and the view of death he develops flows from that christological center. Nonetheless, Barth's argument also manifests a few weaknesses. Engaging those should help us understand both how to apply our christological theses and how best to understand death from a christological perspective.

The greatest strength in Barth's argument is the recognition that a christological anthropology is inherently teleological (thesis 3), and that this almost certainly would have involved some kind of ontological transformation of the human person even if the fall had never happened. Although we should be careful about speculating

---

42. *CD* III/2, 633.
43. *CD* III/4, 580.

252 | ReSourcing Theological Anthropology

too much on the nature of eschatological humanity from what we see in the postresurrection appearances of Jesus, most affirm that some kind of transformation has taken place. This accords with what we saw in chapter 2, where Paul talks about the "spiritual" body as being significantly different from the "natural" body of Adam in the garden. Consequently, it seems reasonable to conclude that the ontological transformation of creational humanity was always part of God's plan.

Nonetheless, I think we need to challenge Barth's conclusion that this means death itself is intrinsic to human nature. The mere fact that eschatological consummation requires ontological transformation does not entail that death has to be a part of this equation. Returning to the analogy above, imagine that God awaits us in another room and that it has always been a part of God's plan for us to enter the room in some way. Yet there are many ways of getting into a room. We can walk calmly through the door, or someone could smash our bodies through the wall with a tractor. The transition takes place either way, but the *means* differs significantly. Similarly, we could affirm the necessity of the ontological transformation of humanity, but contend that death only becomes the means by which we undergo this transformation as a consequence of the fall.[44] To maintain that death itself is intrinsic to humanity, we will need something further.

Barth seeks to provide precisely this with his christological focus on the fact that even Jesus died. However, his argument runs into a different problem here. Barth routinely affirms Jesus's sinlessness, emphasizing this as a way of establishing that Jesus's death points to a creational reality. Yet we saw in chapter 4 that Barth is also one of the theologians who maintains that Jesus assumed a fallen human nature. Although Jesus was personally sinless, his nature was fallen. This makes it difficult for Barth to claim that Jesus's ability to die

---

44. We could address this by adopting Barth's practice of using the term *death* to refer to any kind of transition regardless of whether that transition involves the cessation of biological life. Yet it seems clearest and most consistent with the Bible's own use of terminology to restrict our use of death in this context to biological death.

demonstrates that death is intrinsic to creational humanity. We could easily maintain that this ability flows from his fallen nature instead. Granted, we should not simply assume that death is a consequence of fallenness any more than we should assume the same about eating and drinking. Given his position on the fallenness debate, though, neither can Barth assume that death is a creational reality merely because Jesus experiences it. Since I have argued that the primary focus of a christological anthropology should be on understanding how to live humanly in the midst of a broken world (thesis 11), we need to exercise caution about using this argument to speculate about the condition of humanity before the fall.

An even more critical flaw arises with Barth's conclusions regarding the goodness of death. The key here is that Barth's arguments all depend on the connection between death and finitude, each of which has implications for understanding the eschatological state of humanity. If temporal finitude is necessary for the well-being of the creature, then we have to reject the idea that humans have any kind of continued "history" in the eschaton. Whatever we might want or need to say about me after I die, we must say that my history has concluded. The time between my birth and death is the *only* time I have, which is why I must live it with urgency. Barth offers a christological argument for this conclusion as well, maintaining that even Jesus lived a finite, human life. Although Barth spends a fair bit of time discussing Jesus's resurrection, the "Easter time" between the resurrection and the ascension, and the nature of his own eternal life,[45] he rejects the conclusion that we should view any of this as suggesting that Jesus "was given further time beyond the unique time of his given life on earth back then."[46] Instead, the human life lives forever in the sense that it is drawn up into and preserved in God's eternal love.[47]

---

45. See esp. *CD* III/2, 437–511.

46. *CD* III/2, 477; cf. *CD* I/2, 53.

47. We cannot deal with the specific details of how Barth views the eschatological state of the human person. For a good overview, see Nathan Hitchcock, *Karl Barth and the Resurrection of the Flesh: The Loss of the Body in Participatory Eschatology* (Eugene, OR: Pickwick, 2013).

We do not have the space to adequately address Barth's lengthy discussions of Jesus's "Easter time," but we do need to take seriously the fact that the biblical material presents Jesus as having a continued, historical existence after his biological death. He walks with the disciples, gives them further instruction, eats meals, and even goes fishing (kind of). Even after he ascends to the right hand of the Father, we see him engaging in the kind of meaningful behavior that we would normally associate with temporal existence: he continues to serve as priest for God's people such that "he always lives to intercede for them" (Heb 7:25), and he can even be described as waiting for the completion of God's plans (Heb 10:13). All of this suggests that Jesus's temporal history did *not* come to an end at the cross. Fully aware of this material, Barth affirms that there is a sense in which "Jesus has a further history beginning on the third day after His death and therefore after the time of His first history had clearly come to an end."[48] However, Barth rejects the conclusion that we should take this as warrant for affirming the postmortem history of the human person since this subsequent time is "simply the time of the revelation of the mystery of the preceding time of the life and death of the man Jesus."[49] At this point, however, it is difficult to avoid the impression that rather than beginning with Jesus's death and resurrection to understand humanity, a certain conception of temporal finitude is driving the christological analysis here. If we had not already determined that humans could have no history after death, would we really draw the conclusion that this was anything other than a continued history of the incarnate Christ?

Similar questions arise when we consider Jesus's state *between* his death and resurrection. If human persons have no continued existence after death, must we affirm a cessation of the incarnation immediately following his death on Good Friday? This is one of the difficult questions faced by any physicalist account of the human person. If Christ's human time comes to an end at death, so must

---

48. *CD* III/2, 441.
49. *CD* III/2, 455.

the incarnation. Granted, on this interpretation, the incarnation would resume with the resurrection, but such a temporal gap in the incarnation would run counter to long-standing convictions about the permanence of Christ's incarnate state. And it would also generate some interesting questions about whether we should talk instead about *two* incarnations rather than merely the continuation of the same incarnation. Barth himself would not likely have found such objections convincing. He would probably respond by appealing to the idea that human persons are sustained in God's love after their death. Thus, even on Holy Saturday, the incarnation "continues" in much the same way that all human persons continue to exist in eternity. To do this, however, he must contend that the resurrection does not affect any real change on Jesus's ontological condition. At death, Jesus had already entered the postmortem state of inclusion in God's time. As important as the resurrection might be in Barth's theology, it would seem to constitute a revelation of the truth of Jesus's historical existence rather than transformation of his human condition. Once again, then, we must ask if this is really the only, or even the most likely, conclusion to draw from the christological material. If we had not already drawn conclusions about the necessary finitude of the human person, would we really read the resurrection narratives in this way? To me, that seems unlikely.

In other words, I wonder here if Barth has failed to deal adequately with *all* of the details of Christ's historic existence (thesis 7), which includes the details surrounding his own death, resurrection, and ascension. Close attention to those narratives demonstrates that Jesus's death did *not* bring the story of his human life to an end. If Jesus's history continued, we have good reason to believe that ours will as well. Although we do need to be reminded of our finitude, and consequently of our moment-by-moment dependence on God's grace, Barth errs in thinking that *temporal* finitude is the only way of establishing this.

Focusing on Jesus's resurrection and ascension in this context also helps us think more clearly about life both before and after our deaths. Barth worries that unending time would undermine the significance of any particular segment of our lives. Once again, though, that does not seem to be the conclusion that we would draw from analyzing Jesus's own history. If the biblical material portrays Jesus as continuing to have a history after his death, as I have suggested above, then we must account for the fact that the biblical authors have no difficulty emphasizing the climactic significance of his life between Christmas and Easter. Regardless of how we understand the state of human persons in eternity, he will always be the one who was born to Mary, who befriended sinners, who walked on water, and who gave his life on the cross. Eternity does not minimize either the importance or the urgency of history. Barth also fears that unending time would undermine personal identity; since our stories never come to an end, our identities would remain forever indeterminate. Yet here again the resurrection and ascension of Christ point in a different direction. Jesus remains *Jesus* forever. The author of Hebrews vehemently emphasizes the eternal identity of our risen Lord. Consequently, it does not seem to be the case that having a history beyond our deaths renders our identities vague or insecure. Instead, we see in Jesus that the eschatological state involves the discrete identities of human persons and the continued development of their personal histories. We do not need to speculate about the events that will comprise those histories to be confident that we will have them.

CONCLUSION

What can we conclude from all of this? Barth's theology provides an excellent model of thinking christologically about something as important to the human experience as death. We cannot claim to know what death means and how it relates to God's purposes for humanity until we have seen death through the life of Jesus. We could say much more, of course. A complete christological analysis of death would need to look as well at Jesus's healing ministry, the stories in which Jesus raised people from the dead (particularly

Lazarus), and the importance of *life* and *resurrection* in his own teaching—not to mention the significance of the Spirit as the source of life for God's people. Yet we have seen enough to illustrate how Barth uses Christology to frame and answer an important question: Is death itself a natural part of human existence?

In the end, though, I think we have found that the christological answer to this question is ambiguous at best. Since a christological anthropology is committed to a teleological account of humanity in which eschatological consummation is an intrinsic part of our story, it stands to reason that some form of ontological transformation would also be an essential aspect of that story. This is precisely what we see in Jesus, so it would not be too much of a stretch to maintain that death and resurrection are simply the means by which God always intended to bring about this ontological transformation. Nonetheless, whether Jesus assumed a fallen nature or merely assumed the "symptoms" of such a nature, we have to deal with the possibility that Jesus being "able to die" is a consequence of fallenness and not a part of the natural order. If this is the case, then it becomes difficult to take the claim "even Jesus died" as the fundamental starting point for speculating about human death before the fall. Barth's additional arguments for the goodness of death all center on the necessity of temporal finitude for all creatures, including humans. Yet these arguments all struggle to account for the descriptions of Jesus's life after his resurrection and ascension, which describe him having the kind of postmortem history Barth denies for human persons.

Consequently, it does not seem like Barth's christological argument gives us a decisive answer on whether death is intrinsic to human nature or something that we only experience as a consequence of the fall. Perhaps, then, it is fitting for us to end this study with a healthy dose of chastened humility. Although I think we have seen considerable reason to affirm that Christology is fundamental for understanding humanity, we should be careful not to press this claim too far. While a christological anthropology should maintain

258 | ReSourcing Theological Anthropology

that Christology is central to anthropology in such a way that we need to interpret and understand all anthropological data in light of the humanity we see revealed in Christ, we should not go so far as to claim that this will offer us the definitive answers to all anthropological questions. Instead, as we see in this chapter, some questions, particularly those about creational or eschatological humanity, may well remain opaque even when viewed in the light of Christ. Given the complexity and mystery of the human person, it should come as no surprise that not even this approach to anthropology offers unmitigated access to everything there is to know about humanity.

Nonetheless, the basic conviction of a christological anthropology remains. Only the person and work of Jesus Christ offer the necessary vantage point for understanding humanity. He is the paradigm and the revelation of true humanity, the one who radically reorients all anthropological claims, reshaping our understanding of what it means to be truly human.

Afterword

RECENT YEARS HAVE WITNESSED a rising tide of interest in theological anthropology. Scientific developments like the Human Genome Project alongside pressing societal debates about things like sexuality, personhood, and racism push us to reflect further on the nature and destiny of the human creature. *Who* are we? *What* are we? *How* should we live? Even when we bury such questions beneath the weight of everyday realities like figuring out what to eat for breakfast, scraping together enough money to cover next month's rent, or dealing with the loss of a loved one, they do not recede entirely. Instead, like the superstructure of a building, even when we are not consciously aware of them, such questions continue to shape the visible, human world. Theologians are increasingly mindful of the power and complexity of such questions, a development that seems unlikely to fade any time soon.

The goal of this book has been to resource those discussions with greater emphasis on the significance, indeed the *centrality*, of Jesus Christ for understanding what it means to be human. If Jesus is the true *anthrōpos*, the last Adam, the perfect image of God, and the revelation of true humanity, how can we hope to understand what it means to be human apart from close and careful consideration of the humanity revealed in him? Correspondingly, if such a christologically informed vision is necessary for a right understanding of humanity, this must also serve as the basis for reflecting further on those pressing anthropological debates mentioned above. Apart from robust christological reflection on the nature of humanity, we lose the one sure vantage point from which we can begin to discern the shape and texture of what it means to be human in the midst of this flawed and fragile world.

This book makes no attempt to address *all* of the issues and concerns associated with developing a christological anthropology. Consequently, much work remains to be done. At the very least, others may well choose to explore different paths than the ones I have chosen, either because they disagree with some of the conclusions I have drawn in these discussions or because they choose to prioritize other theological turning points. Such alternate approaches to developing christologically shaped anthropologies would be a welcome addition to the conversation.

Other possibilities for further work lie in pressing more deeply into the anthropological issues addressed in chapters 6–8. Since the discussions presented here merely scratched the surface, much remains to be considered when exploring the resources of Christology for understanding sexuality, race, and death. But why stop there? Although Christology has already played a prominent role in discussions of things like free will and suffering, other areas of investigation remain somewhat thin in the application of christological insights to anthropological topics (e.g., work, creativity, family, aging, uniqueness).

Finally, one of those most notable ways in which the present work falls short is that it has not pressed further into the importance of things like pneumatology and ecclesiology for understanding the human person. Although I have argued that a christological anthropology will necessarily be robustly shaped by these realities as well, since we should in no way divorce Christology itself from either of these doctrines, I have not had the space to develop their anthropological significance in any meaningful way. The time is ripe for studies that not only explore the pneumatological and ecclesiological shape of human existence but that also engage the relationship between these loci and the christological starting point developed here.

I'm sure there are many other possibilities that I have not even considered. However pursued, such further studies in understanding the human person christologically would deepen contemporary theological anthropology immeasurably, demonstrating the breadth and depth of the possibilities that arise from such a starting point. As Karl Barth famously declared, "The ontological determination of humanity is grounded in the fact that one man among all others is the man Jesus."[1]

Ecce homo.

---

1. *CD* III/2, 132.

Bibliography

Aalen, Sverre. "Δόξα." In *The New International Dictionary of New Testament Theology,* edited by Colin Brown, vol. 2, 44–52. Grand Rapids: Zondervan, 1986.

Adams, Marilyn McCord. *Christ and Horrors: The Coherence of Christology.* Cambridge: Cambridge University Press, 2006.

———. "Julian of Norwich on the Tender Loving Care of Mother Jesus." In *Our Knowledge of God,* 197–213. Dordrecht, Netherlands: Kluwer, 1992.

Allen, David Lewis. *Hebrews.* Nashville: B&H, 2010.

Allen, R. Michael. "Calvin's Christ: A Dogmatic Matrix for Discussion of Christ's Human Nature." *International Journal of Systematic Theology* 9, no. 4 (2007): 382–97.

Anderson, Ray S. *Theology, Death and Dying.* Oxford: Basil Blackwell, 1986.

Appiah, Anthony. *In My Father's House: Africa in the Philosophy of Culture.* New York: Oxford University Press, 1992.

Arx, Urs von. "The Gender Aspects of Creation from a Theological, Christological, and Soteriological Perspective: An Exegetical Contribution." *Anglican Theological Review* 84, no. 3 (2002): 519–54.

Attridge, Harold W. *The Epistle to the Hebrews: A Commentary on the Epistle to the Hebrews.* Philadelphia: Fortress, 1989.

Bailey, Lloyd R. *Biblical Perspectives on Death.* Philadelphia: Fortress, 1979.

Balthasar, Hans Urs von. *Mysterium Pachale: The Mystery of Easter.* Translated by Adrian Nichols. Edinburgh: T&T Clark, 1990.

Banton, Michael. "The Idiom of Race: A Critique of Presentism." In *Theories of Race and Racism: A Reader,* 2nd ed., edited by Les Back and John Solomos, 55–67. London: Routledge, 2009.

Bantum, Brian. *Redeeming Mulatto: A Theology of Race and Christian Hybridity.* Waco, TX: Baylor University Press, 2010.

———. *The Death of Race: Building a New Christianity in a Racial World.* Minneapolis: Fortress, 2016.

Barr, James. "Is God a Liar? (Genesis 2–3)—and Related Matters." *The Journal of Theological Studies* 57, no. 1 (2006): 1–22.

———. "The Image of God in the Book of Genesis—A Study of Terminology." *Bulletin of the John Rylands Library* 51, no. 1 (1968): 11–26.

Barrett, C. K. *A Commentary on the Second Epistle to the Corinthians.* New York: Harper & Row, 1973.

———. *The First Epistle to the Corinthians.* Peabody, MA: Hendrickson, 1968.

———. *The Gospel according to St. John: An Introduction with Commentary and Notes on the Greek Text.* New York: Macmillan, 1955.

Barrosse, Thomas. "The Seven Days of the New Creation in St. John's Gospel." *Catholic Biblical Quarterly* 21, no. 4 (1959): 507–16.

Barth, Karl. *Church Dogmatics.* Translated by Geoffrey W. Bromiley and Thomas F. Torrance. 13 vols. Edinburgh: T&T Clark, 1956.

Bathrellos, Demetrios. "The Patristic Tradition on the Sinlessness of Jesus." In *Studia Patristica*, vol. 61, edited by Jonathan Yates, 235–41. Leuven: Peeters, 2013.

Bauckham, Richard. "The Divinity of Jesus Christ in the Epistle to the Hebrews." In *Epistle to the Hebrews and Christian Theology*, edited by Richard Bauckham, Trevor A. Hart, Daniel R. Driver, and Nathan MacDonald, 15–36. Grand Rapids: Eerdmans, 2009.

Baudzej, Julia. "Re-Telling the Story of Jesus: The Concept of Embodiment and Recent Feminist Reflections on the Maleness of Christ." *Feminist Theology* 17, no. 1 (2008): 72–91.

Beek, Abraham van de. "Evolution, Original Sin, and Death." *Journal of Reformed Theology* 5, no. 2 (2011): 206–20.

Beetham, Christopher A. *Echoes of Scripture in the Letter of Paul to the Colossians.* Boston: Brill, 2008.

Berkhof, Louis. *Systematic Theology.* London: Banner of Truth, 1984.

Berkouwer, G. C. *Man: The Image of God.* Grand Rapids: Eerdmans, 1962.

Black, C. Clifton. "God's Promise for Humanity in the New Testament." In *God and Human Dignity*, edited by R. Kendall Soulen and Linda Woodhead, 179–95. Grand Rapids: Eerdmans, 2006.

Blocher, Henri. *In The Beginning: The Opening Chapters of Genesis.* Downers Grove, IL: InterVarsity, 1984.

Blomberg, Craig L. "'But We See Jesus': The Relationship between the Son of Man in Hebrews 2.6 and 2.9 and the Implications for English Translations." In *A Cloud of Witnesses: The Theology of Hebrews in Its Ancient Context*, edited by Richard Bauckham, Daniel Driver, Trevor Hart, and Nathan MacDonald, 28–39. London: T&T Clark, 2008.

Böhler, Dieter. "'Ecce Homo!' (Joh 19,5) ein Zitat aus dem Alten Testament." *Biblische Zeitschrift* 39, no. 1 (1995): 104–8.

Bonhoeffer, Dietrich. *Creation and Fall: A Theological Interpretation of Genesis 1–3*. Translated by John C. Fletcher. New York: Macmillan, 1959.

Bonilla-Silva, Eduardo. *Racism without Racists: Color-Blind Racism and the Persistence of Racial Inequality in America*. 4th ed. Lanham, MD: Rowman & Littlefield, 2014.

Borchert, Gerald L. *John 12–21: An Exegetical and Theological Exposition of Holy Scripture*. Nashville: Holman Reference, 2002.

Bowker, John Westerdale. *The Targums and Rabbinic Literature; an Introduction to Jewish Interpretations of Scripture*. London: Cambridge University Press, 1969.

Branick, Vincent P. "The Sinful Flesh of the Son of God (Rom 8:3): A Key Image of Pauline Theology." *The Catholic Biblical Quarterly* 47, no. 2 (1985): 246–62.

Brotherton, Joshua R. "The Integrity of Nature in the Grace-Freedom Dynamic: Lonergan's Critique of Bañezian Thomism." *Theological Studies* 75, no. 3 (2014): 537–63.

Brown, Jeannine K. "Creation's Renewal in the Gospel of John." *Catholic Biblical Quarterly* 72, no. 2 (2010): 275–90.

Brown, Michael Joseph. "Black Theology and the Bible." In *The Cambridge Companion to Black Theology*, edited by Edward P. Antonio and Dwight N. Hopkins, 169–83. New York: Cambridge, 2012.

Brown, Raymond E. *The Gospel according to John*. Garden City, NY: Doubleday, 1966.

Bruce, F. F. *The Epistle to the Hebrews*. Rev. ed. The New International Commentary on the New Testament. Grand Rapids: Eerdmans, 1990.

Buell, Denise Kimber. *Why This New Race: Ethnic Reasoning in Early Christianity*. New York: Columbia University Press, 2008.

Bultmann, Rudolf. *The Gospel of John: A Commentary*. Translated by G. R. Beasley-Murray. Philadelphia: Westminster, 1971.

Byrne, Brendan. *Romans*. Sacra Pagina. Collegeville, MN: Liturgical, 1996.

Caird, G. B. "Son by Appointment." In *New Testament Age: Essays in Honor of Bo Reicke*, edited by William C. Weinrich, 73–81. Macon, GA: Mercer University Press, 1984.

Cameron, Daniel J. *Flesh and Blood: A Dogmatic Sketch Concerning the Fallen Nature View of Christ's Human Nature*. Eugene, OR: Wipf & Stock, 2016.

Canceran, Delfo. "Image of God: A Theological Reconstruction of the Beginning." *The Asia Journal of Theology* 25, no. 1 (2011): 3–23.

Caneday, Ardel B. "The Eschatological World Already Subjected to the Son: The Οἰκουμένη of Hebrews 1.6 and the Son's Enthronement." In *A Cloud of Witnesses: The Theology of Hebrews in Its Ancient Contexts,* edited by Richard Bauckham, Daniel Driver, Trevor Hart, and Nathan MacDonald, 28–39. London: T&T Clark, 2008.

Carson, D. A. *The Gospel according to John.* Grand Rapids: Eerdmans, 1991.

Carter, J. Kameron. "Christology, or Redeeming Whiteness: A Response to James Perkinson's Appropriation of Black Theology." *Theology Today* 60, no. 4 (2004): 525–39.

———. *Race: A Theological Account.* New York: Oxford University Press, 2008.

Cassuto, Umberto. *A Commentary on the Book of Genesis.* Translated by Israel Abrahams. Jerusalem: Magnes, 1961.

Chancey, Mark A. *Greco-Roman Culture and the Galilee of Jesus.* New York: Cambridge University Press, 2005.

———. *The Myth of a Gentile Galilee.* New York: Cambridge University Press, 2002.

Chapman, Malcolm, ed. *Social and Biological Aspects of Ethnicity.* New York: Oxford University Press, 1993.

Ciampa, Roy E., and Brian S. Rosner. *The First Letter to the Corinthians.* The Pillar New Testament Commentary. Grand Rapids: Eerdmans, 2010.

Ciraulo, Jonathan Martin. "Sacraments and Personhood: John Zizioulas' Impasse and a Way Forward." *Heythrop Journal* 53, no. 6 (2012): 993–1004.

Cleage, Albert B. *The Black Messiah.* New York: Sheed and Ward, 1968.

Clines, David J. A. "The Image of God in Man." *Tyndale Bulletin* 19 (1968): 53–103.

———. "Themes in Genesis 1–11." *The Catholic Biblical Quarterly* 38, no. 4 (1976): 483–507.

Coakley, Sarah. *Powers and Submissions: Spirituality, Philosophy, and Gender.* Oxford: Blackwell, 2002.

Coloe, Mary L. "The Structure of the Johannine Prologue and Genesis 1." *Australian Biblical Review* 45 (1997): 40–55.

———. "Theological Reflections on Creation in the Gospel of John." *Pacifica* 24, no. 1 (2011): 1–12.

Cone, James H. *A Black Theology of Liberation,* 40th anniv. ed. Maryknoll, NY: Orbis, 2012.

———. *Black Theology and Black Power.* New York: Seabury, 1969.

———. *God of the Oppressed.* Maryknoll, NY: Orbis, 2014.

Corrigan, Kevin. *Evagrius and Gregory: Mind, Soul, and Body in the Fourth Century.* Ashgate Studies in Philosophy and Theology in Late Antiquity. Burlington, VT: Ashgate, 2009.

Cortez, Marc. *Christological Anthropology in Historical Perspective: Ancient and Contemporary Approaches to Theological Anthropology.* Grand Rapids: Zondervan, 2016.

———. *Embodied Souls, Ensouled Bodies: An Exercise in Christological Anthropology and Its Significance for the Mind/Body Debate.* London: T&T Clark, 2008.

———. "Idols, Images, and a Spirit-ed Anthropology: A Pneumatological Account of the *Imago Dei.*" In *Third Article Theology: A Pneumatological Dogmatics,* edited by Myk Habets, 267–82. Minneapolis: Fortress, 2016.

———. "The Madness in Our Method: Christology as the Necessary Starting Point for Theological Anthropology." In *The Ashgate Research Companion to Theological Anthropology,* edited by Joshua Farris and Charles Taliaferro, 15–26. Aldershot, England: Ashgate, 2015.

———. *Theological Anthropology: A Guide for the Perplexed.* New York: T&T Clark, 2009.

———. "What Does It Mean to Call Karl Barth a 'Christocentric' Theologian?" *Scottish Journal of Theology* 60, no. 2 (2007): 127–43.

Crisp, Oliver D. "Did Christ Have a Fallen Human Nature?" *International Journal of Systematic Theology* 6, no. 3 (2004): 270–88.

———. *Divinity and Humanity: The Incarnation Reconsidered.* Current Issues in Theology. Cambridge: Cambridge University Press, 2007.

———. *God Incarnate: Explorations in Christology.* New York: T&T Clark, 2009.

———. "Incarnation without the Fall." *Journal of Reformed Theology* 10, no. 3 (2016): 215–33.

Crockett, W. V. "Ultimate Restoration of All Mankind: 1 Corinthians 15:22." In *Studia Biblica 1978, 3: Papers on Paul and Other New Testament Authors,* 83–87. Sheffield: JSOT Press, 1980.

Cullmann, Oscar. *The Christology of the New Testament.* Philadelphia: Westminster, 1959.

Culver, Robert D. "A Neglected Millennial Passage from Saint Paul." *Bibliotheca Sacra* 113, no. 450 (1956): 141–52.

Curtis, Edward Mason. "Man as the Image of God in Genesis in the Light of Ancient Near Eastern Parallels." PhD diss., University of Pennsylvania, 1984.

Daley, Brian E. "'The Human Form Divine': Christ's Risen Body and Ours according to Gregory of Nyssa." In *Studia Patristica, Vol. 41*, 301–18. Leuven: Peeters, 2006.

Daly, Mary. *Gyn/Ecology: The Metaethics of Radical Feminism*. Boston, MA: Beacon, 1979.

Dearborn, Kerry. "The Crucified Christ as the Motherly God: The Theology of Julian of Norwich." *Scottish Journal of Theology* 55, no. 3 (2002): 283–302.

de Boer, Martinus C. *The Defeat of Death: Apocalyptic Eschatology in 1 Corinthians 15 and Romans 5*. Journal for the Study of the New Testament 22. Sheffield: JSOT Press, 1988.

Delitzsch, Franz. *A New Commentary on Genesis*. Translated by Sophia Taylor. Edinburgh: T&T Clark, 1899.

Derrett, J. Duncan M. "Ecce Homo Ruber (John 19,5 with Isaiah 1,18; 63,1–2)." *Bibbia E Oriente* 32, no. 4 (1990): 215–29.

DeSilva, David A. *Perseverance in Gratitude: A Social-Rhetorical Commentary on the Epistle "to the Hebrews."* Grand Rapids: Eerdmans, 2000.

Dick, Michael B. *Born in Heaven, Made on Earth: The Making of the Cult Image in the Ancient Near East*. Winona Lake, IN: Eisenbrauns, 1999.

Dodd, C. H. *The Interpretation of the Fourth Gospel*. Cambridge: Cambridge University Press, 1953.

Du Bois, W. E. B. *The Souls of Black Folk*. New York: Penguin, 1994.

Dunn, James D. G. "1 Corinthians 15:45—Last Adam, Life-Giving Spirit." In *Christ and Spirit in the New Testament: Studies in Honour of Charles Franscis Digby Moule*, edited by Barnabas Lindars and Stephen S. Smalley, 127–41. Cambridge: Cambridge University Press, 1973.

———. "Christ, Adam, and Preexistence." In *Where Christology Began: Essays on Philippians 2*, 74–83. Louisville: Westminster John Knox, 1998.

———. *Christology In The Making: A New Testament Inquiry Into the Origins of the Doctrine of the Incarnation*. Philadelphia: Westminster, 1980.

———. *The Epistles to the Colossians and to Philemon: A Commentary on the Greek Text*. The New International Greek Testament Commentary. Grand Rapids: Eerdmans, 1996.

Dunning, Benjamin H. *Christ without Adam: Subjectivity and Sexual Difference in the Philosophers' Paul*. New York: Columbia University Press, 2014.

Du Rand, Jan A. "The Creation Motif in the Fourth Gospel: Perspectives on Its Narratological Function within a Judaistic Background." In

Theology and Christology in the Fourth Gospel: Essays by the Members of the SNTS Johannine Writings Seminar, 21–46. Leuven: Leuven University Press, 2005.

Eliav-Feldon, Miriam, Benjamin Isaac, and Joseph Ziegler, eds. *The Origins of Racism in the West*. New York: Cambridge University Press, 2013.

Elizondo, Virgilio P. *A God of Incredible Surprises: Jesus of Galilee*. Lanham, MD: Rowman & Littlefield, 2003.

———. *Galilean Journey: The Mexican-American Promise*. Maryknoll, NY: Orbis, 2000.

———. "Jesus the Galilean Jew in Mestizo Theology." *Theological Studies* 70, no. 2 (2009): 262–80.

———. *The Future Is Mestizo: Life Where Cultures Meet*. Boulder: University Press of Colorado, 2000.

———. "What Good Can Come out of Galilee?" *Church & Society* 93, no. 4 (2003): 56–64.

Ellingworth, Paul. *The Epistle to the Hebrews: A Commentary on the Greek Text*. Grand Rapids: Eerdmans, 1993.

Fatum, Lone. "Image of God and Glory of Man: Women in the Pauline Congregations." In *Image of God and Gender Models in Judaeo-Christian Tradition*, edited by Kari Elisabeth Børresen, 50–133. Minneapolis: Fortress, 1995.

Faur, José. "The Biblical Idea of Idolatry." *The Jewish Quarterly Review* 69, no. 1 (1978): 1–15.

Fee, Gordon D. *God's Empowering Presence: The Holy Spirit in the Letters of Paul*. Peabody, MA: Hendrickson, 1994.

———. *Pauline Christology: An Exegetical-Theological Study*. Peabody, MA: Hendrickson, 2007.

———. "Praying and Prophesying in the Assemblies: 1 Corinthians 11:2–16." In *Discovering Biblical Equality : Complementarity without Hierarchy*, edited by Ronald W. Pierce, Rebecca Merrill Groothuis, and Gordon D. Fee, 2nd ed., 142–71. Downers Grove, IL: InterVarsity, 2005.

———. *The First Epistle to the Corinthians*. The New International Commentary on the New Testament. Grand Rapids: Eerdmans, 1987.

Feingold, Lawrence. *The Natural Desire to See God According to St. Thomas and His Interpreters*. 2nd ed. Ave Maria, FL: Sapientia, 2004.

Fenton, John. *Passion According to John*. London: SPCK, 1961.

Fergusson, David. "Humans Created according to the Imago Dei: An Alternative Proposal." *Zygon* 48, no. 2 (2013): 439–53.

Flender, Otto. "Εἰκών." In *The New International Dictionary of New Testament Theology*, edited by Colin Brown, vol. 2, 286–88. Grand Rapids: Zondervan, 1986.

Frerichs, Wendell W. "Death and Resurrection in the Old Testament." *Word & World* 11, no. 1 (1991): 14–22.

Freyne, Seán. *Galilee and Gospel: Collected Essays*. Boston: Brill Academic, 2002.

Garland, David E. *1 Corinthians*. Baker Exegetical Commentary on the New Testament. Grand Rapids: Baker Academic, 2003.

Garr, W. Randall. *In His Own Image and Likeness: Humanity, Divinity, and Monotheism*. Leiden: Brill, 2003.

Gathercole, Simon J. *The Preexistent Son: Recovering the Christologies of Matthew, Mark, and Luke*. Grand Rapids: Eerdmans, 2006.

Gillman, Florence Morgan. "Another Look at Romans 8:3: 'In the Likeness of Sinful Flesh.'" *The Catholic Biblical Quarterly* 49, no. 4 (1987): 597–604.

Glicksman, Andrew T. "Beyond Sophia: The Sapiential Portrayal of Jesus in the Fourth Gospel and Its Ethical Implications for the Johannine Community." In *Rethinking the Ethics of John: "Implicit Ethics" in the Johannine Writings*, 83–101. Tübingen: Mohr Siebeck, 2012.

Golash-Boza, Tanya Maria. *Race & Racisms: A Critical Approach*. New York: Oxford University Press, 2016.

Gonzalez, Michelle A. *Created in God's Image: An Introduction to Feminist Theological Anthropology*. Maryknoll, NY: Orbis, 2007.

Gordon, Robert. *Hebrews*. Sheffield: Sheffield Academic, 2000.

Green, Elizabeth E. "More Musings on Maleness: The Maleness of Jesus Revisited." *Feminist Theology* 20 (1999): 9–27.

Gregory of Nyssa. "On the Making of Man." In *A Select Library of the Nicene and Post-Nicene Fathers*, edited by Philip Schaff, vol. 5, series 2. Grand Rapids: Eerdmans, 1978.

———. *On the Soul and the Resurrection*. Crestwood, NY: St. Vladimir's Seminary Press, 1993.

Grenz, Stanley J. *The Social God and the Relational Self: A Trinitarian Theology of the Imago Dei*. Philadelphia: Westminster, 2001.

Griffiths, Jonathan. *Hebrews and Divine Speech*. London: Bloomsbury, 2014.

Grogan, Geoffrey W. "Christ and His People: An Exegetical and Theological Study of Hebrews 2.5–18." *Vox Evangelica* 6 (1969): 245–76.

Grumett, David. "De Lubac, Grace, and the Pure Nature Debate." *Modern Theology* 31, no. 1 (2015): 123–46.

Gundry-Volf, Judith M. "Gender and Creation in 1 Corinthians 11:2–16: A Study in Paul's Theological Method." In *Evangelium, Schriftauslegung, Kirche: Festschrift für Peter Stuhlmacher zum 65. Geburtstag*, edited by Scott Jack Hafemann, Jostein Ådna, and Otfried Hofius, 151–71. Göttingen: Vandenhoeck & Ruprecht, 1997.

Guthrie, George H., and Russell D. Quinn. "A Discourse Analysis of the Use of Psalm 8:4–6 in Hebrews 2:5–9." *Journal of the Evangelical Theological Society* 49, no. 2 (2006): 235–46.

Hagner, Donald A. "The Son of God as Unique High Priest: The Christology of the Epistle to the Hebrews." In *Contours of Christology in the New Testament*, edited by Richard L. Longenecker, 247–67. Grand Rapids: Eerdmans, 2005.

Hahn, Scott. *The Kingdom of God as Liturgical Empire: A Theological Commentary on 1–2 Chronicles*. Grand Rapids: Baker Academic, 2012.

Hamilton, Victor P. *The Book of Genesis: Chapters 1–17*. Grand Rapids: Eerdmans, 1990.

Hamm, Dennis. "Faith in the Epistle to the Hebrews: The Jesus Factor." *The Catholic Biblical Quarterly* 52, no. 2 (1990): 270–91.

Hannaford, Ivan. *Race: The History of an Idea in the West*. Washington, DC: Johns Hopkins University Press, 1996.

Harrison, Nonna Verna. "The Maleness of Christ." *St. Vladimir's Theological Quarterly* 42, no. 2 (1998): 111–51.

Harrison, Verna E. F. "Gender, Generation, and Virginity in Cappadocian Theology." *Journal of Theological Studies* 47 (1996): 38–68.

Hart, David B. "The 'Whole Humanity': Gregory of Nyssa's Critique of Slavery in Light of His Eschatology." *Scottish Journal of Theology* 54, no. 1 (2001): 51–69.

Hays, Richard B. *Echoes of Scripture in the Gospels*. Waco, TX: Baylor University Press, 2016.

Healy, Nicholas J. "Henri de Lubac on Nature and Grace: A Note on Some Recent Contributions to the Debate." *Communio* 35 (2008): 535–64.

Hector, Kevin W. "God's Triunity and Self-Determination: A Conversation with Karl Barth, Bruce McCormack and Paul Molnar." *International Journal of Systematic Theology* 7, no. 3 (2005): 246–61.

Hilkert, Mary Catherine. "Cry Beloved Image: Rethinking the Image of God." In *In the Embrace of God: Feminist Approaches to Theological Anthropology*, edited by Ann Elizabeth O'Hara Graff, 190–205. Maryknoll, NY: Orbis, 1995.

Hitchcock, Nathan. *Karl Barth and the Resurrection of the Flesh: The Loss of the Body in Participatory Eschatology.* Eugene, OR: Pickwick, 2013.

Hoekema, Anthony A. *Created in God's Image.* Grand Rapids: Eerdmans, 1986.

Holleman, Joost. *Resurrection and Parousia: A Traditio-Historical Study of Paul's Eschatology in I Corinthians 15.* Supplements to Novum Testamentum, vol. 84. New York: Brill, 1996.

Hood, Robert E. *Begrimed and Black: Christian Traditions on Blacks and Blackness.* Minneapolis: Augsburg Fortress, 1994.

Hooker, Morna D. "Adam Redivivus: Philippians 2 Once More." In *Old Testament in the New Testament: Essays in Honour of J. L. North*, 220–34. Sheffield: Sheffield Academic, 2000.

Hopkins, Dwight N. *Being Human: Race, Culture, and Religion.* Minneapolis: Fortress, 2005.

Horan, Daniel P. "How Original Was Scotus on the Incarnation? Reconsidering the History of the Absolute Predestination of Christ in Light of Robert Grosseteste." *Heythrop Journal* 52, no. 3 (2011): 374–91.

Horowitz, Maryanne Cline. "The Image of God in Man: Is Woman Included?" *Harvard Theological Review* 72, no. 3–4 (1979): 175–206.

Houlden, J. L. "John 19:5: 'And He Said to Them, Behold, the Man.'" *The Expository Times* 92, no. 5 (1981): 148–49.

Hunsinger, George. "Election and the Trinity: Twenty-Five Theses on the Theology of Karl Barth." *Modern Theology* 24, no. 2 (2008): 179–98.

———. *How to Read Karl Barth: The Shape of His Theology.* Oxford: Oxford University Press, 1991.

———. *Reading Barth with Charity: A Hermeneutical Proposal.* Grand Rapids: Baker Academic, 2015.

Hurst, Lincoln D. "The Christology of Hebrews 1 and 2." In *The Glory of Christ in the New Testament: Studies in Christology*, edited by Lincoln D. Hurst and N. T. Wright, 151–64. Oxford: Clarendon, 1987.

Irving, Edward. *The Collected Writings of Edward Irving.* Edited by G. Carlyle. Vol. 5. London: Alexander Strahan, 1865.

Jennings, Willie James. *The Christian Imagination: Theology and the Origins of Race.* New Haven, CT: Yale University Press, 2010.

Jenson, Robert W. "Once More the *Logos Asarkos.*" *International Journal of Systematic Theology* 13, no. 2 (2011): 130–33.

———. *Systematic Theology.* 2 vols. New York: Oxford University Press, 1997.

Jobling, David. "A Structural Analysis of Genesis 2:4b–3:24." *SBL Seminar Papers* 1 (1978): 61–69.

John Paul II. *Apostolic Letter Mulieris Dignitatem*. Vatican City: Libreria Editrice Vaticana, 1988.

Johnson, Elizabeth A. "Jesus, the Wisdom of God: A Biblical Basis for Non-Androcentric Christology." *Ephemerides Theologicae Lovanienses* 61, no. 4 (1985): 261–94.

———. "The Incomprehensibility of God and the Image of God Male and Female." *Theological Studies* 45, no. 3 (1984): 441–65.

———. "The Maleness of Christ." In *Special Nature of Women*, 108–16. London: SCM, 1991.

Johnson, Keith L. "When Nature Presupposes Grace: A Response to Thomas Joseph White, O.P." *Pro Ecclesia* 20, no. 3 (2011): 264–82.

Johnston, George. "Ecce Homo: Irony in the Christology of the Fourth Evangelist." In *Glory of Christ in the New Testament: Studies in Christology in Memory of George Bradford Caird*, 125–38. Oxford: Clarendon, 1987.

Julian of Norwich. *Showings*. Translated by Edmund Colledge and James Walsh. The Classics of Western Spirituality. New York: Paulist, 1978.

Jüngel, Eberhard. *Death, the Riddle and the Mystery*. Philadelphia: Westminster, 1975.

Kapic, Kelly M. "The Son's Assumption of a Human Nature: A Call for Clarity." *International Journal of Systematic Theology* 3, no. 2 (2001): 154–66.

Kärkkäinen, Veli-Matti. "The Human Prototype: With Jesus, We See What We Were Created to Be." *Christianity Today* 56, no. 1 (2012): 28–31.

Keener, Craig S. *The Gospel of John*. Grand Rapids: Baker Academic, 2010.

Kelley, Shawn. *Racializing Jesus: Race, Ideology, and the Formation of Modern Biblical Scholarship*. New York: Routledge, 2002.

Kelsey, David H. *Eccentric Existence: A Theological Anthropology*. 2 vols. Louisville: Westminster John Knox, 2009.

Kennedy, Rebecca F., C. Sydnor Roy, and Max L. Goldman, eds. *Race and Ethnicity in the Classical World: An Anthology of Primary Sources in Translation*. Indianapolis: Hackett, 2013.

Kilner, John. *Dignity and Destiny: Humanity in the Image of God*. Grand Rapids: Eerdmans, 2014.

Koester, Craig R. and R. Bieringer, eds. *The Resurrection of Jesus in the Gospel of John*. Wissenschaftliche Untersuchungen zum Neuen Testament 222. Tübingen: Mohr Siebeck, 2008.

Köstenberger, Andreas J. *A Theology of John's Gospel and Letters*. Biblical Theology of the New Testament. Grand Rapids: Zondervan, 2009.

Kraeling, Carl H. *Anthropos and Son of Man: A Study in the Religious Syncretism of the Hellenistic Orient*. Columbia University Oriental Studies, vol. 25. New York: Columbia University Press, 1927.

Kreitzer, L. Joseph. "Christ and Second Adam in Paul." *Communio Viatorum* 32, no. 1–2 (1989): 55–101.

Krimsky, Sheldon and Kathleen Sloan, eds. *Race and the Genetic Revolution: Science, Myth, and Culture*. New York: Columbia University Press, 2011.

Kutsko, John F. *Between Heaven and Earth: Divine Presence and Absence in the Book of Ezekiel*. Winona Lake, IN: Eisenbrauns, 2000.

Ladd, George Eldon. *A Theology of the New Testament*. Rev. ed. Grand Rapids: Eerdmans, 1993.

Lamp, Jeffrey S. "Wisdom in Col 1:15–20: Contribution and Significance." *Journal of the Evangelical Theological Society* 41, no. 1 (1998): 45–53.

Lane, William L. *Hebrews 1–8*. Waco, TX: Word, 1991.

Leithart, Peter J. *A Son to Me: An Exposition of 1 & 2 Samuel*. Moscow, ID: Canon, 2003.

Levison, John R. *Portraits of Adam in Early Judaism: From Sirach to 2 Baruch*. Sheffield: JSOT Press, 1988.

Lewis, C. S. *Mere Christianity*. Rev. ed. San Francisco: HarperOne, 2015.

Lightfoot, J. B. *Saint Paul's Epistles to the Colossians and to Philemon*. Grand Rapids: Zondervan, 1968.

Lincoln, Andrew T. *Paradise Now and Not Yet: Studies in the Role of the Heavenly Dimension in Paul's Thought with Special Reference to His Eschatology*. Society for New Testament Studies Monograph Series 43. New York: Cambridge University Press, 2004.

———. *The Gospel according to Saint John*. Black's New Testament Commentaries 4. New York: Hendrickson, 2005.

Lindars, Barnabas. *The Theology of the Letter to the Hebrews*. Cambridge: Cambridge University Press, 2010.

Lindholm, Stefan. "Would Christ Have Become Incarnate Had Adam Not Fallen? Jerome Zanchi (1516–1590) on Christ as Mediator." *Journal of Reformed Theology* 9, no. 1 (2015): 19–36.

Lindsay, Dennis R. "*Pistis* and '*Emunah*: The Nature of Faith in the Epistle to the Hebrews." In *A Cloud of Witnesses: The Theology of Hebrews in Its Ancient Contexts*, edited by Richard Bauckham, Daniel Driver, Trevor Hart, and Nathan MacDonald, 158–69. London: T&T Clark, 2008.

Lints, Richard. *Identity and Idolatry: The Image of God and Its Inversion.* New Studies in Biblical Theology 36. Downers Grove, IL: InterVarsity, 2015.

Litwa, Matthew David. "Behold Adam: A Reading of John 19:5." *Horizons in Biblical Theology* 32, no. 2 (2010): 129–43.

Long, D. Stephen. "Natura Pura: On the Recovery of Nature in the Doctrine of Grace." *Modern Theology* 27, no. 4 (2011): 695–98.

Long, Steven A. *Natura Pura: On the Recovery of Nature in the Doctrine of Grace.* Moral Philosophy and Moral Theology. New York: Fordham University Press, 2010.

Lossky, Vladimir. *The Mystical Theology of the Eastern Church.* Crestwood, NY: St. Vladimir's Seminary Press, 1976.

Lubac, Henri de. *Augustinianism and Modern Theology.* Translated by Lancelot Sheppard. London: Chapman, 1969.

———. *Surnaturel.* Paris: Aubier, 1946.

———. *The Mystery of the Supernatural.* Translated by Rosemary Sheed. New York: Herder and Herder, 1967.

Ludlow, Morwenna. *Gregory of Nyssa, Ancient and (Post)modern.* Oxford: Oxford University Press, 2007.

Malik, Kenan. *The Meaning of Race: Race, History, and Culture in Western Society.* Washington Square, NY: New York University Press, 1996.

Marsh, John. *The Gospel of St. John.* The Pelican Gospel Commentaries. Harmondsworth, England: Penguin, 1968.

Mason, Eric Farrel. *"You Are a Priest Forever": Second Temple Jewish Messianism and the Priestly Christology of the Epistle to the Hebrews.* Leiden; Boston: Brill, 2008.

Mathews, Kenneth A. *Genesis.* 2 vols. Nashville, TN: Broadman & Holman, 1996.

McConville, J. Gordon. *Being Human in God's World: An Old Testament Theology of Humanity.* Grand Rapids: Baker Academic, 2016.

McCormack, Bruce L. "Grace and Being: The Role of God's Gracious Election in Karl Barth's Theological Ontology." In *The Cambridge Companion to Karl Barth,* edited by John B. Webster, 92–110. Cambridge: Cambridge University Press, 2000.

———. "The Identity of the Son: Karl Barth's Exegesis of Hebrews 1.1–4 (and Similar Passages)." In *Christology, Hermeneutics, and Hebrews: Profiles from the History of Interpretation,* 155–72. London: T&T Clark, 2012.

———. "'With Loud Cries and Tears': The Humanity of the Son in the Epistle to the Hebrews." In *Epistle to the Hebrews and Christian*

Theology, edited by Richard Bauckham, Daniel R. Driver, Trevor A. Hart, and Nathan MacDonald, 37–68. Grand Rapids: Eerdmans, 2009.

McCready, Douglas. *He Came Down from Heaven: The Preexistence of Christ and Christian Faith*. Downers Grove, IL: InterVarsity, 2005.

McCruden, Kevin B. *Solidarity Perfected: Beneficent Christology in the Epistle to the Hebrews*. New York: de Gruyter, 2008.

McDowell, Catherine L. *The Image of God in the Garden of Eden: The Creation of Humankind in Genesis 2:5–3:24 in Light of the mīs pî pīt pî and wpt-r Rituals of Mesopotamia and Ancient Egypt*. Winona Lake, IN: Eisenbrauns, 2015.

McFarland, Ian A. "Fallen or Unfallen? Christ's Human Nature and the Ontology of Human Sinfulness." *International Journal of Systematic Theology* 10, no. 4 (2008): 399–415.

———. *The Divine Image: Envisioning the Invisible God*. Minneapolis: Fortress, 2005.

McKinley, John E. *Tempted for Us: Theological Models and the Practical Relevance of Christ's Impeccability and Temptation*. Colorado Springs: Paternoster, 2009.

McLaughlin, Eleanor. "Feminist Christologies: Re-Dressing the Tradition." In *Reconstructing the Christ Symbol: Essays in Feminist Christology*, 118–49. New York: Paulist, 1993.

Meeks, Wayne A. *The Prophet-King. Moses Traditions and the Johannine Christology*. Leiden: Brill, 1967.

Middleton, J. Richard. *The Liberating Image: The Imago Dei in Genesis 1*. Grand Rapids: Brazos, 2005.

Minear, Paul Sevier. *Christians and the New Creation: Genesis Motifs in the New Testament*. Louisville: Westminster John Knox, 1994.

Moberly, R. W. L. "Did the Serpent Get It Right?" *The Journal of Theological Studies* 39, no. 1 (1988): 1–27.

Moeller, Henry R. "Wisdom Motifs and John's Gospel." *Bulletin of the Evangelical Theological Society* 6, no. 3 (1963): 92–99.

Moffitt, David M. *Atonement and the Logic of Resurrection in the Epistle to the Hebrews*. Leiden: Brill, 2011.

Molnar, Paul D. *Divine Freedom and the Doctrine of the Immanent Trinity: In Dialogue with Karl Barth and Contemporary Theology*. Edinburgh: T&T Clark, 2002.

Molnar, Stephen. *Human Variation: Races, Types, and Ethnic Groups*. 6th ed. Upper Saddle River, NJ: Pearson Prentice Hall, 2006.

Moloney, Francis J. *The Johannine Son of Man*. Rome: Libreria Ateneo Salesiano, 1976.

Montagu, Ashley. *Man's Most Dangerous Myth: The Fallacy of Race*. New York: Columbia University Press, 1942.

Moo, Douglas J. *The Letters to the Colossians and to Philemon*. The Pillar New Testament Commentary. Grand Rapids: Eerdmans, 2008.

Moreland, J. P. *The Recalcitrant Imago Dei: Human Persons and the Failure of Naturalism*. London: SCM, 2009.

Morris, Thomas V. *The Logic of God Incarnate*. Ithaca, NY: Cornell University Press, 1986.

Mouw, Richard J. "Another Look at the Infra/Supralapsarian Debate." *Calvin Theological Journal* 35, no. 1 (2000): 136–51.

Mukhopadhyay, Carol Chapnick, Rosemary C. Henze, and Yolanda T. Moses. *How Real Is Race? A Sourcebook on Race, Culture, and Biology*. 2nd ed. Lanham, MD: AltaMira, 2014.

Mulcahy, Bernard. *Aquinas's Notion of Pure Nature and the Christian Integralism of Henri de Lubac: Not Everything Is Grace*. New York: Peter Lang, 2011.

Nellas, Panayiotis. *Deification in Christ: The Nature of the Human Person*. Crestwood, NY: St. Vladimir's Seminary Press, 1987.

Nicholson, Philip Yale. *Who Do We Think We Are? Race and Nation in the Modern World*. Armonk, NY: M. E. Sharpe, 1999.

Novello, Henry. *Death as Transformation*. Burlington, VT: Ashgate, 2011.

Oakes, Edward T. *A Theology of Grace in Six Controversies*. Grand Rapids: Eerdmans, 2016.

Oakes, Kenneth. "The Question of Nature and Grace in Karl Barth: Humanity as Creature and as Covenant-Partner." *Modern Theology* 23, no. 4 (2007): 595–616.

O'Brien, Peter T. *Colossians, Philemon*. Waco, TX: Word, 1982.

———. *God Has Spoken in His Son: A Biblical Theology of Hebrews*. Downers Grove, IL: IVP Academic, 2016.

———. *The Letter to the Hebrews*. The Pillar New Testament Commentary. Grand Rapids: Eerdmans, 2010.

O'Collins, Gerald. *Christology*. New York: Oxford University Press, 1995.

Omi, Michael, and Howard Winant. *Racial Formation in the United States: From the 1960s to the 1990s*. 2nd ed. New York: Routledge, 1994.

Ormerod, Neil. "The Grace-Nature Distinction and the Construction of a Systematic Theology." *Theological Studies* 75, no. 3 (2014): 515–36.

Osborn, Ronald E. *Death Before the Fall: Biblical Literalism and the Problem of Animal Suffering*. Downers Grove, IL: IVP Academic, 2014.

Osborne, Grant R. "The Christ of Hebrews and Other Religions." *Journal of the Evangelical Theological Society* 46 (2003): 249–67.

Painter, John. "Earth Made Whole: John's Rereading of Genesis." In *Word, Theology and Community in John*, 65–84. St Louis: Chalice, 2002.

———. "The Enigmatic Johannine Son of Man." In *Four Gospels 1992: Festschrift Frans Neirynck*, 1869–87. Louvain: Peeters, 1992.

Palliser, Margaret Ann. *Christ, Our Mother of Mercy: Divine Mercy and Compassion in the Theology of the "Shewings" of Julian of Norwich*. New York: de Gruyter, 1992.

Panackel, Charles. *Idou o Anthrōpos (John 19:5b): An Exegetico-Theological Study of the Text*. Rome: Pontificia Università Gregoriana, 1988.

Pannenberg, Wolfhart. *Anthropology in Theological Perspective*. Translated by Matthew J. O'Connell. Edinburgh: T&T Clark, 1985.

———. *Jesus—God and Man*. Translated by Lewis L. Wilkins and Duane A. Priebe. 2nd ed. Philadelphia: Westminster John Knox, 1977.

———. *Systematic Theology*. Translated by Geoffrey W. Bromiley. Grand Rapids: Eerdmans, 1991.

Peeler, Amy L. B. *You Are My Son: The Family of God in the Epistle to the Hebrews*. New York: Bloomsbury, 2015.

Pelphrey, Brant. *Christ Our Mother: Julian of Norwich*. Way of the Christian Mystics. Wilmington, DE: Michael Glazier, 1989.

Peterson, David. *Hebrews and Perfection: An Examination of the Concept of Perfection in the "Epistle to the Hebrews."* Cambridge: Cambridge University Press, 1982.

Pickstock, Catherine. "The One Story: A Critique of David Kelsey's Theological Robotics." *Modern Theology* 27, no. 1 (2011): 26–40.

Porter, Stanley E. "Allusions and Echoes." In *As It Is Written: Studying Paul's Use of Scripture*, edited by Stanley E. Porter and Christopher D. Stanley, 29–40. Atlanta: Society of Biblical Literature, 2008.

Postell, Seth D. *Adam as Israel: Genesis 1–3 as the Introduction to the Torah and Tanakh*. Cambridge: James Clarke, 2012.

Rahner, Karl. *On the Theology of Death*. Translated by Charles H. Henkey. New York: Herder and Herder, 1961.

Rajagopalan, Kumar. "What Is the Defining Divide? False Post-Racial Dogmas and the Biblical Affirmation of 'Race.'" *Black Theology* 13, no. 2 (2015): 166–88.

Ratzinger, Joseph. *Eschatology, Death and Eternal Life*. Translated by Johann Auer. Washington, DC: Catholic University of America Press, 1988.

Rhee, Victor. *Faith in Hebrews: Analysis within the Context of Christology, Eschatology and Ethics*. New York: Peter Lang, 2001.

Richard, Earl J. "Expressions of Double Meaning and Their Function in the Gospel of John." *New Testament Studies* 31, no. 1 (1985): 96–112.

Richardson, Christopher A. *Pioneer and Perfecter of Faith: Jesus' Faith as the Climax of Israel's History in the Epistle to the Hebrews*. Wissenschaftliche Untersuchungen zum Neuen Testament 2. Reihe 338. Tübingen: Mohr Siebeck, 2012.

Routledge, Robin L. "Death and Afterlife in the Old Testament." *Journal of European Baptist Studies* 9, no. 1 (2008): 22–39.

Ruether, Rosemary Radford. *Sexism and God-Talk: Toward a Feminist Theology*. London: SCM, 1983.

———. "The Liberation of Christology from Patriarchy." *Religion and Intellectual Life* 2, no. 3 (1985): 116–28.

———. *To Change the World: Christology and Cultural Criticism*. New York: Crossroad, 1981.

Scharlemann, Martin H. "'In the Likeness of Sinful Flesh.'" *Concordia Theological Monthly* 32, no. 3 (1961): 133–38.

Schenck, Kenneth L. "A Celebration of the Enthroned Son: The Catena of Hebrews 1." *Journal of Biblical Literature* 120, no. 3 (2001): 469–85.

———. "God Has Spoken: Hebrews' Theology of the Scriptures." In *Epistle to the Hebrews and Christian Theology*, edited by Daniel R. Driver, Richard Bauckham, Trevor Hart, and Nathan MacDonald, 321–36. Grand Rapids: Eerdmans, 2009.

———. "Keeping His Appointment: Creation and Enthronement in Hebrews." *Journal for the Study of the New Testament* 66 (1997): 91–117.

Schillebeeckx, Edward. *Jesus: An Experiment in Christology*. Translated by Hubert Hoskins. New York: Seabury, 1979.

Schleiermacher, Friedrich. *The Christian Faith*. Edited by H. R. Mackintosh and J. S. Stewart. Berkeley: Apocryphile, 2011.

———. "On Colossians 1:15–20 (1832)." Translated by Esther D. Reed and Alan Braley. *Neues Athenaeum* 5 (1998): 48–80.

Schnackenburg, Rudolf. "Die Ecce-Homo-Szene und der Menschensohn." In *Jesus und der Menschensohn: Für Anton Vögtle*, 371–86. Freiburg im Bresgau: Herder, 1975.

———. *The Gospel according to St. John*. New York: Seabury, 1980.

Schüle, Andreas. "Made in the 'Image of God': The Concepts of Divine Images in Gen 1–3." *Zeitschrift für die Alttestamentliche Wissenschaft* 117, no. 1 (2005): 1–20.

Schüssler Fiorenza, Elisabeth. *Jesus: Miriam's Child, Sophia's Prophet : Critical Issues in Feminist Christology*. 2nd ed. New York: Bloomsbury, 2015.

Schwarz, Hans. *The Human Being: A Theological Anthropology*. Grand Rapids: Eerdmans, 2013.

Scroggs, Robin. *The Last Adam; a Study in Pauline Anthropology*. Philadelphia: Fortress, 1966.

Sevenster, G. "Remarks on the Humanity of Jesus in the Gospel and Letters of John." In *Studies in John: Presented to Professor Dr. J. N. Sevenster on the Occasion of His Seventieth Birthday*, 185–93. Leiden: Brill, 1970.

Siker, Jeffrey S. "Historicizing a Racialized Jesus: Case Studies in the 'Black Christ,' the 'Mestizo Christ,' and White Critique." *Biblical Interpretation* 15, no. 1 (2007): 26–53.

Small, Brian C. *The Characterization of Jesus in the Book of Hebrews*. Boston: Brill, 2014.

Smedes, Lewis. *My God and I: A Spiritual Memoir*. Grand Rapids: Eerdmans, 2003.

Smith, D. Moody. *John*. Nashville: Abingdon, 1999.

Smith, Justin E. H. *Nature, Human Nature, and Human Difference: Race in Early Modern Philosophy*. Princeton, NJ: Princeton University Press, 2015.

Snowden, Frank M. *Before Color Prejudice: The Ancient View of Blacks*. Cambridge, MA: Harvard University Press, 1983.

Sosa Siliezar, Carlos Raúl. *Creation Imagery in the Gospel of John*. London: T&T Clark, 2015.

Stamm, Raymond Thomas. "Creation and Revelation in the Gospel of John." In *Search the Scriptures: New Testament Studies in Honor of Raymond T. Stamm*, 13–32. Leiden: Brill, 1969.

Steenberg, M. C. *Of God and Man: Theology as Anthropology from Irenaeus to Athanasius*. London: T&T Clark, 2009.

Steinberg, Stephen. *The Ethnic Myth: Race, Ethnicity, and Class in America*. 3rd ed. Boston: Beacon, 2001.

Still, Todd D. "*Christos* as *Pistos*: The Faith(fulness) of Jesus in the Epistle to the Hebrews." In *A Cloud of Witnesses: The Theology of Hebrews in Its Ancient Contexts*, edited by Richard Bauckham, Daniel Driver, Trevor Hart, and Nathan MacDonald, 40–50. London: T&T Clark, 2008.

Suggit, John N. "Jesus the Gardener: The Atonement in the Fourth Gospel as Re-Creation." *Neotestamentica* 33, no. 1 (1999): 161–68.

———. "John 19:5: 'Behold the Man.'" *The Expository Times* 94, no. 11 (1983): 333–34.

Sumner, Darren O. "Fallenness and Anhypostasis: A Way Forward in the Debate over Christ's Humanity." *Scottish Journal of Theology* 67, no. 2 (2014): 195–212.

Sussman, Robert W. *The Myth of Race: The Troubling Persistence of an Unscientific Idea.* Cambridge, MA: Harvard University Press, 2014.

Tanner, Kathryn. *Christ the Key.* Current Issues in Theology. New York: Cambridge University Press, 2010.

———. "In the Image of the Invisible." In *Apophatic Bodies: Negative Theology, Incarnation, and Relationality,* edited by Chris Boesel and Catherine Keller, 117–34. New York: Fordham University Press, 2009.

Thiselton, Anthony C. *The First Epistle to the Corinthians: A Commentary on the Greek Text.* The New International Greek Testament Commentary. Grand Rapids: Eerdmans, 2000.

———. "Realized Eschatology at Corinth." *New Testament Studies* 24, no. 4 (1978): 510–26.

Thompson, James. *Hebrews.* Grand Rapids: Baker Academic, 2008.

Thompson, Marianne Meye. *Colossians and Philemon.* The Two Horizons New Testament Commentary. Grand Rapids: Eerdmans, 2005.

Tidball, Derek. "Completing the Circle: The Resurrection according to John." *Evangelical Review of Theology* 30, no. 2 (2006): 169–83.

Torrance, Thomas F. *Incarnation: The Person and Life of Christ.* Edited by Robert T. Walter. Wilton Keynes, UK: Paternoster, 2008.

———. *The Trinitarian Faith: The Evangelical Theology.* Edinburgh: T&T Clark, 1988.

Vander Beek, William L. "Hebrews: A 'Doxology' of the Word." *Mid-America Journal of Theology* 16 (2005): 13–28.

Van der Watt, J. G. "Double Entendre in the Gospel according to John." In *Theology and Christology in the Fourth Gospel: Essays by the Members of the SNTS Johannine Writings Seminar,* 463–81. Leuven: Leuven University Press, 2005.

Van Driel, Edwin Chr. *Incarnation Anyway: Arguments for Supralapsarian Christology.* New York: Oxford University Press, 2008.

VanMaaren, John. "The Adam-Christ Typology in Paul and Its Development in the Early Church Fathers." *Tyndale Bulletin* 64, no. 2 (2013): 275–97.

von Rad, Gerhard. *Genesis: A Commentary.* Philadelphia: Westminster, 1961.

Wade, Nicholas J. *A Troublesome Inheritance: Genes, Race and Human History.* New York: Penguin, 2014.

Wallis, Wilber B. "Problem of an Intermediate Kingdom in I Corinthians 15:20–28." *Journal of the Evangelical Theological Society* 18, no. 4 (1975): 229–42.

Wanamaker, Charles A. "Philippians 2:6–11: Son of God or Adamic Christology?" *New Testament Studies* 33, no. 2 (1987): 179–93.

Ware, Bruce A. "Male and Female Complementarity and the Image of God." *Journal for Biblical Manhood and Womanhood* 7 (2002): 14–23.

Webster, John. "One Who Is Son: Theological Reflections on the Exordium to the Epistle to the Hebrews." In *Epistle to the Hebrews and Christian Theology*, edited by Richard Bauckham, Daniel R. Driver, Trevor Hart, and Nathan MacDonald, 69–94. Grand Rapids: Eerdmans, 2009.

Weinandy, Thomas G. *In the Likeness of Sinful Flesh: An Essay on the Humanity of Christ*. New York: T&T Clark, 2000.

Wellum, Stephen J. *God the Son Incarnate: The Doctrine of Christ*. Wheaton, IL: Crossway, 2016.

Wenham, Gordon J. *Genesis 1–15*. Waco: Word, 1987.

Westermann, Claus. *Creation*. Philadelphia: Fortress, 1974.

———. *Genesis 1–11: A Commentary*. Minneapolis: Augsburg, 1984.

Weyermann, Maja. "The Typologies of Adam-Christ and Eve-Mary and Their Relationship to One Another." *Anglican Theological Review* 84, no. 3 (2002): 609–26.

Wilson-Kastner, Patricia. "Contemporary Feminism and Christian Doctrine of the Human." *Word & World* 2, no. 3 (1982): 234–42.

Wolff, Hans Walter. *Anthropology of the Old Testament*. Translated by Margaret Kohl. London: SCM, 1974.

Wood, Susan. "The Nature-Grace Problematic within Henri de Lubac's Christological Paradox." *Communio* 19 (1992): 389–403.

Woodhead, Linda. "Apophatic Anthropology." In *God and Human Dignity*, edited by R. Kendall Soulen and Linda Woodhead, 233–46. Grand Rapids: Eerdmans, 2006.

Wright, N. T. *The Climax of the Covenant: Christ and the Law in Pauline Theology*. Minneapolis: Fortress, 1992.

Young, Frances M. "God's Image: The 'Elephant in the Room' in the Fourth Century?" In *Studia Patristica*, vol. 50, 57–71. Leuven: Peeters, 2011.

Zathureczky, Kornél. "Jesus' Impeccability: Beyond Ontological Sinlessness." *Science et Esprit* 60, no. 1 (2008): 55–71.

Ziebertz, Hans-Georg. *The Human Image of God*. Leiden: Brill, 2001.

Zimmerman, Ruben. "Symbolic Communication between John and
    His Reader: The Garden Symbolism in John 19–20." In *Anatomies of
    Narrative Criticism: The Past, Present, and Futures of the Fourth Gospel as
    Literature*, edited by Tom Thatcher and Stephen D. Moore, 221–35.
    Atlanta: Society of Biblical Literature, 2008.
Zizioulas, John D. "Human Capacity and Human Incapacity: A Theo-
    logical Exploration of Personhood." *Scottish Journal of Theology* 28,
    no. 5 (1975): 401–48.

Subject Index

Scripture Index

Author Index

Christological Anthropology in Historical Perspective

Ancient and Contemporary Approaches to Theological Anthropology

Marc Cortez

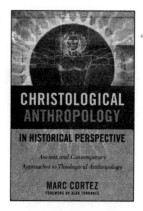

What does it mean to be "truly human?" *In Christological Anthropology in Historical Perspective*, Marc Cortez looks at the ways several key theologians—Gregory of Nyssa, Julian of Norwich, Martin Luther, Friedrich Schleiermacher, Karl Barth, John Zizioulas, and James Cone—have used Christology to inform their understanding of the human person. Based on this historical study, he concludes with a constructive proposal for how Christology and anthropology should work together to inform our view of what it means to be human.

Available in stores and online!